THOMSON
COURSE TECHNOLOGY ™

PAINT SHOP PRO® 8

P O W E R !

By Lori J. Davis

Paint Shop Pro® 8 Power!

Senior Vice President, Professional, Trade, and Reference Group: Andy Shafran

Publisher: Stacy L. Hiquet

Credits: Senior Marketing Manager, Sarah O'Donnell; Marketing Manager, Heather Hurley; Manager of Editorial Services, Heather Talbot; Senior Acquisitions Editor, Kevin Harreld; Senior Editor, Mark Garvey; Associate Marketing Manager, Kristin Eisenzopf; Retail Market Coordinator, Sarah Dubois; Production Editor, Karen A. Gill; Copy Editor, Laura Gabler; Technical Editor, Sarah Arnott; Proofreader, Kathy Marshall; Cover Designer, Nancy Goulet; Interior Design and Layout, Shawn Morningstar; Indexer, Sharon Shock.

Technology and the Internet are constantly changing, and by necessity of the lapse of time between the writing and distribution of this book, some aspects might be out of date. Accordingly, the author and publisher assume no responsibility for actions taken by readers based upon the contents of this book.

Library of Congress Catalog Number: 2003108381

ISBN: 1-929685-38-6

5 4 3 2 1

Educational facilities, companies, and organizations interested in multiple copies or licensing of this book should contact the publisher for quantity discount information. Training manuals, CD-ROMs, and portions of this book are also available individually or can be tailored for specific needs.

MUSKA&LIPMAN

Muska & Lipman Publishing,
a Division of Course Technology
25 Thomson Place
Boston, MA 02210
http://www.courseptr.com/
publisher@muskalipman.com

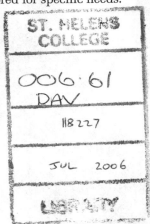

About the Author

Lori J. Davis is a technical writer and former college teacher who developed a passion for Paint Shop Pro in the mid 1990s while creating a gardening Web site. She has taught many Paint Shop Pro online courses and has been a beta tester for several versions of Paint Shop Pro and various plug-in filters. She has contributed articles on Paint Shop Pro to *Digital Camera Magazine* and is the author of several books on Paint Shop Pro, including *Paint Shop Pro 8 Solutions*. When she's not writing or exploring computer graphics, Lori enjoys photography, knitting, painting, gardening, finding and drinking good but inexpensive wine, and walking on the beach.

Dedication

To Patti, Joyce, Lily, and Mei for your generosity and caring in troubled times.

Acknowledgments

My sincere thanks to everyone who helped make this book possible, whether or not I dealt with you directly. In particular, I wish to thank Sarah Arnott, Laura Gabler, and Karen Gill. As in the past, Sarah caught my slips and pointed out ways to expand on or clarify the various topics covered. Laura did an excellent job keeping me on the editorial straight and narrow. And Karen not only held it all together, but through her patience, cajoling, prodding, and encouragement helped get me through the rough spots.

I seldom thank by name my many colleagues in the Paint Shop Pro community, for fear of inadvertently leaving someone out. I admire their knowledge and creativity and appreciate their sense of sharing and camaraderie. But this time, in addition to the unnamed many, I'd also like to single out Sally and Porter for their support and good wishes inside and outside the graphics sphere.

And a very big thank you to Lar for once more putting up with my hours and hours cloistered away tapping keys and scratching on a graphics tablet.

iv

Contents

5—Mastering Selections, Masks, and Channels 97

6—Working with Vectors 111

7—Paint Shop Pro 8 Effects   131

8—Photo Editing and Enhancement   163

Introduction

Paint Shop Pro is a powerful yet easy-to-use graphics editor that is also surprisingly affordable. Whether you're creating your own images from scratch, editing clip art, or retouching digital photos, Paint Shop Pro has the tools you need. *Paint Shop Pro 8 Power!* helps you explore these tools and provides examples of advanced techniques that illustrate the power of Paint Shop Pro.

Who This Book Is For

This book is for intermediate and advanced users of Paint Shop Pro. It can also be useful for experienced users of other image editors who are new to Paint Shop Pro.

For this book to be most useful to you, you should either be somewhat familiar with Paint Shop Pro's interface and tools or be ready and willing to use the Paint Shop Pro documentation to look up any of the basics that you're not clear on. Some basic information is provided in the early chapters of this book, but the book's central purpose is to examine techniques that go beyond the basics.

Assumptions

As just mentioned, this book assumes that you are already somewhat familiar with Paint Shop Pro's interface or that you are ready to consult Paint Shop Pro's documentation if you come across something basic that you're unclear about.

This book also assumes that you have Paint Shop Pro version 8 and an interest in using advanced techniques in creating and editing digital images. Following are a few other assumptions made in the book:

- ▶ **You're running Windows 98, NT 4 SP6a, 2000, Me, or XP.** Paint Shop Pro is available only for the PC platform. You should also be familiar with how to install and run programs on your PC.

- ▶ **You're familiar with the peripherals used with your computer.** This book will help you use Paint Shop Pro to edit scanned images and digital photos and to print your images. But you will need to be familiar with how to install and use your particular peripherals (your scanner, digital camera, and printer).

- ▶ **You want to learn and explore.** This book has been written to show you what can be done with Paint Shop Pro. You'll find many specific techniques that you can employ in your own work, but what is presented here should be seen as a springboard, inspiring you to explore Paint Shop Pro even more on your own.

How This Book Is Organized

Paint Shop Pro 8 Power! is divided into 12 chapters and 5 appendixes, and also has a section of color plates:

▶ **Chapter 1, "Basic Drawing and Painting Tools."** This chapter focuses on the Paint Brush, Airbrush, Eraser, and Preset Shapes tools. You'll also take a first look at the Pen tool and the Text tool.

▶ **Chapter 2, "More Painting Tools."** In this chapter, you'll take a look at some of the other painting tools, including the Eye Dropper and Color Replacer tools, the Picture Tube tool (which enables you to paint with ready-made pictures), and the Flood Fill tool. You'll also take a first look at the Clone Brush, Warp Brush, and Mesh Warp tools.

▶ **Chapter 3, "Being Selective."** Being able to isolate parts of an image and modify only those parts makes many image editing tasks easier. This chapter shows you how to do just that, using Paint Shop Pro's selection tools.

▶ **Chapter 4, "Mastering Layers and Blend Modes."** In this chapter, you'll learn about the power of layers. Layers let you manipulate part of a complex image while leaving the rest untouched. Layers enable you to easily blend one image into another and to produce many effects that would be difficult or close to impossible to do without layers.

▶ **Chapter 5, "Mastering Selections, Masks, and Channels."** Masks enable you to modify transparency on other layers without actually affecting the data on those layers. In this chapter, you'll discover the power of masks, and you'll also explore some advanced selection techniques.

▶ **Chapter 6, "Working with Vectors."** Drawing with vectors allows you to deform a shape or change its attributes again and again, all without degrading image quality in the least. Discover how vectors can help you create great drawings that you can change easily whenever you like.

▶ **Chapter 7, "Paint Shop Pro 8 Effects."** Paint Shop Pro 8 has many built-in special effects. This chapter catalogs them all and gives an in-depth look at some of the most useful and powerful effects.

▶ **Chapter 8, "Photo Editing and Enhancement."** Now that scanners and digital cameras are becoming more affordable, the number of people needing the digital equivalent of a darkroom is on the rise. Paint Shop Pro fits the bill by providing you with a wide range of photo editing tools and filters. In this chapter, you'll learn how to edit and enhance your photos.

▶ **Chapter 9, "Web Tools."** Paint Shop Pro has lots of tools for the Web graphics designer, including built-in Web optimizers, an image slicer, and an image map utility. In this chapter, you'll learn about these and more.

▶ **Chapter 10, "Tricks and Techniques."** This chapter features a potpourri of advanced techniques. Create dynamic Web graphics, striking text effects, digital drawings and paintings, and more.

▶ **Chapter 11, "Adding to Your Toolkit."** Paint Shop Pro comes with a large collection of textures, patterns, Picture Tubes, gradients, brushes, and other resource files. But why be limited to what's there already? In this chapter, you'll learn how to create your own resource files.

▶ **Chapter 12, "Scripting."** One of the most powerful new additions in Paint Shop Pro 8 is its scripting engine. Scripts enable you to record a series of operations and play them again whenever you need to. You can also write scripts that do much more than just replay a set of operations. In this chapter, you'll begin to explore the power of scripts.

▶ **Appendix A, "Paint Shop Pro 8 Menus, Toolbars, and Palettes."** This appendix includes illustrations of Paint Shop Pro's basic interface elements.

▶ **Appendix B, "Configuring Paint Shop Pro 8."** This appendix outlines the various ways in which you can make Paint Shop Pro work the way you want it to.

▶ **Appendix C, "Adjusting Color Depth."** In this appendix, the issue of color depth and the fine points of adjusting an image's color depth are examined.

▶ **Appendix D, "Printing."** This appendix gives a brief discussion of printing your images.

▶ **Appendix E, "Resources."** This appendix lists a few online resources for Paint Shop Pro.

Conventions Used in This Book

The following conventions are used in this book:

▶ All Web page *Uniform Resource Locators* (URLs) mentioned appear in **boldface**, such as **http://www.jasc.com**.

▶ Hot keys in commands and menu options are shown in **boldface**, such as **Edit > Copy**.

▶ Labels for controls in a dialog box or palette are shown in **boldface**, such as **Match mode**.

▶ In the running text, all *Hypertext Markup Language* (HTML) tags and attributes appear in full monospace capital letters so that the HTML code stands out from the rest of the text. In expanded examples, HTML code is presented in lowercase. (Today's Web browsers don't pay attention to case in HTML code. Keep in mind, though, that specifications for HTML coding are being considered that include a preference, if not a requirement, that HTML tags and attributes appear only in lowercase.)

In addition to these typographical conventions, this book features the following special displays for different types of important text:

TIP

Text formatted like this offers a helpful tip relevant to the topic discussed in the main text.

NOTE

Text formatted like this highlights other interesting or useful information that relates to the topic discussed in the main text.

CAUTION

Cautions highlight actions or commands that can make irreversible changes to your files or that can cause other serious problems. Read cautions carefully; they can help you avoid confusion or loss of work.

Keeping the Book's Content Current

Everyone involved with this book has worked hard to make it complete and accurate. But as we all know, mistakes sometimes find a way of creeping in. If you discover any errors or want to make suggestions for future editions, please contact Muska & Lipman Publishing at **http://www.courseptr.com/**. You might also find updates, corrections, and other information related to this book on the Muska & Lipman site.

1

Basic Drawing and Painting Tools

The first tools that you're likely to use in Paint Shop Pro are the basic drawing and painting tools, such as the Paint Brush, Airbrush, Preset Shape tool, Eraser, Pen tool, and Text tool. In this chapter, you'll explore these simple drawing and painting tools by looking at both the basic functions and the more advanced features of each one. For now, you'll examine painting and drawing only on raster layers. In Chapter 6, "Working with Vectors," you'll examine vector drawing.

Throughout this chapter, keep in mind that many of the painting tools behave differently depending on whether you use them with the left mouse button or the right mouse button. If you paint with the left mouse button depressed, the current Foreground material is used. If you paint with the right mouse button depressed, however, the current Background material is used. (Refer to the Paint Shop Pro documentation if you're unsure how to select the Foreground and Background colors in the Materials palette.)

Here's what you'll be exploring in this chapter:

▶ Using brushes
▶ Drawing lines and shapes
▶ Adding text to images

The Paint Brush and Airbrush

The Paint Brush and Airbrush are the most basic painting tools. They differ from each other only in the way they apply "paint" to an image. The Paint Brush applies paint in dabs. When you keep your mouse in one place while holding down either mouse button, you get the same effect as you do when simply single-clicking the mouse button. The Airbrush, on the other hand, applies paint like an aerosol spray can. If you keep the mouse in one place and hold down one of the mouse buttons, paint is applied until you release the mouse button. In other respects, however, these two tools are similar.

Basic Brush Settings

Let's take a look at the settings you can use with the Paint Brush and Airbrush.

TIP

Although you usually do freehand painting when you use the Paint Brush or Airbrush tool, you can also use these tools to draw straight lines. To draw a straight line, click where you want to begin the line. Hold down the Shift key and click where you want the line to end—left-click to produce a line in the Foreground material, or right-click to produce a line in the Background material. As explained a bit later in this chapter, you can also use the Pen tool, with somewhat different effects, to create straight lines.

With the Paint Brush selected, open the Tool Options palette (if the palette isn't already visible) by pressing F4 to see the controls shown in Figure 1.1. (Most of these controls are also present in the Tool Options palette of the Airbrush.)

When using either the Paint Brush or the Airbrush, you can control the brush shape and size, the width and rotation of the brush or spray, the density and hardness of the brush or spray, and the "steps" between the dabs or spray bursts painted when you drag the mouse. You can also control the opacity of the paint and how the paint is blended with whatever is already on the image canvas. Here's what the basic brush settings control:

▶ **Shape.** Sets the basic shape of the brush. Available basic brush shapes are Square and Round.

▶ **Size.** Sets the diameter of the brush. Available brush sizes range from 1 to 500 pixels.

▶ **Hardness.** Controls how hard or how diffuse the edges of the brush are. Ranges from 0 (most diffuse) to 100 (completely hard).

▶ **Step.** Controls how the brush shape is repeated as you drag the mouse while you're painting. The lower the Step value, the smoother and more continuous the line that's drawn with the brush. As the Step value increases, the repeated brushstrokes or spray bursts that form the line become more pronounced individually and less continuous as a line, as demonstrated in Figure 1.2. Ranges from 1 (closest) to 200 (farthest apart).

▶ **Density.** Controls how solid the brush is. Ranges from 1 (least dense) to 100 (completely solid).

▶ **Thickness.** Controls the width of the brush in its narrowest dimension. Create an Oval brush by reducing the thickness of a Round brush. Create a Rectangular brush by reducing the thickness of a Square brush. Ranges from 1 (minimum thickness) to 100 (maximum thickness).

▶ **Rotation.** Controls the angle of the brush. Ranges from 0 degrees to 359 degrees. Rotation has no effect on a Round brush at maximum width. Use it to adjust the angle of an Oval, a Square, or a Rectangular brush.

▶ **Opacity.** Controls the opacity of the paint applied. Ranges from 1 (least opaque) to 100 (most opaque).

▶ **Blend Mode.** Controls how the new paint blends together with existing paint on the image.

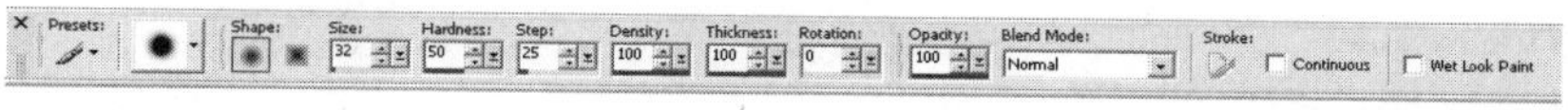

Figure 1.1
The Tool Options palette
for the Paint Brush.

Figure 1.2
Step set to 1, 25, 50, 75,
100 (from top to bottom).

TIP

To see the effect that these settings have on your brush, keep an eye on the preview
window just to the left of the **Shape** controls in the Tool Options palette.

Clicking the brush preview or the button next to it opens a drop-down list of custom brush shapes
(shown in Figure 1.3). And to the left of the custom brush control is a drop-down list of brush
presets. You can use both the custom brush shapes and the presets to load custom brushes. And,
as you'll see in Chapter 11, "Adding to Your Toolkit," you can create your own custom brushes.

To get a feel for what effect the different brush options have, let's try a few variations. Figure 1.4
shows what you get with the Charcoal preset, the Highlighter preset, and the Squeaky Marker
preset. When you load a brush preset, be sure to see what settings are used to produce the
particular brush effect.

Other controls available with the Paint Brush (but not the Airbrush) are **Wet Look Paint**,
Continuous, and **Stroke**. The Highlighter example in Figure 1.4 shows the effect of **Wet Look
Paint**. With **Wet Look Paint**, paint applied with a soft brush (that is, a brush with a low Hardness
setting) resembles a watercolor or ink wash (semitransparent with a more opaque edge).

Figure 1.3
Custom brush drop-down
list.

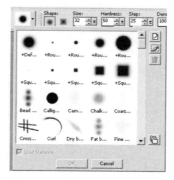

Figure 1.4
Examples of Charcoal
(top), Highlighter
(middle), and Squeaky
Marker (bottom).

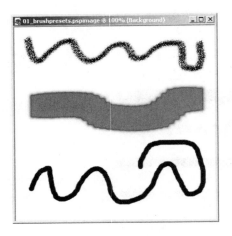

To understand **Continuous** and **Stroke**, you first have to keep in mind how the Paint Brush normally applies paint. Paint applied in a single stroke produces a uniform effect, even where part of the stroke overlaps another part. When **Continuous** is not checked, if you release the mouse button and begin a new stroke, any semitransparent paint that overlaps another area of semitransparent paint affects the previously painted area. If you instead want the paint for a series of strokes to behave as paint does for a continuous stroke, check **Continuous**. And if at some point you want the paint to be applied as a new stroke when **Continuous** is in effect, just click the **Stroke** button.

Brush Variance

The basic brush characteristics aren't the only ones that you can change to create different effects with the Paint Brush and Airbrush tools. You can also get some complex effects with Brush Variance. If the Brush Variance palette isn't showing on your workspace, press F11 or choose **View** > **Palettes** > **Brush** Variance. You'll then see the Brush Variance palette, shown in Figure 1.5.

With Brush Variance, you can create a brush that uses paint that varies in color, hue, saturation, lightness, or opacity. Or the brush itself can be made to vary in size, thickness, rotation, or density. You can make the variations dependent on several different conditions, such as the direction of the stroke or the stylus pressure (if you're using a pressure-sensitive stylus and graphics tablet). With the **Jitter** controls, the variations can also be created more or less randomly.

Figure 1.5
The Brush Variance
palette.

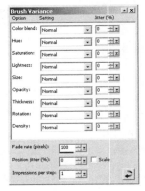

Here's a brief overview of the settings available for each brush or paint characteristic that can be controlled with Brush Variance:

- ▶ **Normal.** No variance at all, except for any random variance introduced by **Jitter**.
- ▶ **Pressure.** Varies according to the amount of pressure applied with a stylus on a pressure-sensitive graphics tablet.
- ▶ **Altitude.** Available only with a graphics tablet. Varies according to the up-and-down tilt of a stylus on a graphics tablet.
- ▶ **Azimuth.** Available only with a graphics tablet. Varies according to the right-to-left tilt of a stylus on a graphics tablet.
- ▶ **Twist.** Available only with a graphics tablet. Varies as a stylus on a graphics tablet twists.
- ▶ **Fingerwheel** and **Z Wheel.** Available only with input devices that have these features.
- ▶ **Direction.** Varies with the direction of the brushstroke.
- ▶ **Fade In.** Begins at 0 and fades to the value set in the Tool Options palette.
- ▶ **Repeating Fade In.** Like Fade In, but in a repeating pattern.
- ▶ **Fade Out.** Begins at the value set in the Tool Options palette and fades to 0.
- ▶ **Oscillating Fade.** Repeatedly fades in and out.

Several other controls appear in the bottom pane of the Brush Variance palette. **Fade rate (pixels)** determines the length of a fade-in or fade-out in pixels. For example, if you set the fade rate of **Size** to fade out at 300, then the brush will completely fade out after it has been dragged a length of 300 pixels.

Position jitter (%) determines whether and to what extent the position of a brush impression is random. At a setting of 0, the position of an impression is precisely where the cursor is when you click your mouse button. At a high setting, the position of the impression varies from the cursor position. This control yields particularly interesting results when used in conjunction with **Impressions per step**. With **Impressions per step** set to 1, you get exactly one impression at each step interval as you drag the brush. With higher settings, you get multiple impressions at each step.

Several of the presets make use of Brush Variance. For example, Figure 1.6 shows the effects of Chenille, Confetti, and Ink Wash.

In Chapter 11, we'll take a closer look at brush variance.

Figure 1.6
Brush Variance examples: Chenille (top), Confetti (middle), and Ink Wash (bottom).

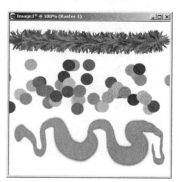

The Eraser

The first editing tool that you should get to know well is the Eraser, which is much more versatile than a pencil eraser.

In unlayered images, the Eraser acts like the Paint Brush in reverse: If you paint with the left mouse button depressed, the pixels that you paint over become the current Background color. If you paint with the right mouse button depressed, the pixels become the current Foreground color.

In layered images (discussed in Chapter 4, "Mastering Layers and Blend Modes"), the Eraser has a more interesting use. On any layer except for Background, painting with the Eraser makes the pixels transparent, and using the Eraser with the right mouse button depressed reapplies any paint that was previously removed.

NOTE

If you right-drag the Eraser on a layer, the paint that you reapply might look somewhat different than it looked originally. The settings for Opacity, Density, and Hardness in the Tool Options palette or the setting for Texture in the Materials palette can produce different effects from the original.

The Tool Options palette for the Eraser has most of the same controls and settings as the Paint Brush: presets and a custom brush drop-down list, as well as controls for **Shape**, **Size**, **Hardness**, **Step**, **Density**, **Thickness**, **Rotation**, and **Opacity**. The Eraser can also be used with a texture (as set in the Materials palette). So, for example, you could choose a **Texture** and set the **Opacity** of the Eraser to 50 to reduce a layer's opacity and add a texture to it, restricting the change to areas you paint on.

We'll look more at using the Eraser on layered images in Chapter 4. In that chapter, we'll also examine the Eraser's more powerful cousin, the Background Eraser.

The Preset Shape Tool

With the Preset Shape tool, you can draw simple and complex shapes precisely. The available shapes, which you choose from the tool's Tool Options palette, can be as simple as basic geometric shapes—like Rectangle, Ellipse, Pentagon, Hexagon, Octagon, and several types of stars—but more complex shapes are also available. As you'll see in Chapter 11, anything that you can draw with the vector tools can be saved as a preset shape. Figure 1.7 shows some of the preset shapes that come with Paint Shop Pro, and Figure 1.8 shows the Tool Options palette for the Preset Shape tool.

To define a vector shape, check **Create as vector** in the Tool Options palette for the Preset Shapes tool. To define a raster shape, uncheck **Create as vector**.

If you uncheck **Retain style**, the Foreground/Stroke material set in the Materials palette is used for the outline of the shape and the Background/Fill material is used for the inside of the shape. (Set Stroke to Transparent if you don't want an outline, or set Fill to Transparent if you want only an outline.) If you check Retain style, then the stroke and fill match those of the original shape, as shown in the thumbnail displayed in the Shapes drop-down list.

Figure 1.7
Some of the shapes
available with the Preset
Shape tool.

Figure 1.8
The Tool Options palette
for the Preset Shape tool.

Another option that you can set for the Preset Shape tool is whether or not the shape is antialiased. Aliasing is the stepped effect produced when a line is drawn on a computer screen. Antialiasing is a method of smoothing this jagged effect by adding pixels along the edge of the line, in colors that are intermediate between the color of the line and the Background color. To use antialiasing, check the **Anti-alias** check box.

NOTE

Antialiasing is available only with greyscale images and 16-million color images.

Figure 1.9 shows a zoomed-in view of a portion of a circle created without antialiasing in effect. Figure 1.10 shows a zoomed-in view of a portion of a circle created with antialiasing. As you can see, the jagged edges of the circle appear to be much smoother in the antialiased version.

CAUTION

Antialiasing does a great job smoothing lines, but you have to be careful when you manipulate antialiased elements. If you paste an antialiased figure into an image or Flood Fill around an antialiased figure, an edge of the original surrounding color will appear around the figure along the area where the blended pixels are located.

The remaining controls—**Line Style**, **Width**, **Join**, and **Miter limit**—all affect the stroke. If you want the stroke to be something other than an unbroken line with no variation, leave **Line Style** set to **+Solid**. If you want a fancier line, choose one from the drop-down list. To set the width of your stroke, supply a nonzero value for **Width**. (If you want no stroke, even if Stroke in the Materials palette is set to something other than Transparent, set **Width** to 0.)

Figure 1.9
A circle without
antialiasing.

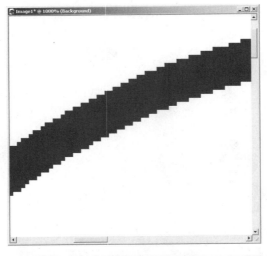

Figure 1.10
A circle with antialiasing.

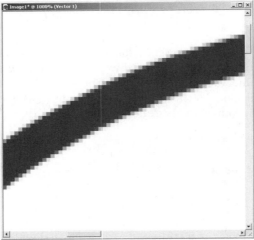

Join and **Miter limit** control how the corners of a shape look. You can set **Join** to one of three types: Miter, for mitered corners; Round, for rounded corners; or Bevel, for beveled corners. When **Join** is set to Miter, corners are mitered when lines meeting at a corner are within the miter limit and are beveled otherwise.

You define the shape in any of the following ways:

▶ Click the left mouse button and drag to draw the shape corner to corner.

▶ Hold down the Shift key as you drag to draw the shape from the center out.

▶ Click the right mouse button and drag to maintain the aspect ratio of the original shape.

▶ Hold down the Shift key as you drag with the right mouse button down to maintain the original aspect ratio and rotate the image at the same time.

The controls for **Line Style**, **Width**, **Join**, and **Miter Limit** are available only when Retain Style is unchecked.

If you drag from the top down, the shape is drawn as it appears in the **Shapes** drop-down list. If you drag from the bottom up, the shape is flipped from top to bottom.

TIP

As you draw a shape, look on the right of the Status bar. You'll see several sets of numbers in the following form:

(x: n1 y: n2) n3°

where n1, n2, and n3 are all numbers. The pair of numbers enclosed in the parentheses indicate the x- and y-coordinates of the cursor position, while the third number indicates the number of degrees the shape is rotated.

The Pen Tool

The Pen tool is the tool of choice when you want to create either straight lines or smooth curves. To start drawing, click the Drawing Mode button on the Tool Options palette when the Pen tool is active. You can then select any of three **Segment Types**: **Line Segments**, **Point to Point**, or **Freehand**. Use Line Segments for straight lines drawn singly or in a series of connected lines. Use Point to Point to create complex, smooth curves. Use Freehand to create curves you draw by hand, simply by dragging the mouse.

For simple raster lines and curves, it's easiest to use **Simple Mode**. In **Simple Mode**, the only Pen tool mode available to you is **Drawing Mode**. If you want each mouse click or drag to add to a single line or curve, also select **Contiguous**. If instead you want mouse clicks to draw separate lines or curves, keep **Contiguous** unchecked.

NOTE

You don't have to use **Simple Mode** when you're drawing on a raster layer, but as the name of the mode implies, it will be much simpler if you do. Without **Simple Mode**, raster drawing behaves much more like vector drawing. However, I strongly urge you not to do raster drawing without **Simple Mode** selected. Instead, if you want to graduate beyond **Simple Mode**, jump right into vectors. Vectors give you much more flexibility and are readily editable—even after you save your image.

As with the Preset Shape tool, you control the width of the line's stroke with **Width**. Keep in mind that a line's or curve's stroke is what you think of as the line or curve itself. The fill for a line or curve is the area contained "under" the set of lines or curve—that is, the area contained within the shape defined by the lines or curve(s).

To draw lines or curves only, with no fill, set the style mode for the Foreground/Stroke box on the Materials palette to any mode other than Transparent, and set the style mode for Fill to Transparent. If you set the Fill to anything other than Transparent, the area between the start point and endpoint of your curve or series of lines will be filled with paint. If you want to draw a handmade shape without an outline, set the Stroke to Transparent and the Fill to anything other than Transparent. To create a handmade shape that is both outlined and filled, set both the Stroke and the Fill to anything other than Transparent. Figures 1.11 through 1.13 show each of these variations.

Figure 1.11
Shape drawn with Stroke set to Solid Color and Fill set to Transparent.

Figure 1.12
Shape drawn with Stroke set to Transparent and Fill set to Pattern.

Figure 1.13
Shape drawn with Stroke set to Solid Color and Fill set to Gradient.

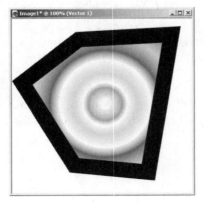

Let's now take a quick look at the three types of segments you can draw with the Pen tool. In Chapter 6, we'll work through all the ins and outs of the Pen tool (in vector mode).

Line Segments

To draw a straight line, choose **Line Segments** as the **Segment Type** in the Tool Options palette, select the **Width** you'd like, and check **Anti-alias** if you want antialiasing to be in effect. Then in the image canvas, click the left mouse button at the spot where you want the line to begin and drag to where you want the line to end. Figure 1.14 shows a line being drawn.

Figure 1.14
Drawing a line with the Pen tool.

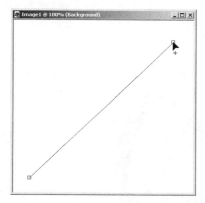

As long as you hold down the mouse button, what you'll see are the line's start and end nodes and a single-pixel line. When you release the mouse button, your line will be rendered without the nodes and at the width that is specified in the Tool Options palette.

When you want to restrict your line drawing to horizontal lines, vertical lines, and other lines at 45-degree increments, hold down the Shift key while you drag to draw your line. And if you want to draw a series of connected lines, be sure that Contiguous is selected.

Point to Point Lines and Curves

Point to Point provides a lot of control when drawing lines and shapes. A pair of nodes defines each line or curve, and complex shapes are created by defining a series of nodes. Let's take a look at a simple raster example of **Point to Point**. To draw a shape made up of a series of straight line segments, set **Segment Type** to **Point to Point** in the Tool Options palette, and then simply click at the endpoints of each segment, as shown in Figure 1.15.

To close the shape, click the **Close selected open contours** button in the Tool Options palette (just to the right of the **Tracking** drop-down list).

To create curves, click to define a node (the start point) and drag. As you drag away from the node, you'll see an arrow-shaped control. Dragging away from the node increases the length of the arrow and adds to the length of the segment between this node and the next node you define. Swiveling the arrow changes the curvature of the segment at the node. Add more nodes by clicking or clicking and dragging. Figure 1.16 shows a curved path being drawn in this way.

Figure 1.15
Shape drawn with
straight line segments
using Point to Point.

Figure 1.16
Shape drawn with curved
segments using Point to
Point Lines.

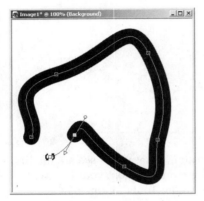

NOTE
Figures 1.15 and 1.16 show **Point to Point** being drawn with **Simple Mode** toggled off. With **Simple Mode** on, the rendered portions of the shape would show only the rendered lines and curves. The nodes and segment lines would not be shown.

If you want to close the curve, click the **Close selected open contours** button. Figure 1.17 shows an example of a shape drawn with **Point to Point**.

Freehand Lines and Curves

To draw freehand instead of drawing a set of straight lines or smooth curves, choose **Freehand** as the **Segment Type**. Be sure to set **Curve tracking**, too. Freehand lines are made from a continuous set of line segments, and **Curve tracking** determines the length of each segment. The smaller the value for **Curve tracking**, the shorter the component line segments and the smoother the curves.

Figure 1.18 shows an example of a simple drawing created with Freehand lines and curves.

Figure 1.17
Shape drawn with Point
to Point (Stroke: Solid
Color; Fill: Gradient;
Width: 10).

Figure 1.18
A simple drawing created
with Freehand lines and
curves.

CHAPTER 1

The Text Tool A

It's easy to add text to your images in Paint Shop Pro with the Text tool.

To use the Text tool, choose the tool from the Tool palette, and in its Tool Options palette choose
a setting for **Create as** (either **Floating**, **Selection**, or **Vector**). Click within your image at the point
where you want your text block to appear. The Text Entry dialog box then opens. Adjust the settings
for the Text tool in the Tool Options palette, and in the Materials palette select the materials for the
text (and for a stroke, if you want one). Then enter your text in the Text Entry dialog box.

Here's a summary of the **Create as** options:

▶ **Floating.** Select this to create your text as a floating selection. The text "floats"
above the active layer and is filled with whatever material is currently set as
the Background/Fill material in the Materials palette. If you drag a floating text
selection with the Text tool, the colored text is moved and the pixels of the layer
beneath the selection remain untouched.

▶ **Selection.** Select this if you want an empty text selection. This gives you a standard (nonfloating) selection in the shape of the text you specify. If you drag a standard text selection with the Text tool, the pixels within the selection move and the area left behind is filled either with the current Background material (if the text is on a Background layer) or with transparency (if the text is on a true layer). (For more information on floating selections and standard selections, see Chapter 3, "Being Selective.")

▶ **Vector.** Select this if you want to create text on a vector layer rather than on a raster layer. You'll explore vector text in Chapter 6.

Figure 1.19 shows the Tool Options palette for the Text tool.

Figure 1.19
The Tool Options palette for the Text tool.

In addition to **Create as**, the Text tool's Tool Options palette has what might seem to be quite a lot of controls, but they're all pretty straightforward.

▶ **Font.** In this drop-down list, you select the font face for your text.

▶ **Size.** In this drop-down list, you select the point size for your text. Alternatively, you can enter the point size in the text box above this list, which enables you to select a point size that isn't included in the list. For example, although 100 isn't included in the scroll list, you can set the font size to 100 points by entering 100 in this text box.

▶ **Stroke width (pixels).** Here you set the width of the stroke (that is, the outline) that you want around each character of your text. Usually it's best to keep this set to 0.

▶ **Anti-alias.** Antialiasing works with text as it does with shapes and lines. If you select **Anti-alias**, the jagged edges of your text will be made smooth by blending the text color with the Background color. Keep in mind that checking this box has an effect only if your image is a greyscale image or a 16- million color image.

▶ **Warp Text.** This control is active only when you make text conform to a path. We'll look at this control in Chapter 6.

▶ **Alignment.** These buttons—Align Left, Center, and Right Align—determine where your text is placed and how multiple lines of text are aligned relative to one another.

    Align Left. All text is left-aligned. The block of text is placed in your image so that the left edge of the first line of text is placed at the point you clicked on when you activated the Text tool.

    Center. All text is centered. The block of text is placed in your image so that the first line of text is centered horizontally around the point you clicked on when you activated the Text tool.

    Right Align. All text is right-aligned. The block of text is placed in your image so that the right edge of the first line of text is placed at the point you clicked on when you activated the Text tool.

Figure 1.20 illustrates the different alignments.

CHAPTER 1

- ▶ **Font Style.** There are styles for bold, italics, underline, and strikethrough. You can select any combinations of these attributes or none at all. Only attributes available for the chosen font will have an effect.

- ▶ **Line Style**, **Join,** and **Miter Limit.** These are all like their counterparts for Preset Shape.

- ▶ **Kerning.** This affects the spacing between adjacent characters. The **Kerning** control is active only if the cursor is placed in the Text Entry box between two characters (or in front of or after a single character) or if a string of text is selected.

  Positive values for kerning increase the amount of spacing, and negative values decrease the spacing. Set the kerning by selecting text (by dragging across the text). Then adjust the **Kerning** control.

  To automatically set the kerning appropriately for the current font, toggle Auto Kern on instead of setting the kerning yourself. When Auto Kern is on, the **Kerning** control becomes inactive and is greyed out. (This control may not be visible on the Tool Options palette until you click the appropriate expansion arrow on the palette.)

- ▶ **Leading.** The **Leading** control affects the amount of space between lines of text. Enter positive values to increase the spacing, and enter negative values to decrease the spacing. Set the leading by selecting the relevant lines of text in the Text Entry box and adjusting the **Leading** control. (This control might not be visible in the Tool Options palette until you click the appropriate expansion arrow on the palette.)

NOTE

"Leading" rhymes with "heading." In old-fashioned typesetting, strips of lead were used to increase the distance between lines of type.

The Text Entry dialog box is where you enter your text. You have all sorts of options here. You can simply enter text of a single color and font size, but you can also do a lot more. For example, suppose you start out by entering the text shown in Figure 1.21 with Trebuchet MS as the font and 36 as the point size.

Figure 1.20
Examples of Align Left (top), Center (middle), and Right Align (bottom).

Figure 1.21
36-point Trebuchet MS
text.

You can change the properties of any portion of the text by highlighting that portion and then adjusting the appropriate settings. For instance, in this example, you can change the font, font size, and the color of just the word "fine."

1. Select the word by dragging across it.
2. Set the font and size.
3. Click the Background/Fill material box on the Materials palette; then choose a new material in the Materials dialog box. Figure 1.22 shows the results.

Figure 1.22
Changing the word "fine"
to 48-point Times New
Roman and setting a
different color.

When your text is as you want it, click the **Apply** button.

TIP

After you click the **Apply** button in the Text Entry dialog box, you can reposition the text by dragging it with the Text tool. Place the Text tool over the text. When the cursor is in the proper place, the cursor changes to a pair of crossed double-headed arrows, just like the Mover tool. Click and drag the text to the desired position.

For floating text or a text selection, you can anchor your text in place by clicking the right mouse button while using the Text tool and then selecting Select None from the context menu. You can also deselect the text with **S**elections > Select None or by pressing Ctrl+D. If you anchor your text and then notice that it isn't quite where you want it, you can get the text selection back by clicking the Undo button, by pressing Ctrl+Z, or by choosing **E**dit > **U**ndo.

Now you have the basics for adding text to your images. In several of the examples later in this book, you'll explore advanced text manipulation techniques, such as making text conform to a curved path, modifying the shape of characters entered as vector text, and adding special effects to text.

2
More Painting Tools

In this chapter, you will learn about the remaining painting tools. These include the Eye Dropper, Flood Fill, and Picture Tube tools and some editing tools that people who are new to Paint Shop Pro sometimes miss. We'll also look at a couple of tools that are new in Paint Shop Pro 8: the Warp Brush and Mesh Warp tool.

Here's what you'll be exploring in this chapter:

▶ Using the Eye Dropper and Color Replacer tools
▶ Mastering the Clone Brush
▶ Painting with the Picture Tube tool
▶ Flood filling
▶ A first look at the Warp Brush and Mesh Warp tool

The Eye Dropper

The Eye Dropper (or Dropper) isn't a painting tool in itself. What it does is enable you to "pick up" a color from an image—or anywhere on your screen—to set the Foreground or Background material for use with tools like the Paint Brush, Airbrush, and Flood Fill tool. To set the Foreground color, click with the left mouse button. To set the Background color, click with the right mouse button.

When you select the Eye Dropper, its Tool Options palette shows two controls: a drop-down list labeled **Sample Size** and a check box labeled **Active layer only**.

Sample Size can be **1×1 Pixel**, **3×3 Pixels**, **5×5 Pixels**, **7×7 Pixels**, or **11×11 Pixels**. When you're sampling a uniform solid-colored area, all of these settings are equivalent and you'll get whatever image color is under the cursor. When you're sampling a nonuniformly colored area, Paint Shop Pro will calculate an average of the colors within whatever sampling range you've set. For example, if **Sample Size** is set to **3×3 Pixels** and the 3×3 pixel area surrounding the pixel under the cursor contains more than one color, the color that is picked up will be an average of those colors.

With **Active layer only** unchecked, Paint Shop Pro samples any image color under the cursor, no matter what layer the color is on. When this check box is checked, Paint Shop Pro samples only colors that are on the currently active layer.

TIP

When any tool is active, you can temporarily change it to the Dropper tool by holding down the Ctrl key. You can then click on a color to set the Foreground color or right-click to set the Background color. To go back to the normal functioning of the active tool, just release the Ctrl key.

With this method, the last used settings for **Sample Size** and **Active layer only** will be in effect.

TIP

If you are using Windows 2000 or later, you can pick up a color that appears on your screen somewhere other than in an image canvas. With any tool selected, place the cursor over one of the material boxes in the Materials palette. Press the Ctrl key and, with the Ctrl key still held down, move the mouse to the area of color that you want to sample. Click when the cursor is over the color you want. If you started from the Foreground material box or Foreground solid-color box, the Foreground color is set. If you started from the Background material box or Background solid-color box, the Background color is set.

This technique also works with any material box appearing in a dialog box.

The Color Replacer

The Color Replacer appears in the same family of tools as the Dropper. You use the Color Replacer to replace an existing color in your image with another color—either by changing the current Background color to the current Foreground color or vice versa, depending on whether you use the tool with the left mouse button or the right mouse button.

The Color Replacer's Tool Options palette is much like the one for the Paint Brush, an important difference being that the Color Replacer has a **Tolerance** control. If you set **Tolerance** to 0, the pixels to be replaced must match the specified color exactly. Setting the **Tolerance** to a higher number tells Paint Shop Pro to also change pixels that closely match the specified color. With a **Tolerance** setting of 200, all the pixels are changed.

Compare Figures 2.1 and 2.2. In Figure 2.1, the Foreground color is set to white and the Background color is set to a brownish color found in the original coins image, with **Tolerance** set to 10. In Figure 2.2, the Foreground and Background colors are the same, but this time **Tolerance** is set to 40.

TIP

Painting with the Color Replacer is convenient when you want to replace a color in only certain parts of your image. But if you want to replace *all* instances of a certain color in your image, you can take a shortcut.

To change all instances of the current Background color to the current Foreground color, double-click your image with the left mouse button. To change all instances of the current Background color with the current Foreground color, double-click your image with the right mouse button.

Figure 2.1
Color Replacer with **Tolerance** set to 10.

Figure 2.2
Color Replacer with **Tolerance** set to 40.

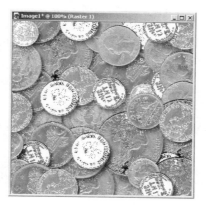

You can create some interesting effects by using the Color Replacer with a high **Tolerance** setting to replace a color. After you've replaced the color, use the Color Replacer again, but this time with a low **Tolerance** and with the Foreground and Background colors switched to change the altered pixels *back* to the original source color. Figure 2.3 shows the result of changing the white areas of Figure 2.2 to dark brown, with **Tolerance** set to 0.

Figure 2.3
Coins image with new white areas changed to brown.

By increasing the areas of brown, you've given the coins a somewhat tarnished look. The effect isn't all that refined in this particular example, but this gives you an idea of what you might achieve.

The Clone Brush

The Clone Brush is a particularly handy tool, especially if you need to modify a photo. You use the Clone Brush to apply portions of an image as "paint." The source image can be either the image that you're modifying or some other image.

NOTE
The Clone Brush works only with greyscale images and 16-million color images.

The Tool Options palette for the Clone Brush is almost identical to the one for the Paint Brush, having controls that determine the brush characteristics and the opacity of the paint. The Clone Brush also has two other controls: a check box labeled **Aligned mode** and a check box labeled **Sample Merged**. (You won't explore **Sample Merged** here, but we'll return to it in Chapter 4, "Mastering Layers and Blend Modes.")

The **Aligned mode** check box controls where the Clone Brush begins to pick up paint from your source each time you begin to paint with the Clone Brush.

> ▶ **Aligned mode checked.** The starting point of your cloning shifts to the point at which you stopped painting, relative to your original starting point (unless you first choose a new starting point).

> ▶ **Aligned mode unchecked.** The Clone Brush returns to the original source point each time that you stop painting and then start again (unless you first choose a new starting point).

To begin painting with the Clone Brush, right-click in the source image at the point where you want to begin picking up paint. How the Clone Brush then behaves depends on whether **Aligned mode** is checked or not.

Aligned Mode

Here's an example with **Aligned mode**. Suppose that you want to clone the image in Figure 2.4 so that part of the image is opaque on a smooth surface and the rest of the image is semitransparent and textured.

1. Open both the original image and a new image with the same dimensions and with a white background.

2. In the Tool Options palette, set **Size** to a moderately large size (about 30 to 50) and **Shape** to Round. Set **Opacity** to 100, **Density** to 100, and **Hardness** to 0. This produces a solid, round brush with diffuse edges. Be sure that **Aligned mode** is checked and that **Texture** on the **Foreground** material box in the Materials palette is toggled off.

Figure 2.4
Source image to be
cloned.

3. Now, right-click the area in the source image where you want to begin picking up the paint. When you start painting in the target image, you'll see a crosshair in the source image that shows where the paint is being picked up, as shown in Figure 2.5.

NOTE
When you right-click with the Clone Brush, you'll hear a click from your PC's speaker. This click is to alert you that you've changed the start point for the cloning.

Figure 2.5
The cloned image in
progress.

4. When the solid area in the target image is the way you like it, go back to the Tool Options palette and change the setting for **Opacity** to about 50. Click the Foreground material box in the Materials palette. In the Materials dialog box, check **Texture** and choose a texture. (Coarse Canvas is used in this example.)

5. Start painting around the edge of your completely opaque area in the target, and click around the edges of this new textured area, creating a gradual fade to the edge of the image. Notice that, because the Clone mode is Aligned, your paint in the source starts out in an area aligned with where you restart in your target. The results are shown in Figure 2.6.

Here's another example of how to use the Clone Brush with **Aligned mode**. Suppose you have a photo that has an imperfection or an object that's obstructing the main figure of your image. The Clone Brush can be used to paint out the imperfection or the obstructing object.

Figure 2.7 shows a photo of a chapel. Very pretty, but the headstones in the foreground give the image a rather bleak look. Fortunately, if you want a lighter mood, you can remove the headstones with the Clone Brush.

1. This time, open just the marred photo image. Choose the Clone Brush tool and set the brush **Shape** to Round or Square, the **Size** to about 2 or 3, and the **Step** fairly low.

2. Set all the other Brush Tip controls to their maximums. Check **Aligned mode** and be sure that the **Foreground** texture is toggled off in the Materials palette.

3. Right-click several pixels away from an object you want to remove, being sure that the area you click in has enough of the snow or other material that you want for your paint. Then carefully start painting over the object you want to remove. It's usually better to paint in dabs rather than to drag.

    If you make a mistake, click the **Undo** button on the standard toolbar or press Ctrl+Z. Because you're in **Aligned mode**, you'll pick up your paint in the right place when you start to paint again. Figure 2.8 shows the edits of the chapel image in progress.

Figure 2.6
The completed cloned image.

Figure 2.7
An image with objects to remove.

Figure 2.8
Painting out objects.

4. Continue in this way until all of what you want removed is painted out. If you need to adjust the source point at any time in the process, just right-click again at the point where you want to start picking up paint next. Also adjust the brush settings as needed. The finished product is shown in Figure 2.9.

Figure 2.9
The corrected image.

This method is useful not only for painting out intrusive objects but also for correcting imperfections in a photo, such as dust spots or scratches. It can even be used to make fantasy images (for example, by cloning an animal's head onto a human body).

Nonaligned Cloning

Cloning with **Aligned mode** toggled off is most useful when you want to add multiple copies of a single object or pattern, perhaps overlapping the copies with one another. For instance, clone a single horse to get a whole herd of horses, or clone a tree to create a forest.

Figure 2.10 shows a simple example of this mode.

NOTE
The grey-and-white checkerboard pattern in the sphere image isn't actually part of the image. It's the default pattern that Paint Shop Pro uses to indicate transparency in an image with a transparent background. You'll sometimes want to use an image with a transparent background as the source for cloning because an image with an opaque background might accidentally pick up the Background color as well as the areas that you want to clone.

Picture Tubes

One of Paint Shop Pro's most popular features is Picture Tubes. A PspTube file is a collection of image elements, such as a series of flowers or other objects, that can be painted onto your image. A tube can have a single element or many elements.

Tubes are used to repeatedly apply an object or a set of objects to your image. This can be useful for creating a matched set of buttons and icons for a Web site, as in Figure 2.11, or for creating

Figure 2.10
Cloning with **Aligned
mode** toggled off.

bouquets, forests, crowds, or other massed figures in computer-displayed or print images, as
in Figure 2.12. Tubes with a low **Step** setting can also be used to create 3-D–looking effects, as in
Figure 2.13.

The Tool Options palette for tubes has a drop-down selection list with a preview thumbnail of the
currently selected tube, a **Settings** button, and four other controls: one for **Scale**, one for **Step**, and
two others, labeled **Placement mode** and **Selection mode** (see Figure 2.14).

Figure 2.11
Matched Web elements
made with a tube.

Figure 2.12
An aquarium scene made
with tubes.

Figure 2.13
3-D–looking effect made
with a tube.

Figure 2.14
The Tool Options palette
for Picture Tubes.

The **Scale** control adjusts the size of the Picture Tube elements. You can set the **Scale** anywhere from 10 percent to 250 percent, with 100 percent being the default.

In conjunction with **Step**, **Placement mode**—which can be set to either Random or Continuous—determines how the tube elements are placed as you paint with the Picture Tube tool. **Step** (measured in pixels) determines either exactly how far apart the center of one tube element is from the next (if **Placement mode** is set to Continuous) or what the maximum distance is between tube elements (if **Placement mode** is set to Random).

Selection mode determines how the different elements in the tube are selected as you paint with the Picture Tube tool. The following are the settings available for **Selection mode**:

▶ **Random.** Tube selection is (as you might suspect) random.

▶ **Incremental.** Each tube element is selected sequentially, and then the sequence is repeated.

▶ **Angular.** Tube selection is determined by the direction in which you drag the mouse as you paint.

▶ **Pressure.** This is effective only if you are painting with a pressure-sensitive graphics tablet and have Paint Shop Pro set up to recognize different pen pressures.

▶ **Velocity.** Tube selection is dependent on the speed of your mouse drag.

For example, Jasc's Beetles tube (see Figure 2.15) has both **Placement mode** and **Selection mode** set to Random. Draw a line across an image canvas once with this tube, release the mouse button, and then draw again. Repeat as many times as you like. You'll see that all the lines are quite different, as shown in the figure.

Compare this with Jasc's Arachnophobia tube (see Figure 2.16), in which **Placement mode** is set to Continuous and **Selection mode** is set to Incremental. Draw one line with this tube and you produce a series of evenly spaced figures. Release the mouse button, draw another line, and you continue in the series. Repeat the process, and you'll see that you get the same series of figures again and again, as shown in the figure.

Figure 2.15
A tube that has both **Placement mode** and **Selection mode** set to Random.

Figure 2.16
A tube with **Placement mode** set to Continuous and **Selection mode** set to Incremental.

CHAPTER 2

None of the tubes now included with Paint Shop Pro 8 has a default **Selection mode** of Angular, but if you have Paint Shop Pro 6 or 7, the Pointing Hands tube is one of these. In Figure 2.17, I've changed the settings for the Pine Cone tube to show how Angular works. This figure shows the result of dragging clockwise with this tube set to Angular.

The remaining control on the Picture Tube Tool Options palette is the **Settings** button.

Clicking the **Settings** button opens up the Picture Tube Settings dialog box, shown in Figure 2.18.

When you're using (as opposed to creating or installing) Picture Tubes, you should adjust only the **Placement options** on the right of the Picture Tube Settings dialog box. You should not change the **Cell arrangement** text boxes on the left side of the Picture Tube Settings dialog box. You use these controls only to create your own tubes (as described in Chapter 11, "Adding to Your Toolkit").

You might wonder why you'd ever want to use the **Settings** button, because the controls you'd normally use in the Picture Tube Settings dialog box are the same as those available in the Tool Options palette itself. The difference is that you can adjust the default settings for the tube when using the Picture Tube Settings dialog box. To make your adjusted settings the new defaults, check the box labeled **Save as default for this Picture Tube**.

Setting Up Third-Party Tubes

To use third-party tubes that were created in Paint Shop Pro 7 or 8, all you need to do is put the TUB or PspTube file in Paint Shop Pro's Picture Tubes subfolder. The next time you access the **Tube** drop-down list in the Picture Tube Tool Options palette, you'll find the name of your new tube included in the list.

Figure 2.17
Using a tube with **Selection mode** set to Angular.

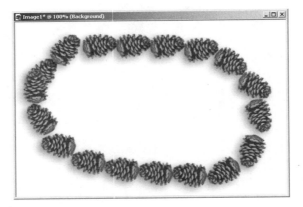

Figure 2.18
Picture Tube Settings dialog box.

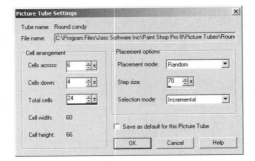

TIP

If Paint Shop Pro is open and the Picture Tube tool is active when you add a new tube, you may need to select another tool and then reselect the Picture Tube tool before the new tube shows up in the Tool Options palette.

One thing you need to keep in mind, though, if you're adding tubes created in Paint Shop Pro 5 or 6, is that the format of tube files created in these older versions is not the same as the format for Paint Shop Pro 8 tubes. Old tubes that you want to use in Paint Shop Pro 8 need to be converted. To make old tubes available in Paint Shop Pro 8, you need to open the tube image and then export the image as a tube.

To export an older TUB file as a Paint Shop Pro 8 tube, follow these steps:

1. Select **File > B**rowse from Paint Shop Pro's menu bar, and navigate to the folder that contains the tube that you want to convert.

2. Double-click on the thumbnail of the tube file. The file opens up in an image window, showing the tube elements on a transparent layer, with the elements arranged in columns and rows, as in Figure 2.19.

3. Choose **File > Export > P**icture Tube, which opens the Picture Tube Settings dialog box. Fill in the number of rows and columns for the tube file. The total number of cells is calculated automatically. Set the **Placement options** as you'd like them, and enter the name of the tube as you'd like it to appear in the drop-down list in the Tool Options palette. Click OK. The next time you use the Picture Tube tool, your new tube will be available for you to use.

For now, don't worry too much about the details of the Picture Tube settings. It's only if you decide to create your own tubes that you'll really need to know about all the options. You'll see how to create your own tubes in Chapter 11.

TIP

You can find tubes for downloading from Jasc Software at **http://www.jasc.com**. The site also lists several other sources of downloadable tubes.

Figure 2.19
A Picture Tube file opened in Paint Shop Pro.

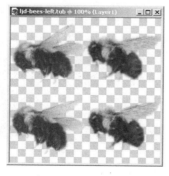

CHAPTER 2

Flood Fill

The Flood Fill tool in its simplest form is like a paint bucket from which you can pour paint onto your image. And by using different settings in the Tool Options palette for **Match Mode**, **Tolerance**, **Blend Mode**, and **Opacity**, you can create quite complex effects.

Figure 2.20 shows the Tool Options palette for the Flood Fill tool, and Figures 2.21 through 2.23 show a few of the effects that you can produce with various materials and Flood Fill settings.

Figure 2.20
The Tool Options palette for the Flood Fill tool.

Figure 2.21
Grey, beveled text filled with a pattern (Material: Pattern; Texture toggled off; **Match Mode**: All Opaque; **Opacity**: 100; **Blend Mode**: Overlay).

Figure 2.22
Solid color applied with a Texture on grey, beveled text (Material: Solid Color; Texture: Granite2; **Match Mode**: All Opaque; **Opacity**: 100; **Blend Mode**: Screen).

Figure 2.23
Jasc Software's Rainbow gradient applied to the image in Figure 2.22 (Material: Sunburst Gradient; Texture toggled off; **Match Mode**: None; **Opacity**: 40; **Blend Mode**: Normal).

You can alter the effect of fill by adjusting **Tolerance, Opacity, Blend Mode,** and **Match Mode** and by adding a texture to your material. **Blend Mode,** which you will explore in Chapter 4, controls how the pixels of your fill are blended in with the pixels that the fill covers. Used with **Match Mode** set to None and/or with **Opacity** set to less than 100, the various blend modes can produce some interesting effects.

Using Different Materials with Flood Fill

As with the Paint Brush and Airbrush, you can use solid colors, patterns, and gradients—with or without an added texture—to good effect with Flood Fill.

You can use a pattern as your material to fill an image or a selection with a ready-made pattern or with the contents of another image. For example, open an image to use as the source of your pattern. Then click the Foreground material box in the Materials palette to open the Material dialog box. Go to the Pattern tab, click the pattern preview to open the pattern selection list, and select the thumbnail for your source image (which will be at the top of the selection list). After selecting your pattern, click in your target image to fill it with the pattern.

You can also get some interesting effects using a gradient as your fill. Click the Foreground material box in the Materials palette to open the Material dialog box. Go to the Gradient tab and click one of the gradient style buttons: **Linear, Rectangular, Sunburst,** and **Radial** (from left to right in the **Style** pane). Then choose a gradient transition in the **Gradient** drop-down list.

TIP
You can reverse the direction of the gradient transition by checking Invert on the Gradient tab of the Material dialog box.

When the gradient style is Linear, you can adjust the angle of the gradient either by dragging the pointer in the gradient preview or by entering the angle number directly in the **Angle** text box. You can also select how many times to repeat the gradient transition by setting **Repeats.**

For Rectangular gradients, you also have the option of changing the gradient's **Center Point** and the **Focal Point.** When the **Link center and focal points** check box is checked, only **Center Point** is available, and when this value is adjusted, both the center point and focal point are modified in tandem. When this check box is unchecked, you can adjust the center point and focal point separately. **Center Point** controls the point from which the gradient radiates. With a Rectangular gradient, **Focal Point** controls the axis around which the gradient is rotated when **Angle** is set to a nonzero value.

Center Point and **Focal Point** are also available with Sunburst gradients. With a Sunburst gradient, **Focal Point** controls the shape of repeated gradient transitions when **Repeats** is set to a nonzero value.

With a Radial gradient, all the gradient controls except **Focal Point** are available.

Figures 2.24 through 2.26 show a few examples of gradient fills, with the Foreground-Background gradient selected.

Figure 2.24
Rectangular gradient fill with **Angle** set to 30, **Repeats** set to 0, **Center Point Horizontal** set to 20 and **Vertical** set to 30, and **Link Center and Focal Points** checked.

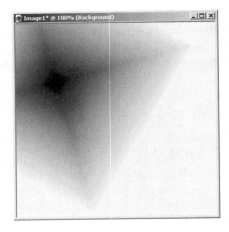

Figure 2.25
Sunburst gradient fill with **Repeats** set to 2, **Center Point Horizontal** set to 30 and **Vertical** set to 20, **Focal Point Horizontal** set to 15 and **Vertical** set to 58.

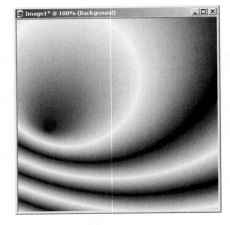

Figure 2.26
Radial gradient fill with **Angle** set to 180, **Repeats** set to 5, **Center Point Horizontal** set to 50 and **Vertical** set to 15.

That's just the beginning of the variations in what you can achieve with Flood Fill. Now let's take a look at the settings available in the Tool Options palette when Flood Fill is active.

Flood Fill Settings

When you click with the Flood Fill tool in your image, pixels surrounding the spot where you click are filled according to the current **Match Mode. Match Mode** has seven different options:

▶ **None.** All areas are filled, regardless of what the characteristics are of the pixel that you click. The entire image canvas or selection is filled, no matter where you click inside the image.

▶ **RGB Value.** Surrounding pixels that match the Red-Green-Blue (RGB) color value of the target pixel are filled.

▶ **Color.** Surrounding pixels that match the target pixel in terms of hue and saturation are filled.

▶ **Hue.** Pixels that are filled match the Hue value (for example, where 0 is red, 90 is green, 180 is blue, 225 is red-violet, and 255 is red again).

▶ **Brightness.** Pixels are filled according to their level of brightness.

▶ **All Opaque.** All surrounding nontransparent areas are filled.

▶ **Opacity.** Surrounding pixels that match the target pixels in level of opacity are filled.

Figures 2.27 through 2.30 illustrate how the match modes affect the behavior of Flood Fill. Figure 2.27 shows the original image. Figure 2.28 shows the result of clicking the center pixel with the Flood Fill tool, with the following settings:

Material: Solid Color

Match Mode: RGB Value

Tolerance: 20

Opacity: 100

Figure 2.29 shows the result of clicking the same pixel with the same settings, except that **Match Mode** is set to Hue. Figure 2.30 shows the result of clicking on the same pixel with the same settings, except that **Match Mode** is set to Brightness.

Figure 2.27
Original image.

Figure 2.28
Match Mode set to RGB
Value.

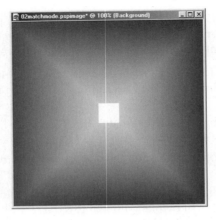

Figure 2.29
Match Mode set to Hue.

Figure 2.30
Match Mode set to
Brightness.

Tolerance, which can be set from 0 to 200, determines how similar to the target pixel surrounding pixels must be in order to be filled. With **Tolerance** set to 0, only pixels that exactly match the target pixel (according to the **Match Mode**) are filled. The higher the **Tolerance** settings, the less closely the pixels need to match the target pixel to be among those that are filled.

> **TIP**
>
> If you try to fill the seemingly solid center of an antialiased outlined shape, you might find a fuzzy fringe of pixels between the edge of your fill and the inside edge of the outline. To fill the entire center of the outlined shape, increase the **Tolerance** for the fill so that the antialiasing pixels are also included as target pixels of the fill.

Opacity can be set from 0 to 100 (percent). A setting of 100 makes the fill completely opaque. Lower values make the fill less opaque (that is, more transparent), letting some of the original color show through.

The **Sample Merged** check box is relevant only for layered images. With **Sample Merged** unchecked, only pixels on the current layer determine what areas are to be filled. With **Sample Merged** checked, the pixels of all layers are examined to see what areas are to be filled, just as if the layers were merged. Only areas on the current layer are actually affected, however. You'll explore **Sample Merged** in more detail in Chapter 4.

The Warp Brush and Mesh Warp Tool

Paint Shop Pro 8 has two new tools that enable you to warp an image: the Warp Brush and the Mesh Warp tool. These tools aren't painting tools per se, but they affect existing painted areas. Each of these tools allows you to move pixels around in a controlled way.

The Warp Brush

Let's look first at the Warp Brush, whose Tool Options palette is shown in Figure 2.31.

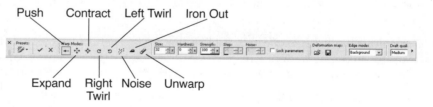

Figure 2.31
The Tool Options palette for the Warp Brush.

In addition to some of the controls also available with the Paint Brush, the Warp Brush has several **Warp Modes**:

> ▶ **Push.** Pushes pixels, moving them in the direction of the brushstroke.
>
> ▶ **Expand.** Enlarges the area under the brush. The effect increases the longer you hold down the mouse button.
>
> ▶ **Contract.** Shrinks the area under the brush. The effect increases the longer you hold down the mouse button.
>
> ▶ **Right Twirl.** Swirls the pixels under the brush to the right, as if the image were a thick liquid being stirred. The effect increases the longer you hold down the mouse button.

▶ **Left Twirl.** Swirls the pixels under the brush to the left, as if the image were a thick liquid being stirred. The effect increases the longer you hold down the mouse button.

▶ **Noise.** Warps the pixels under the brush pseudo-randomly. Use this mode to give a more natural look to the edges of drawn or painted objects.

▶ **Iron Out.** Undoes the effects of a previous warp. In order for this to have an effect, you must drag the mouse across an area of warped pixels (much like using a real iron).

▶ **Unwarp.** Undoes the effect of a previous warp. Unlike **Iron Out**, **Unwarp** has an effect as soon as you click with the mouse. The effect increases the longer you hold down the mouse button.

The various other settings for Warp Brush affect how each **Warp Mode** modifies your image. The size of your brush and the setting for **Strength** are perhaps the most important. In general, a large brush produces a more subtle effect than a small one. And a time-dependent brush like **Push** or **Unwarp** has a stronger effect more quickly when **Strength** has a high value.

The **Noise** setting that is active when **Warp Mode** is set to **Noise** affects how sharp or jagged the introduced randomness effect appears. Higher values produce a more jagged effect, while lower values produce a smoother effect.

You might think that the Warp Brush is just a toy, good for torturing photos of your friends or pets. You certainly can use the Warp Brush in this way, and it definitely is fun to do so. For example, starting with the photo in Figure 2.32, you can produce wickedly warped versions like the one in Figure 2.33.

However, the Warp Brush has more practical and benign uses as well. Using much more subtle modifications, you can change a person's age or expression, for example. Compare the original portrait in Figure 2.32 with the version in Figure 2.34, where the friendly young man is warped into an angry young man.

To get these more subtle effects, try using a rather large brush (so that the warping effects are not abrupt) with **Strength** set relatively low. And remember to take advantage of **Iron Out** and **Unwarp** to selectively undo some of the effects you get with the other **Warp Modes**.

You'll explore the Warp Brush more in some of the examples later in this book.

The Mesh Warp Tool

With Mesh Warp, a mesh is superimposed on your image. When you move the nodes of this mesh, the image is warped.

▶ Move individual nodes by dragging them. This warps the image area near the node in the direction in which the node is moved.

▶ When the Shift key is down, all the nodes in the row or column move together in a line, pulling all the pixels in the row or column in the direction in which the nodes are moved. See Figure 2.35, where a Picture Frame on a layer is being resized with Mesh Warp.

Figure 2.32
A normal photographic
portrait.

Figure 2.33
A completely warped
variation.

Figure 2.34
A friendly fellow warped
into an angry guy.

▶ To move a whole row or column of nodes to form a curve, hold down the Ctrl key as you drag. When the Ctrl key is down, the pixels at the node you drag are moved more than the adjacent nodes, which are moved more than the nodes farther out from them, so that a curved warping is produced. See Figure 2.36, where text is being warped into an egg shape.

Figure 2.35
Moving a column of pixels in a straight line.

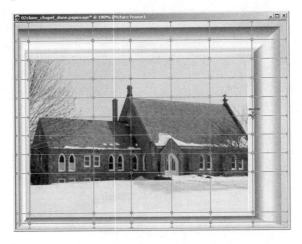

Figure 2.36
Forming a curved effect along a row of pixels.

Do some warping, change the warp grid, and do some more warping, if you wish. When you have an effect you like, click the **Apply** button in the Tool Options palette. If you make a mistake, click the **Undo** button on the menu bar. And if you think it would be better to go back to the drawing board, click the **Cancel** button on the Tool Options palette and start again. As you get more and more comfortable with the Mesh Warp tool, you'll find that you can achieve quite complex warp effects without a whole lot of effort.

TIP

You can save the warping effects of either the Mesh Warp tool or the Warp Brush as a deformation map, and any deformation map can be loaded in either one of these tools. To save a deformation map, click the **Save** icon in the **Deformation map** segment of the Mesh Warp or Warp Brush's Tool Options palette and enter a name for your deformation map. To load a deformation map, click the **Load** icon there and select the deformation map you want.

3

Being Selective

Now let's look at the basic tools and techniques for making and using selections. We'll see how to modify the shape of a selection, how to copy and paste a selection, and how to move the content of a selection or eliminate it entirely.

Here's what you'll be exploring in this chapter:

▶ Using the selection tools

▶ Making standard selections and floating selections

▶ Using operations in the Selections menu to alter or create selections

▶ Using the Edit operations to cut, copy, and paste selections

▶ Using Clear to fill a selection or image with color or transparency

Making Selections

You can restrict image editing to a part of your image by making a selection. Some selection functions are performed with the Selections menu, which is shown in Figure 3.1, and you also can make a selection from a mask. You'll probably make most selections, however, by using one of the selection tools.

Figure 3.1
The Selections menu.

Following are the three tools that you can use to make selections:

▶ **Selection tool.** Use this tool to define a regularly shaped selection by dragging the cursor.

▶ **Freehand Selection tool.** Use this tool to define an irregularly shaped selection by dragging the cursor. Good for isolating a figure in an image.

▶ **Magic Wand.** Use this tool to define a selection based on color, hue, brightness, or opacity. Excellent for selecting a solid-colored area, such as a background in a drawing.

The edges of a selection are marked with a marquee, a flashing line of dashes popularly referred to as "marching ants." Notice the selection marquee in Figure 3.2, which shows a star-shaped selection on a solid-colored image.

The edge of a selection can be sharp or soft. To soften the edges of a selection, you can feather the selection. To set the feather, either use the Tool Options palette of a selection tool or, after making a selection, choose **S**elections > **M**odify > **F**eather from the menu bar.

Figure 3.3 shows an example of a nonfeathered selection cut from one image and pasted onto a solid background along with a pasted-in feathered selection. The zoom factor of this example is set to 400 percent so that you can see the difference better. Notice how the edges of the feathered version are softer than the edges of the nonfeathered version.

Figure 3.2
A selection marquee
(a.k.a. "marching ants").

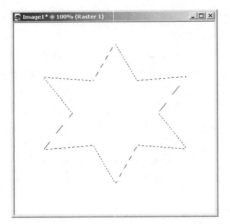

Figure 3.3
A nonfeathered selection
(left) and a feathered
selection (right) pasted
onto a solid background.

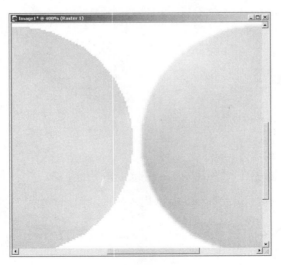

NOTE

Another way to blend the edges of a selection with the background is to check **Anti-alias** in the Tool Options palette of a selection tool. Antialiasing works much like feathering, but the transition between the selection and the background is more limited with antialiasing. Both feathering and antialiasing are covered in more depth later in this chapter, along with cutting and pasting.

You can move selections by clicking inside them and dragging with either a selection tool or the Mover tool (whose icon in the Tool palette looks like two crossed double-headed arrows). Whether the content of the image moves along with the selection depends on whether the selection is a standard selection or a floating selection.

▶ **Standard selection.** A standard selection is like a cookie cutter pressed into your image. Move a standard selection, and the image's contents also move.

▶ **Floating selection.** As its name suggests, a floating selection "floats" above your image. Move a floating selection, and the selection's contents move, but the pixels below the selection remain unaffected.

Figures 3.4 and 3.5 illustrate the difference between standard and floating selections.

Figure 3.4
Moving a standard selection.

Figure 3.5
Moving a floating selection.

CHAPTER 3

Figure 3.4 shows a standard selection that has been moved up and to the right. Notice how the pixels of the original image have been moved, whereas the area from which the selection was moved is filled with the current Background color.

Figure 3.5 shows a floating selection. This selection has also been moved up and to the right. Here, the floating selection and its contents have moved, but the pixels of the original image are unaffected.

NOTE

After you move a standard selection, it automatically becomes a floating selection.

CAUTION

If you try to move a standard selection that contains only transparency, you'll receive the error message "This operation could not be completed because the current layer does not contain any active data within the current selection area."

To reposition the marquee of such a selection, choose the Mover tool, right-click inside the selection area, and drag with the right mouse button depressed. This method of moving only the selection marquee also works when the selection contains pixels—the pixels are unaffected, but the marquee is repositioned.

NOTE

When you have a layer that includes transparency, and you make a selection around a figure on that layer, the selection marquee snaps to the edges of the figure if you move the selection.

To turn off a selection, right-click with a selection tool anywhere on the image canvas, press Ctrl+D, or choose **S**elections > Select **N**one.

What you've seen so far applies to all selections. Now it's time to explore each of the selection tools and take a closer look at the Selections menu. In a few places, some things about layers and selections are mentioned. If you don't yet know much about layers, just skip over those remarks for now. You will return to selections in multilayered images in Chapter 5, "Mastering Selections, Masks, and Channels."

The Selection Tool

The easiest selection tool to use is called, quite appropriately, the Selection tool (see Figure 3.6). You use this tool to define a selection that has any one of several predefined shapes, including Rectangle, Square, Ellipse, Circle, and others. A rectangle, square, or other nonellipsoid selection is defined by dragging from one corner to the diagonally opposite corner, whereas a selection in the shape of an ellipse or circle is defined by dragging from the center outward.

You use the Tool Options palette to set the **Selection Type** (that is, the shape of the selection) and whether the selection is feathered or antialiased. Other controls for this tool include the **Mode** (Replace, Add, or Remove), the **Custom Selection** button, and the **Create selection from** buttons.

Figure 3.6
Defining a selection with
the Selection tool.

The Freehand Selection Tool

You won't always want a regularly shaped selection. To make irregularly shaped selections, use the Freehand Selection tool (also called the lasso).

When the Freehand Selection tool is active, four **Selection Types** are available in the Tool Options palette: Edge Seeker (Figure 3.7), Freehand (Figure 3.8), Point to Point (Figure 3.9), and Smart Edge (Figure 3.10). Except for Smart Edge, there is no real difference in the appearance of the tool in these various modes. The difference in the tool's behavior is significant, though.

Figure 3.7
Edge Seeker enables you
to drag the mouse along
an edge, with the
selection marquee
snapping to the edge.
Excellent for isolating a
figure on a background.

NOTE
To undo the last selection point that you set with Edge Seeker, Point to Point, or Smart Edge, just press the Delete key. Repeat as needed to undo previous selection points.

Figure 3.8
Freehand enables you to drag the mouse to draw a freeform selection.

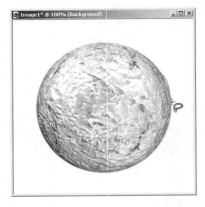

Figure 3.9
Point to Point enables you to click various points, usually around the edges of a figure, to define the edges of your selection. This has the effect of roping off a figure or other area of your image.

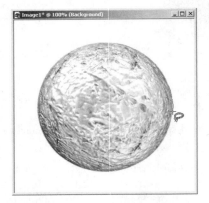

Figure 3.10
Smart Edge enables you to click along the edge of a figure, with Paint Shop Pro defining the selection edge based on differences in contrast. Good for isolating a figure on a background.

In addition to controls for setting **Selection type**, **Mode**, **Feather**, and **Anti-alias**, the Tool Options palette for the Freehand Selection tool in all its selection types has a control for **Smoothing**. Increase the value for **Smoothing** to reduce the jaggedness of the selection edge.

Edge Seeker and Smart Edge also have a control labeled **Sample Merged**. This control is meaningful only for multilayered images. When this control is checked, the selection is made

TIP

If you make your own Picture Tubes, you might find that Edge Seeker and Smart Edge are especially useful for creating tube elements from scanned images. Make sure that the background you use during the scan contrasts with the objects that you're scanning. (You might, for example, cover the objects with a light-colored cloth if the scanner cover provides a background that's too dark.) Then use Edge Seeker or Smart Edge to isolate the scanned objects. You might need to adjust the selection a bit, but Edge Seeker or Smart Edge will do most of the work.

(To make your own Picture Tubes, see Chapter 11, "Adding to Your Toolkit.")

as if all visible layers in the image were merged into a single layer. When this control is *not* checked, the selection is made based only on the pixels on the currently active layer.

Edge Seeker has one other control: **Range**. This control determines how far from the selection point Paint Shop Pro should look for an edge to snap to.

The Magic Wand

One of the handiest of Paint Shop Pro's tools is the Magic Wand, which can truly be magical. The Magic Wand enables you to make selections based on the color, hue, brightness, or opacity of a target pixel that you click on in your image. The pixels that are selected will either match the target pixel exactly or fall within a tolerance range, depending on the settings you select.

The Tool Options palette for the Magic Wand has controls for **Mode**, **Match mode**, **Tolerance**, **Sample Merged**, **Feather**, and **Anti-alias** (see Figure 3.11). You can also choose whether to add the antialiasing inside or outside the selection.

Figure 3.11
Tool Options palette for the Magic Wand.

Match Mode

Match mode determines what the Magic Wand uses as the basis for selection. The following lists the available **Match mode** settings, along with a description of how each setting affects the Magic Wand's selection criteria:

- ▶ **None.** Pixels are selected with no restriction. In other words, all pixels are selected.
- ▶ **RGB Value.** The pixels selected match the Red-Green-Blue color value of the target pixel. This is the mode you undoubtedly will use most often.
- ▶ **Color.** The pixels selected match the color of the target pixel (that is, the hue and saturation only). This enables you to make a selection without regard to the pixel's brightness.
- ▶ **Hue.** The pixels selected match the Hue value of the target pixel (where, for example, 0 is red, 85 is green, and 170 is blue). This enables you to make a selection without regard to the pixel's saturation or brightness.

▶ **Brightness.** The pixels selected match the target pixel's brightness rather than its color. This might be useful, for example, if you want to select a dark figure on a light background.

▶ **All Opaque.** The selection includes all contiguous pixels in nontransparent areas.

▶ **Opacity.** The pixels selected match the target pixel's level of opacity.

Tolerance

Tolerance determines how closely pixels must match the target pixel. A **Tolerance** setting of 0 restricts the selection to pixels that match the target exactly. A **Tolerance** of 200, the maximum, makes your selection match all areas of your image. Different intermediate **Tolerance** values match more or less closely to the target. Figures 3.12 through 3.14 show examples of the selections made by clicking on the same pixel with the Magic Wand with **Match mode** set to Brightness and with **Tolerance** settings of 10, 40, and 90, respectively.

Figure 3.12
Tolerance set to 10.

Figure 3.13
Tolerance set to 40.

Figure 3.14
Tolerance set to 90.

CAUTION
Keep in mind that **Tolerance** and **Match mode** can influence each other. When **Tolerance** is set to 200, all areas are matched regardless of the **Match mode** setting. When **Match mode** is set to None, all areas are matched regardless of the **Tolerance** setting.

Feather and Sample Merged

Feather settings work just as they do with the other selection tools, and **Sample Merged** works just as it does with the Freehand Selection tool. **Feather** settings soften the edges of the selection, blending them in with the background. **Sample Merged** treats all visible layers of a multilayered image as if the layers were merged together as a single layer, operating on the pixels on all the visible layers.

Adding to and Subtracting from a Selection

When you make a complex selection, you normally start with a simple selection and then edit that selection by adding to it or subtracting from it. Paint Shop Pro provides an easy way to add to and subtract from a selection. With any of the selection tools, set the **Mode** to Add to add to a selection or set the **Mode** to Remove to subtract from a selection. (If you want to make a new selection, without regard to any previously defined selection, set the **Mode** to Replace.)

Another way to add to a selection, no matter what the **Mode** is set to, is to hold down the Shift key and click or drag. Unless you've set up Paint Shop Pro to use a precise cursor, a plus sign (+) will appear near the cursor to remind you that you're adding to the selection. To subtract from a selection, no matter what the **Mode** is set to, hold down the Ctrl key and click or drag. A minus sign (-) will appear near the cursor to remind you that you're subtracting from a selection.

Suppose that you start with an image such as the one in Figure 3.15, and you want to select the two lower spheres but not the sphere in the upper-right corner.

Figure 3.15
An image that contains
figures you want to
select.

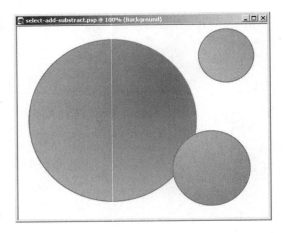

To start, you can choose the Magic Wand, set it to a fairly high **Tolerance** setting, and then click one of the lower spheres. The result might look something like Figure 3.16.

That didn't quite do the trick. What you could do, then, is click the Undo button and try again at a higher **Tolerance** setting, but that really isn't necessary. Instead, just Shift-click with the Magic Wand in one of the unselected areas that you want included in the selection. Continue in this way until you have the entire area that you want selected.

Figure 3.17 shows an intermediate step in adding to the selection, and Figure 3.18 shows the complete selection.

Another approach that you can take with the image in Figure 3.15 is to start by selecting the white background and then inverting the selection with **S**elections > **I**nvert. This produces the selection in Figure 3.19.

Now you want to eliminate the upper sphere from the selection. An easy way to do this is to choose the Freehand Selection tool and set it to **Freehand** mode. Then hold down the Ctrl key and drag around the area that you want to remove from the selection. Figure 3.20 shows this step in progress, with the end result being the same as you saw in Figure 3.18.

Figure 3.16
Beginning the selection.

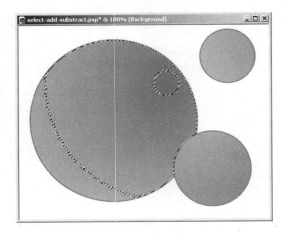

Figure 3.17
Adding to the selection.

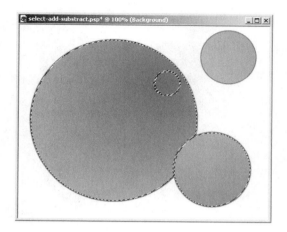

Figure 3.18
The complete selection.

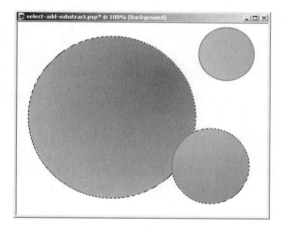

Figure 3.19
Select the figures by selecting the background and inverting the selection.

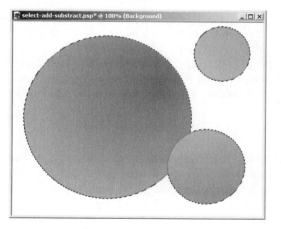

Figure 3.20
Subtracting from the
selection.

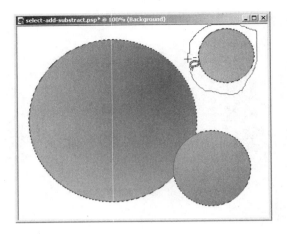

The Selections Menu

The Selections menu enables you to alter a selection, make a selection from a mask, "promote" a selection to a layer, save a selection to disk or to an alpha channel, load a selection from disk or from an alpha channel, and modify or edit a selection.

Many of the items on the Selections menu, such as From Mask, are examined in Chapter 5, but for now take a look at the items that enable you to alter a selection.

Select All and Select None

The first two items on the Selections menu are Select All and Select None, which do exactly as their names suggest. Choosing Select All selects all areas of an image (or, in a multilayered image, all areas on a layer). Choosing Select None turns off a selection and is equivalent to right-clicking your image with a selection tool.

NOTE

In most cases, using **S**elections > Select **A**ll is unnecessary. By default, most Paint Shop Pro operations—including, for example, **E**dit > **C**opy—affect the entire flat image or layer anyway.

Select All is most useful when you don't actually want the entire image or layer selected. To get the selection you want, you might first choose Select All and then choose **S**elections > **M**odify. We'll see an example of this later in this chapter.

Invert

The fifth item on the Selections menu is **Invert**. This is a handy operation, especially when used in combination with the Magic Wand (as you saw earlier in this chapter). When using the Magic Wand, you'll often find that selecting what you *don't* want selected is easier than selecting what you *do* want selected. If you select the areas of your image that you don't want and then choose **S**elections > Invert, the selection is inverted, and the resulting selection is the part of the image that you *did* want selected.

TIP

You can easily invert an existing selection by pressing Shift+Ctrl+I.

Matting

The next Selections menu item, **Matting,** has three subitems: **Defringe, Remove Black Matte,** and **Remove White Matte.** Each of these works only with floating selections (discussed later in this chapter) and only with greyscale or 16-million color images.

NOTE

To use any of the Matting operations on a selection, you must have a floating selection. If you have a standard selection instead, choose **S**elections > **F**loat to change your selection to a floating selection.

Defringe, Remove Black Matte, and **Remove White Matte** are used to remove pixels that are blended into the edge of a selection as a result of feathering or antialiasing. **Remove Black Matte** and **Remove White Matte** are for removing black and white fringe, respectively. **Defringe** is for removing any other Background color fringe.

TIP

You'll probably find that you get much better results if you defringe by hand. Select the area outside your figure using the Magic Wand. Expand the selection by a pixel or so with **S**elections > **M**odify > **E**xpand. Then feather the selection a bit with **S**elections > **M**odify > **F**eather. Press the Delete key, and then turn off the selection with **S**elections > **S**elect **N**one.

Modify

The **Modify** menu selection can be used for all sorts of things. The operations under **Modify** include such operations as **Contract, Expand,** and **Feather,** each of which is pretty much self-explanatory. Use **Contract** to make a selection smaller by a number of pixels, use **Expand** to make a selection larger by a number of pixels, and use **Feather** to feather a selection by a number of pixels. The other operations available under **S**elections > **M**odify are explained here:

▶ **Select Similar.** Expands the selection within the current **Tolerance** setting, which usually changes the basic shape of the selection quite drastically. You can choose to include pixels that are discontiguous with the selected pixels or restrict the expansion to contiguous pixels only. Figures 3.21 through 3.23 illustrate this difference. Figure 3.21 shows the original selection, Figure 3.22 shows the results of applying **Select Similar** with **Tolerance** set to 20 and **Contiguous** selected, and Figure 3.23 shows the result of applying **Select Similar** with the same **Tolerance** setting of 20 and **Discontiguous** selected.

CHAPTER 3

Figure 3.21
Original selection.

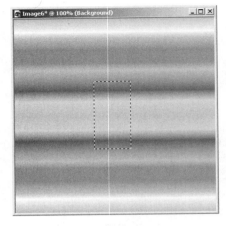

Figure 3.22
Select Similar with
Contiguous selected.

Figure 3.23
Select Similar with
Discontiguous selected.

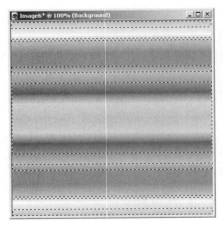

▶ **Select Color Range.** Also expands the selection based on the color of pixels in the current selection, within the current **Tolerance**.

Enables you to add or subtract pixels of a particular color from the current selection. When you choose **S**elections > **M**odify > Select Color Range, the dialog box that appears lets you set the color that you want to add to or eliminate from the selection, within whatever **Tolerance** level you choose. There is also a control for **Softness**, which determines how hard or soft the modified selection edges will be.

Here's one of the times that choosing Select All can come in handy. Suppose that you have black hollow shapes on a multicolored background, as in Figure 3.24, and you want to select everything but the shapes.

You can choose **S**elections > Select **A**ll, followed by **S**elections > **M**odify > Select Color Range with the color set to black and **Subtract color range** selected. The result is shown in Figure 3.25.

This is a good way to isolate either the content of an outlined image or the outline itself. Isolating an outline is just what you want if you're trying to add a metallic texture to a hand-drawn stained-glass window, for example. To select only the outline, use the method just described followed by **S**elections > Invert.

Be careful when you use Select Color Range, however. All instances of the color that you choose will be added to or eliminated from the selection. This might go too far, adding areas that you don't want or eliminating areas of the selection that you do want to include in the selection.

TIP

Remember that with Windows 2000 and later Windows versions you can set the color in any color box to a color sampled from your image (or one appearing elsewhere on your screen). Position the cursor over the color box, holding down the Ctrl key. Then with the Ctrl key down, move the cursor to the color you want to sample and click.

Use this method with Select Color Range to set the target color to a color that appears in your image.

Figure 3.24
Original image with black hollow shapes.

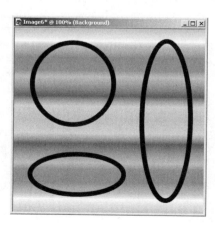

Figure 3.25
Selections > Modify >
Select Color Range
applied after Selections >
Select All.

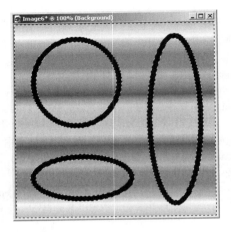

▶ **Inside/Outside Feather.** Enables you to add feathering to your selection.

▶ **Unfeather.** Enables you to remove feathering from your selection.

▶ **Shape-based Anti-alias.** Enables you to add antialiasing to your selection, based on the selection's shape.

▶ **Recover Anti-alias.** Enables you to restore antialiasing to a pasted-in selection.

▶ **Remove Specks and Holes.** Sometimes when you use the Magic Wand to create a selection, or when you use Select Color Range to add to a selection, the selection includes stray specks or has small holes in it. You can eliminate these with Selections > Modify > Remove Specks and Holes.

▶ **Smooth.** Smooths the edges of a hand-drawn selection.

▶ **Select Selection Borders.** Creates a selection from the edges of the current selection. You choose the width of the new selection and whether it is created inside the current selection edge, outside the edge, or straddling the edge.

Hide Marquee

The next item in the Selections menu, Hide Marquee, can be quite useful. In fact, setting Hide Marquee is a good idea when you're defringing by hand; that way, the effect on the edge is clear during the editing, because the marquee isn't covering the edge. Hide Marquee makes the selection marquee invisible until you uncheck Hide Marquee again. The selection border is still there—you just can't see it. Use Hide Marquee whenever you need to see what's happening at the edge of your selection.

CAUTION
After you check Hide Marquee, it's easy to forget that you have a selection! If you're trying to paint in your image and nothing seems to happen, or if your paint is applied only in part of your image, check whether the selection marquee is hidden. You might have a selection set and not know it.

Edit Selection

With Edit Selection toggled on, you can paint a selection onto your image and modify the selection just as you would a greyscale image. Until you toggle Edit Selection off, all changes are made to the selection rather than to the image.

We'll look at Edit Selection in detail in Chapter 5.

Edit Operations

The Edit operations, which are all available both from the Edit menu and through keyboard shortcuts, include **Cut**, **Copy**, several **Paste** operations, and **Clear**. The basic Edit operations—**Cut**, **Copy**, and **Paste as New Image**—are also available as the standard Windows icons on the standard toolbar.

Cut and Copy

Basically, two ways exist to copy pixels to the Windows Clipboard, thereby making those pixels available for insertion elsewhere. Pixels can be either *cut* from an image, which both deletes the pixels from the original image and places them on the Clipboard, or *copied* from the image to the Clipboard, leaving the pixels in the original image as they were.

To cut all the pixels from a flat image or from a layer, choose **E**dit > **C**ut or press Ctrl+X (the standard Windows shortcut for Cut). Alternatively, you can click the standard Windows **Cut** icon on the Paint Shop Pro Standard toolbar. If you want to cut only some of the pixels from the image or layer, first select the area that you want to cut, and then use any of the methods just mentioned to remove the selection from the original and place those pixels on the Clipboard.

You can copy pixels to the Clipboard just as easily—and in just as many ways. To copy all the pixels from a flat image or a layer, choose **E**dit > **C**opy or press Ctrl+C (the standard Windows shortcut for **Copy**). You also can click the standard Windows **Copy** icon on the Paint Shop Pro Standard toolbar. As with **Cut**, you can copy portions of the image or layer by first making a selection and then applying **Copy** in any of the ways just mentioned.

Cut and **Copy** will take only the pixels on a single layer. To copy the pixels from all visible layers in an image, choose **E**dit > **C**opy Merged or press Shift+Ctrl+C. No equivalent way exists to perform a one-step **Cut** on all visible layers. Probably the best approach for cutting a multilayered selection is to do a **Copy Merged** (to create a copy that you can paste later) and then delete the selection on each individual layer by first making one layer active and pressing the Delete key, and then making the next layer active and pressing the Delete key, and so on. Turn off the selection only after you've finished making deletions on all the relevant layers.

When you cut or copy from a selection, keep in mind that any antialiasing or feathering of a selection affects the copy. With antialiasing or feathering, the edges of the copied area will be softened, picking up or blending into the original image's Background color or transparency. You can use this to your advantage when you later paste this material. But if you want a sharp edge on your copied material, be sure to uncheck **Anti-alias** and set **Feather** to 0 in the Tool Options palette *before* you make your selection.

Paste

Five basic Edit operations are available for pasting material from the Clipboard:

▶ **Edit > Paste > Paste As New Image (Ctrl+V).** Creates a new image from whatever material is currently on the Clipboard. The dimensions of the new image will be the minimal rectangle that can surround the pasted-in material, and the color depth will match that of the source of the pasted-in material. Any background areas not covered by the pasted-in material will be transparent if the color depth was 24-bit color or greyscale when Paint Shop Pro was loaded; otherwise, the background areas will be filled with the current Background color set in the Materials palette.

TIP

Here's a convenient way to **Paste As New Image**: Right-click on an empty area of Paint Shop Pro's workspace or on an image's title bar. Then, in the resulting menu, choose **Paste As New Image**.

The menu presented when you right-click on the title bar is more extensive than the one presented when you right-click on the workspace. On the title bar menu you can select any of the **Cut**, **Copy**, or **Paste** operations.

▶ **Edit > Paste > Paste As New Layer (Ctrl+L).** Places the pasted-in material on a new layer in the currently active image canvas. (This option is inactive for images with color depths other than 24-bit color or greyscale.) Any areas on the new layer that are not filled with the pasted-in material will be transparent. If the material is larger than the image canvas, the outer edges of the material "fall off the edges"— the material is still there, but it's outside the canvas area and thus can't be seen. Regardless of whether the material fits completely in the image canvas, it can be repositioned on its layer with the Mover tool.

▶ **Edit > Paste > Paste As New Selection (Ctrl+E).** Pastes the material on the Clipboard into the currently active image as a floating selection above the image's currently active layer. You can position the selection by dragging until you anchor it in place by clicking. You can then manipulate the pasted-in selection like any other floating selection. You can defloat it, reposition it by dragging with a selection tool or the Mover tool, modify it by choosing **S**elections > **M**odify, and so on.

If the pasted-in selection is too large to fit inside the image canvas, it "falls off the edges," just like a pasted-in layer. As long as the selection is kept floating, the material outside the image canvas is not destroyed, and repositioning the selection can reveal hidden areas of the selection. However, once the selection is defloated (by choosing **S**elections > **D**efloat or pressing Shift+Ctrl+F), the areas outside the image canvas are deleted, and the shape of the selection changes to include only the areas visible in the image canvas.

▶ **Edit > Paste > Paste As Transparent Selection (Shift+Ctrl+E).** Similar to choosing Paste As New Selection, except that any pixels in the material on the Clipboard that match the current Background color (as set in the Materials palette) are eliminated from the pasted-in selection. Figure 3.26 shows an example of a pasted-in selection made by choosing Paste As New Selection; Figure 3.27 shows the same material pasted in by choosing Paste As Transparent Selection with white as the current Background color.

Figure 3.26
Results of choosing **E**dit >
Paste > Paste As New
Selection.

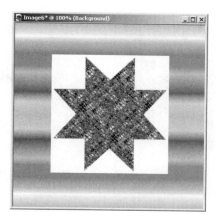

Figure 3.27
Results of choosing
Edit > **P**aste > Paste As
Transparent Selection.

▶ **Edit > Paste > Paste Into Selection (Shift+Ctrl+L).** Great for filling a text selection or other irregularly shaped selection with an image. The pasted-in material is adjusted to fit inside the selection. If the selection is too big, the material is stretched; if the selection is too small, the material is compressed. Figure 3.28 shows both an image that was copied to the Clipboard and a text selection filled with that material by choosing Paste Into Selection.

NOTE

When you fill a selection with a texture, remember that an important difference exists between using Paste Into Selection and filling with a seamless pattern. When you use Paste Into Selection, the copied pattern stretches to fit the dimensions of the selected area. When you add a seamless pattern with the Flood Fill tool, however, the pattern tile maintains its original dimensions and repeats to fill the selection. Compare Figure 3.29 with Figure 3.28.

The method you should choose in any given instance depends on the effect you want to produce.

Figure 3.28
Text selection filled with
material by choosing
Edit > **P**aste > Paste Into
Selection.

Figure 3.29
The text selection filled
with the seamless tile by
using Flood Fill.

Clear

Choosing **E**dit > **C**lear (the keyboard shortcut for which is the Delete key) is an operation that you might find quite useful.

On a flat image or Background layer, Clear replaces pixels with the current Background color set in the Color Palette. On a layer, Clear replaces pixels with transparency. If you want to replace all the pixels in a flat image or layer, make sure that either no selection is active or Select All is in effect, and then invoke Clear. Figure 3.30 shows an example of a text selection on a solid-white layer with all of the selection's pixels deleted with the Delete key, revealing the patterned layer underneath.

Figure 3.30
Using Clear to eliminate
pixels in a selection on a
layer.

This completes your preliminary look at selections. You'll return to the subject of selections in Chapter 5.

SpaceCat.PSPimage.

Background layer.

Yellow Planet layer.

Cat layer.

A text layer above a
pattern-filled layer.

An Invert adjustment layer
applied to both layers.

Invert restricted to the text
layer using a layer group.

A patterned
Background layer.

A gradient layer above the
Background layer.

Blend range affecting Opacity
of gradient layer: visible only
above dark layers of pattern.

Blend range affecting Opacity
of gradient layer: visible only
above light layers of pattern.

Image (upper left) applied as a mask on a dark layer to let a lighter underlying layer show through.

Image with blue color cast.

Cast removed by editing Blue channel.

Examples of recombined or edited channels.

Original photo.

One Step Photo Fix.

Black-and-White Points: Black (8, 3, 9), Grey (58, 49, 51), White (167, 158, 165), Preserve lightness, Balance to grey.

Grey World Color Balance: Temperature 6184.

Manual Color Correction: Source (172, 158, 169), Target (192, 192, 192).

Curves: Points located at (0,0), (29,11), (116, 129), (210, 241), (255, 255).

Histogram Adjustment: Low 5 (0.054%), High 245 (0.002%), Gamma 1.25.

Levels: Input levels 4, 1.19, 244.

Unsharp Mask: Radius 1.40, Strength 100, Clipping 5.

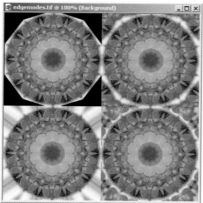

Kaleidoscope effect with different Edge Modes: Color (top left),
Reflect (top right), Repeat (bottom left), and Wrap (bottom right).

Watercolor effect produced with Erode and Edge Preserving Smooth.

First photo to combine in a panorama.

Second photo to add to the panorama.

Third photo to combine in a panorama.

The completed panorama.

Original vector clip art.

Recolored vector clip art.

4

Mastering Layers and Blend Modes

Sometimes you want to be able to manipulate different parts of your image independently of each other, without affecting any other part of your image. In this case, you'll want to make use of layers. In this chapter, you'll explore the layers and how to blend them together.

Here's what you'll be exploring in this chapter:

▶ Manipulating raster layers
▶ Using layer opacity, blend modes, and blend ranges to create various effects
▶ Understanding adjustment layers
▶ Taking a first look at masks

Layer Basics

One of the most popular and powerful features of Paint Shop Pro is layers. You'll probably find that you use layers in the majority of your Paint Shop Pro projects. And if you're a graphic artist whose work involves a lot of compositing, nearly all of your image editing will involve layering.

Layers let you manipulate different components of your image independently. This can enable you to, for example, apply an effect or a filter to only part of your image, reposition or rotate a figure in the image without affecting the background, or blend one part of your image into another.

Paint Shop Pro has four types of layers. In this chapter, we'll look at three of these: raster layers, adjustment layers, and mask layers. You "paint" with pixels on a raster layer. Adjustment layers enable you to affect color, brightness, or contrast on underlying layers without actually changing any data on those layers. Mask layers (also simply called masks) are rather like adjustment layers, except that instead of color, brightness, and contrast, the opacity of underlying layers is affected. We'll explore masks in more detail in Chapter 5, "Mastering Selections, Masks, and Channels." And in Chapter 6, "Working with Vectors," we'll explore the fourth type of layer, vector layers.

Think of a layer as a clear sheet of acetate on which you can paint. A multilayered image is like a stack of these acetate sheets, each with its own image elements. With raster layers, areas of a sheet that are unpainted are transparent, allowing the image elements of lower sheets to show through. Areas of a sheet that are opaque block out image elements on lower sheets. Finally, areas of a sheet that are semitransparent partially reveal image elements on lower sheets.

Extending this analogy further, the order of the sheets in the stack can be changed. One or more sheets can be removed from the stack, either temporarily or permanently, and other sheets can be added to the stack.

Getting Acquainted with Layers

Let's take a look at a simple example of a multilayered image to get a better idea of what layers are. Figure 4.1 shows an image with three layers, one named Background, one named Cat, and one named Yellow Planet.

Figures 4.2 through 4.4 show each of the three layers separately. The layer named Background, which is totally opaque, is filled with a dark, starry sky. The Yellow Planet layer contains a solid-yellow circle, with the rest of the layer transparent. The Cat layer contains the head of a cat, with the rest of the layer transparent (the checkerboard pattern that you see "behind" the cat is what Paint Shop Pro shows by default to indicate transparent areas).

Figure 4.1
Simple multilayered image.

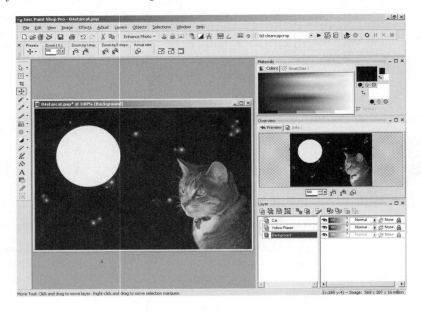

Figure 4.2
The Background layer.

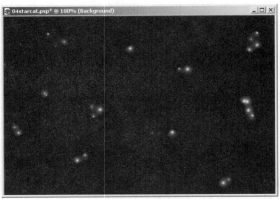

Figure 4.3
The Yellow Planet layer.

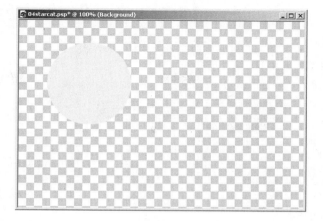

Figure 4.4
The Cat layer.

NOTE
If you want to work through this example, you can find it at
http://www.courseptr.com/downloads.

The palette showing on the bottom right of the screen in Figure 4.1 is the Layer palette, which you can toggle on and off by pressing the F8 key on the keyboard. Although there are quite a few ways to manipulate layers, using the Layer palette is generally the easiest way to control layers. Let's examine the Layer palette, shown in Figure 4.5, more closely.

The left pane of the palette includes a column of rectangular, labeled buttons. These buttons, the layer buttons, correspond to each of the layers in your image. The layer button at the bottom of the column corresponds to the "lowest" layer in the stack of layers, and each layer button up the column corresponds to an increasingly higher layer in the stack.

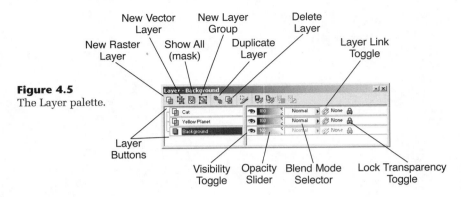

Figure 4.5
The Layer palette.

In the right pane of the Layer palette are several more controls for each layer, including a **Layer Visibility** toggle, which looks like an eye. Above the two panes is a row of clickable icons for various layer commands, including the **New Raster Layer** button (which looks like a pair of acetate sheets) on the far left and the **Delete Layer** button (which looks like a pair of acetate sheets with a red X) located several icons to the right.

The following is a quick summary of what the basic Layer palette controls are used for. You'll try out each of these controls, along with a few others, later in the chapter.

▶ **Layer Button.** Click a layer button to make its layer the active layer. In most cases, Paint Shop Pro tools and operations affect only the active layer.

Double-click a layer button to open the Layer Properties dialog box, which is one means of manipulating a layer.

Right-click a layer button to open a menu that contains most of the commands available on the Layers menu on the Paint Shop Pro menu bar.

Position the mouse cursor over a layer button, without clicking, to see a thumbnail of the button's associated layer. The thumbnail disappears when you move the cursor away from the layer button.

▶ **Opacity Slider.** Nontransparent areas on a layer can be entirely opaque or semitransparent. To adjust the opacity of a layer, move the **Opacity** slider (located in the right pane, just to the right of the **Visibility** toggle). Moving the slider to the left makes pixels on the layer less opaque, and moving the slider to the right increases the opacity of the pixels. (Keep in mind, though, that you can't use the **Opacity** control to make pixels any more opaque than they were when they were painted on the layer.)

▶ **New Raster Layer Button** and **Delete Layer Button.** Click the **New Raster Layer** button on the Layer palette toolbar to create a new, empty layer "above" the current active layer.

Click the **Delete Layer** button on the Layer palette toolbar to delete the current active layer.

NOTE

The Background layer does not have an active **Opacity** slider. This special layer, created when you either open a new image with an opaque background or flatten a layered image, does not have a transparency channel. If you have a Background layer and want it to have a transparency channel, right-click any layer button and in the context menu choose **Promote Background Layer**. The Background layer's name will change from Background to Raster *n*, where *n* is a number determined by the current number of raster layers in the image.

An alternative way of promoting the Background to a layer is to double-click the Background's layer button, which brings up the Layer Properties dialog box. Click OK and the Background is automatically promoted and its name changed to Raster *n*.

TIP

If you're not sure what an icon on the Layer palette toolbar is for, hover the mouse cursor over the icon. A tool tip will appear that shows the descriptive name of the icon.

Working with Layers

Let's now return to the simple three-layer example shown in Figure 4.1. To add a new layer to this image, click the layer button labeled **Yellow Planet** to make this the active layer. Then click the **New Raster Layer** button, which opens the New Raster Layer dialog box, shown in Figure 4.6.

Figure 4.6
The New Raster Layer dialog box.

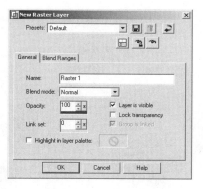

TIP

If you want to add a new layer without opening the Layer Properties dialog box, hold down the Shift key while you click the **New Raster Layer** button.

Any layer that you create in this way will be given a default name of the form Raster 1, Raster 2, and so on. You can always give such a layer a more meaningful name later on by double-clicking the layer's layer button and entering a new name in the Layer Properties dialog box.

Notice that, in addition to the **Name** text box, the New Raster Layer and Layer Properties dialog boxes present quite a few other controls corresponding to controls in the Layer palette. For now, all we're going to do with this dialog box is give a name to the new layer. Enter "Red Planet" in the text box labeled **Name** and then click **OK**.

An empty layer is now above the Yellow Planet layer. Because this layer is empty, the appearance of the image hasn't changed. If you look at the Layer palette, though, you'll see a new layer button labeled **Red Planet** above the layer button labeled Yellow Planet. The new layer automatically becomes the active layer.

CAUTION

Before you use a tool or perform an operation on a layered image, be sure the layer that you want to be affected is the active layer.

NOTE

The layer button of the currently active layer is highlighted.

Now draw on the new layer. Select the Preset Shapes tool and set the Fill color in the Materials palette to a shade of red and set the Stroke mode to Transparent. In the Tool Options palette, be sure that neither **Retain Styles** nor **Create as vector** is selected. Then draw a small circle near the middle of the Red Planet layer.

The image and the Layer palette should now look something like Figure 4.7.

Figure 4.7
Red planet drawn on the Red Planet layer.

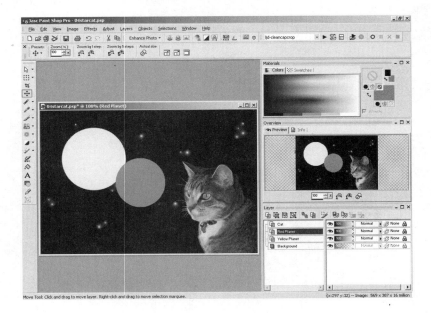

Next, try moving the figure that you just drew. Choose the Mover tool and click with it on the red planet figure. Drag the red planet to a new position. To return the figure to its original position, either click the Undo button on the Paint Shop Pro toolbar or press Ctrl+Z.

CAUTION

If you click the Mover tool on a figure that is on a layer other than the current active layer, the Mover tool affects that figure, and the figure's layer becomes the active layer.

This can be quite handy when you do it intentionally, but be careful. It's easy to click in the wrong place and unintentionally move an image element on the wrong layer. If you do make a mistake, don't forget that you can easily recover by clicking Undo or pressing Ctrl+Z.

To ensure that the Mover tool affects only the current layer, hold down the Shift key while clicking and dragging with the Mover.

Now move the Yellow Planet layer above the Red Planet layer in the layer stack. You can move a layer up and down in the layer stack by dragging the layer's layer button. Click the layer button of the Yellow Planet and drag it to the top of the layer button of the Red Planet, as shown in Figure 4.8. Keep an eye on the black line that shows up at the top or bottom of the moving layer's layer button; this line indicates the position of the moving layer.

After you move the Yellow Planet layer, notice that the yellow planet figure appears to be in front of the red planet figure, as shown in Figure 4.9.

Figure 4.8
Moving the Yellow Planet layer above the Red Planet layer.

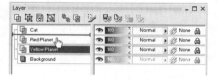

Figure 4.9
The example image after restacking the layers.

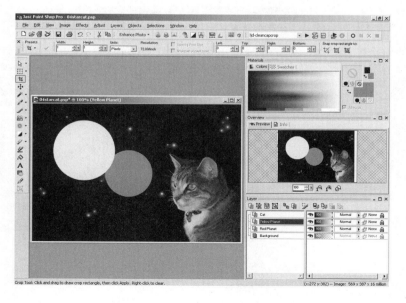

CHAPTER 4

TIP

You also can move layers by using the Layers menu on the Paint Shop Pro menu bar. Click the layer button of the layer you want to move. Then choose Layers > Arrange from the menu bar and choose one of the menu options, such as **Bring to Top**, **Move Up**, **Move Down**, or **Send to Bottom**.

Next, let's copy a layer. Right-click the **Red Planet** layer button and on the context menu choose **Duplicate**. A new layer is created just above the Red Planet layer, and this new layer has a layer button labeled **Copy of Red Planet**. Nothing in the image appears different yet, however, because the copied layer is simply overlaying the original Red Planet layer. To see a difference, choose the Mover tool and drag the uppermost red circle away from the red circle on the original Red Planet layer. Then you'll see something like the image in Figure 4.10.

NOTE

You also can duplicate a layer by using the Layers menu on the Paint Shop Pro menu bar. Click the layer button of the layer that you want to duplicate and then choose Layers > Duplicate.

Another alternative is to click the **Duplicate Layer** button on the Layer palette toolbar.

Now edit the circle on the Copy of Red Planet layer, changing the red circle to blue with Paint Shop Pro's Colorize operation. First, be sure that Copy of Red Planet is the current layer, clicking its layer button if you need to. Then choose **Adjust** > **Hue** and Saturation > **Colorize** from the menu bar, and set **Hue** to 175 and **Saturation** to 255. After you click OK, you'll see something like the image in Figure 4.11.

Figure 4.10
Copy of Red Planet layer with its red circle moved up and to the right.

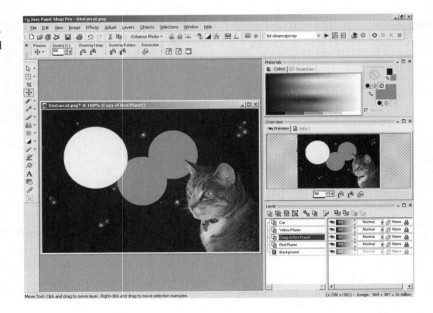

Figure 4.11
Colorize applied to the
Copy of Red Planet layer.

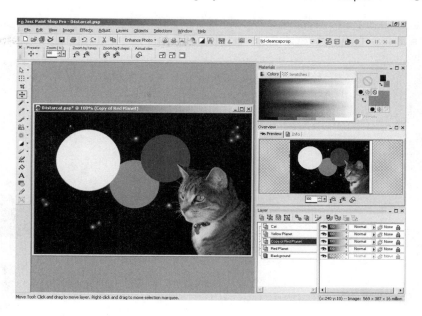

As you see, Colorize affected only the current layer.

This covers the basic Layer operations. The next few sections explore more advanced Layer features and operations.

Layer Visibility and Protect Transparency

Now let's try out the **Layer Visibility** and **Lock Transparency** toggles.

Each layer has an associated **Layer Visibility** toggle, which you use to hide a layer temporarily. One reason to hide a layer is simply to get extraneous material out of your way while you're working on one or more layers of your image. Return to the example image as it was left in Figure 4.11. Suppose that you want to edit the Yellow Planet layer without looking at any of the other elements of your image. You can do so by hiding all the other layers, as in Figure 4.12.

Figure 4.12
Layer palette with all but
the Yellow Planet layer
hidden.

You may want to add some shading to the planet, perhaps by using the Airbrush tool to spray a darker yellow color lightly along the lower-right edge of the planet to create a shadow. You probably want to add color to the planet but not to the transparent area surrounding the planet. You could accomplish this by using the Magic Wand to select the planet. There's an easier way, however, to restrict your painting to the nontransparent areas of a layer: Simply turn on the **Lock Transparency** toggle.

With **Lock Transparency** toggled on, only pixels that are already nontransparent accept paint. With **Lock Transparency** toggled off, any area of the layer accepts paint. Figures 4.13 and 4.14 illustrate the difference.

In the example image, the version made with **Lock Transparency** on was used. If you're working on this example, you should use this version, too. You should then make all the layers visible again by clicking their **Layer Visibility** toggles on.

Figure 4.13
Painting with **Lock Transparency** toggled off.

Figure 4.14
Painting with **Lock Transparency** toggled on.

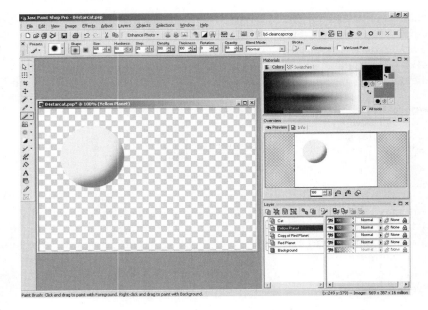

NOTE

You can easily hide all layers except the current one by using the Layers menu on the Paint Shop Pro menu bar. Choose **L**ayers > Vie**w** > **C**urrent Only.

To make all currently hidden layers visible and all currently visible layers hidden, choose **L**ayers > Vie**w** > Invert.

To make all the layers visible again, choose **L**ayers > Vie**w** > **A**ll.

Linked Layers

Layer links are used to keep elements on separate layers together so that when you move an element on one of the layers with the Mover tool, all the elements on the other layers in the link set move along, too. In the example image, you might want to keep the three planets together in the same relative alignment. To do this, add each of the planet layers to a single link set.

Linking a layer to another layer (or set of layers) is easy—just click the layer's **Layer Link** toggle. The **Layer Link** toggle of a layer that is not a linked to any other layer has **None** as its label. If no layers are linked yet, clicking a layer's **Layer Link** toggle changes its label to **1**. Click that same toggle after that to increment the link number and remove the layer from the linked layers labeled **1**. Each click further increments the number until the label returns to **None**. The number of times the link number is incremented until returning to **None** depends on how many layers are present in the image. (You also can decrement the layer group number by right-clicking the **Layer Link** toggle.)

To link each of the planet layers, click once on each planet layer's **Layer Group** toggle so that a **1** shows on each toggle, as in Figure 4.15.

Now, select the Mover tool and drag one of the planets around the image canvas. All three of the planets move together, maintaining their original positions relative to one another (see Figure 4.16).

Figure 4.15
The Planet layers all have link number 1, so they are all linked.

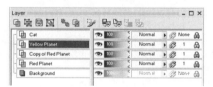

Figure 4.16
Linked layers move together.

You can have more than one set of linked layers. To add a set of linked layers, select the first layer that you want in the linked set of layers and click its **Layer Link** toggle until the label is a number different from any other layer. (If you click too many times, the label returns to **None**, and the layer is removed from any set of linked layers.) Then for the next layer that you want in the new linking, click its **Layer Link** toggle until the number matches that of the layer that you want to link it to.

In our example, suppose that instead of linking all the planets together, you decide that the red and blue planets should be linked and the yellow planet should be linked with the Cat layer. To accomplish this, click the **Layer Link** toggles for the red and blue planets so that both are labeled **1**. Then click the **Layer Link** toggle of the Cat layer until it is labeled **2**. Finally, click the toggle for the Yellow Planet layer until its toggle is also labeled **2**.

Figure 4.17 shows these two sets of linked layers and the effect of dragging the red planet figure after these linkings.

Figure 4.17
You can have multiple
sets of linked layers.

NOTE
You can directly set the Layer Link designation for a layer by using the Layer Properties dialog box. Bring up the dialog box for a layer by double-clicking the layer's layer button or, for the current layer, by choosing **Layers** > **Properties** on the Paint Shop Pro menu bar, or by right-clicking the layer's layer button and choosing Properties on the context menu. In the Layer section of the dialog box, set a value in the text box labeled **Link Set**.

Linked layers are most useful when you have a complex figure with various components on separate layers—maybe a car or a bird in a cage. By keeping the layers of such a figure in their own set of linked layers, you can ensure that the components don't become misaligned if you move any part of the figure.

Layer Groups

Besides linking, multiple layers can be related by grouping. You can group layers that are adjacent to each other in the layer stack to restrict certain operations to those specific layers. As you'll see later in this chapter, layer groups are particularly important when you are using mask layers and adjustment layers. Figure 4.18 shows an example of how a layer group appears in the Layer palette.

Figure 4.18
The Layer palette for an image that includes a layer group.

Notice that associated with the layer group header is a **Visibility** toggle, an **Opacity** slider, and a **Blend Mode** drop-down selection list. These controls can be used to affect all of the layers in the layer group.

You can move layers into or out of an existing layer group. One of the easiest ways to do this is to right-click the layer button of the layer that you want to move and then choose Arrange > Move In or Arrange > Move Out.

Opacity and Blend Modes

You can dynamically adjust the opacity of a layer or the way a layer's pixels are blended with pixels on lower layers by using the layer's **Opacity** control and **Blend Mode** selector. If you save your layered image in a format that preserves layering, such as PSPimage or PSD, such settings are retrieved when you open the image and then are available for further adjustment.

Opacity determines how much the pixels on one layer cover pixels on lower layers. The opacity for a layer can be set on the layer's **Opacity** slider, anywhere from 0 (fully transparent) to 100 (fully opaque). Any layer with an opacity setting of less than 100 allows pixels from lower layers to show through to some extent. Figures 4.19 and 4.20 show a layer with some gold text above a layer that is filled with a pattern. In Figure 4.19, the **Opacity** of the text layer is set to 100, and in Figure 4.20, the **Opacity** is set to 60.

Figure 4.19
Text layer with **Opacity** set at 100.

Figure 4.20
Text layer with **Opacity** set at 60.

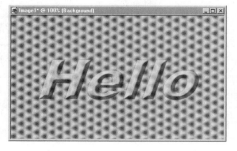

Blend Mode determines how the pixels of a layer are blended with those on lower layers. With **Blend Mode** set to **Normal**, pixels on the layer simply cover the pixels on lower layers. With the other blend modes, the pixels of the layer are combined with the lower pixels in various ways. For example, with **Blend Mode** set to **Lighten**, only the pixels that are lighter than the pixels on lower layers show up, whereas with **Blend Mode** set to Darken, only the pixels that are darker than the pixels on lower layers show up. You set the blend mode for a layer with the layer's **Blend Mode** drop-down selection list, located just to the right of the layer's **Opacity** slider.

TIP

You also can use blend modes with the Flood Fill tool: On the Flood Fill tool's Tool Options palette, set **Blend Mode** to any of the blend modes that are available with layers. This option is particularly useful with the Fill tool's **Match Mode** set to **None**. Refer to Chapter 2, "More Painting Tools," for more information about the Flood Fill tool.

Figure 4.21 shows some of the results that you can create with blend modes, and Table 4.1 summarizes the effects produced by using the different blend modes.

Figure 4.21
Blend Mode examples: (top, left to right) Normal, Multiply, Screen, Dissolve; (bottom, left to right) Hard Light, Overlay, Burn, Difference.

TABLE 4.1 THE EFFECTS OF USING DIFFERENT BLEND MODES

Blend Mode	Effect
Normal	Pixels cover pixels on lower layers; affected only by the Opacity setting.
Lighten	Only a pixel that is lighter than those on lower layers shows up.
Darken	Only a pixel that is darker than those on lower layers shows up.
Hue	Only a pixel's hue is applied to the layer.

Blend Mode	Effect
Hue (Legacy)	Version of Hue that matches the behavior of Paint Shop Pro 7.
Saturation	Only a pixel's saturation level is applied to the layer.
Saturation (Legacy)	Version of Saturation that matches the behavior of Paint Shop Pro 7.
Color	Only a pixel's color (hue and saturation, without luminance) is applied to the layer.
Color (Legacy)	Version of Color that matches the behavior of Paint Shop Pro 7.
Luminance	Only a pixel's luminance level is applied to the layer.
Luminance (Legacy)	Version of Luminance that matches the behavior of Paint Shop Pro 7.
Multiply	The value of a pixel and the value of lower pixels are multiplied and adjusted so that no value exceeds 255. The overall result is darker than the separate layers.
Screen	The inverse of Multiply. The overall result is lighter than the separate layers.
Dissolve	At random intervals, pixels from lower layers are displayed. The degree of the dissolve effect increases as the layer's opacity decreases.
Overlay	Acts like Multiply for pixels with values less than 128, and acts like Screen for all other pixels. Good for "painting" a pattern over a textured layer.
Hard Light	Similar to Overlay. Good for adding highlights and/or shadows.
Soft Light	Acts like Burn for pixels with values less than 128, and acts like Dodge for all other pixels.
Difference	Subtracts the values of the layer's pixels from the values of lower pixels, or vice versa, depending on which pixel value is lower. This modifies the hues of the image.
Dodge	Lightness values lighten underlying pixels. The lighter the areas, the more the resulting lightening. Good for photo correction.
Burn	Lightness values darken underlying pixels. The darker the areas, the more the resulting darkening. Good for photo correction.
Exclusion	A "softer" version of Difference.

CHAPTER 4

Here's a simple example using blend modes. Suppose you start out with some text on a white background, as in Figure 4.22, and then add a new layer and fill it with a wood pattern, as in Figure 4.23.

Figure 4.22
Text on a white background.

Figure 4.23
A wood pattern on a new layer.

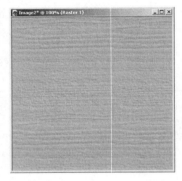

Change the **Blend Mode** setting of the wood pattern layer to Screen, however, and you now have text filled with the wood pattern, as in Figure 4.24. Because Screen does not show up anywhere where the lower layer is white, the background of the lower layer is maintained. Overlay or Soft Light would also yield a nice result here, with no change to the white background. Multiply would meld the two layers together, making it look like the text was painted on the wood.

Figure 4.24
The result with **Blend Mode** set to Screen.

Merging Layers

The three basic layer-merge operations are Merge Down, Merge All (Flatten), and Merge Visible. You can access these operations either by choosing **L**ayers > **M**erge or by right-clicking a layer's layer button in the Layer palette and choosing Merge in the context menu.

Merge Down merges the currently active layer with the layer just below it in the layer stack, creating a single layer from the two.

Merge All (Flatten) merges all the layers in an image and makes the image nonlayered, or "flat." Any areas in the image that had been transparent are filled with white.

CAUTION

For most file formats, saving automatically flattens layers. When you open such a file again, you'll find that the layers are gone and cannot be retrieved.

If you want to save your file with the layers intact, use a file format that preserves layering: PSPimage (Paint Shop Pro native format) or PSD (Photoshop format).

Merge Visible merges only those layers that are visible, so it can be used to merge one or more layers while leaving other layers untouched. Merge Visible can be used when all layers or only some layers are visible.

Figure 4.25 shows an image with three layers. Compare Figure 4.26, in which Merge Visible has been applied with all the layers visible, with Figure 4.27, in which Merge All (Flatten) has been applied.

Figure 4.25
A three-layered image with no Background layer.

Figure 4.26
Merge Visible applied to all layers.

Figure 4.27
Merge All (Flatten)
applied.

Notice that after Merge Visible, the appearance of the image doesn't change, only its layer structure changes—where there had been three layers, there's now only one. With Merge All (Flatten), the layers are collapsed into one, transparent areas are changed to solid white, and the one remaining layer is a Background layer rather than a true layer.

NOTE
If you choose Merge Visible when the current active layer is a member of a layer group, the visible layers in that layer group are the only layers that are merged. If you have one or more layer groups and want to merge all the visible layers in the image, first select a layer outside any layer group (or the "highest" layer group header if there are no layers outside any layer group). Then with this layer (or layer group header) as the active layer, choose Merge Visible.

Some of Paint Shop Pro's operations can behave as if layers were merged even when they're not. For example, **E**dit > **C**opy Merged copies all visible layers as if they were a single, nonlayered image. And the Selection tool in some of its modes, the Magic Wand, the Clone Brush, several of the retouching tools, and the Flood Fill tool can each be used on a layered image as if the image were nonlayered—just check **Sample Merged** in the tool's Tool Options palette before using the tool. When using **Sample Merged**, keep in mind that although data is sampled as if the layers were merged, no actual changes to data are made to any layer except the active layer.

Suppose that you choose the Magic Wand to make a selection in an image that contains the two layers shown in Figures 4.28a and 4.28b.

If the Square layer is active and **Sample Merged** is checked in the Magic Wand's Tool Options palette, clicking the square results in the selection shown in Figure 4.29. Clicking the square when **Sample Merged** is unchecked, however, results in the selection shown in Figure 4.30.

Blend Ranges

Blend Ranges are a rather advanced—and often overlooked—feature. You use **Blend Ranges** to determine which pixels show up on a layer and which ones don't based either on the brightness of the pixels themselves or on the brightness of pixels below the current layer.

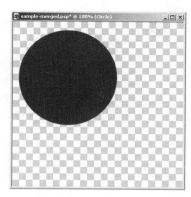

Figure 4.28a
Circle layer visible.

Figure 4.28b
Square layer visible.

Figure 4.29
Selection with Magic Wand set to **Sample Merged**—pixels in both the circle and the square are selected.

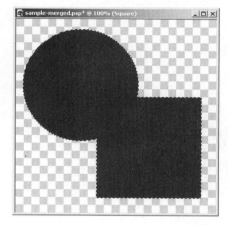

Figure 4.30
Selection when **Sample Merged** is not checked—only pixels in the square are selected.

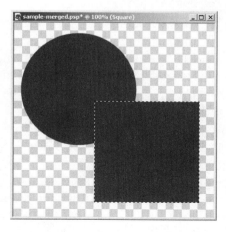

To understand blend ranges, it's easiest to look at specific examples. Let's begin with a single-layer image where the layer is filled with Paint Shop Pro's "Animal zebra" pattern, as in Figure 4.31.

Figure 4.31
A layer filled with a zebra-striped pattern.

Add a new raster layer and fill it with the "Metal brass" gradient, as shown in Figure 4.32.

Figure 4.32
A higher layer filled with a metallic gradient.

Now access **Blend Ranges** for the gradient layer. Either choose **Layers > Properties** while the gradient layer is the active layer, or right-click on the layer's layer button and choose Properties from the context menu, or double-click the layer's layer button. In the Properties dialog box, click the **Blend Ranges** tab, shown in Figure 4.33.

There are three **Blend Ranges** controls. In the drop-down list labeled **Blend channel**, you can select whether to restrict the blend range to the Grey Channel (luminance) or to any of the three color channels (Red, Green, or Blue). In the examples here, we'll stick with Grey Channel.

The other two controls each have two pairs of arrows, one at the top of the box and one at the bottom of the box. These arrows are used to define opacity ranges for the current layer and the underlying layers. The box labeled **This layer** can be used to restrict the blending based on the brightness values of the pixels on the current layer. The box labeled **Underlying layer** can be used to restrict the blending based on the brightness values of the pixels below the current layer.

Figure 4.33
The **Blend Ranges** tab of the Layer Properties dialog box.

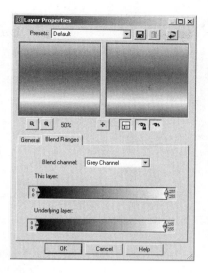

In both controls, the top arrows are used to set the range for pixels that are to be treated as 100 percent opaque. The bottom arrows are used to set the points at which opacity begins to be 0 percent. Values along the bar range from 0 on the left to 255 on the right. Dark pixels (shadows) are represented at the left end of the range, and light pixels (highlights) at the right end, with intermediate values (midtones) in between.

First, let's try out **This layer**. Click the **Reset** button to set all values to their defaults. Then slide the upper-right arrow to 99, leaving the other arrows alone, as shown in Figure 4.34.

This tells Paint Shop Pro to treat all pixels on the current layer that have brightness values greater than or equal to 99 as if they were semitransparent, the brightest pixels being completely transparent. The result is shown in Figure 4.35.

Figure 4.34
Setting Blend Range values for **This layer**.

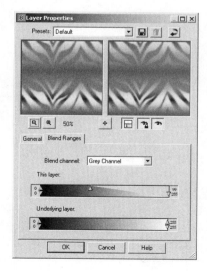

Figure 4.35
The result: Bright areas of
the current layer appear
semitransparent.

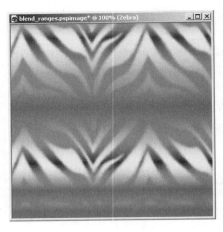

Now let's look at a couple examples using **Underlying layer**. Click the **Reset** button, and then set
the upper-right arrow to 59 and the lower-right arrow to 165, as shown in Figure 4.36.

This tells Paint Shop Pro to treat areas on the current layer as if they were semitransparent
wherever the brightness levels of the underlying layer are greater than or equal to 59 (with pixels
whose brightness is at least 165 producing complete transparency). See Figure 4.37 for the result.

In this example, what we've done is make the gradient show up only in the dark stripes, leaving
the light background alone.

Now we'll do the opposite, leaving the stripes as they were and letting the gradient show through
only in the light background. With all other settings at their defaults, set the upper-left arrow for
Underlying layer to 178 and the lower-left arrow to 43, as in Figure 4.38.

The result, shown in Figure 4.39, is just what we wanted.

Figure 4.36
Setting values for
Underlying layer.

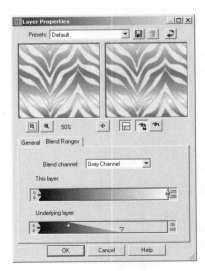

Figure 4.37
The result: The stripes take on the colors of the gradient.

CHAPTER 4

Figure 4.38
Another example using **Underlying layer**.

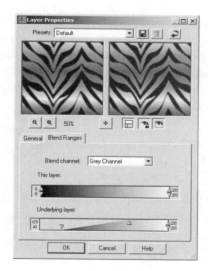

Figure 4.39
The result: The gradient shows up in place of the light background.

You can use blend ranges for all sorts of effects. Maybe you want to restrict colorizing to a specific tonal range, as we've done here in the **Underlying layers** examples. Or maybe you have fireworks against a dark sky and want only the fireworks to show up. Or perhaps you want to dodge or burn only those areas of a photo that are within a specific tonal range. Once you give blend ranges a try, you're sure to find quite a few uses for them.

CAUTION

Paint Shop Pro versions 8.0 and 8.01 have a bug that involves **Blend Ranges**. If you set **Blend Ranges** for a layer and then leave the Properties dialog box, you can't go back to the dialog box later to change the ranges reliably. This problem has been fixed in version 8.10.

Adjustment Layers

An adjustment layer differs significantly from a raster layer. Instead of adding pixels to your image, an adjustment layer seems to modify the brightness, contrast, or color of pixels on lower layers. The word "seems" is important here. No pixels on lower layers are actually changed; it only appears that they are. This is a crucial distinction, because it means that adjustment layers enable you to fine-tune your adjustment at any time, even in a later editing session (provided you save your image in PSPimage format or in another format that supports layers).

Adding an Adjustment Layer

There are nine available adjustment layers: Brightness/Contrast, Channel Mixer, Color Balance, Curves, Hue/Saturation/Lightness, Invert, Levels, Posterize, and Threshold. Each of these is entirely equivalent to the corresponding adjustment available in the Adjust menu.

To add an adjustment layer, choose **Layers > New Adjustment Layer** and choose the adjustment that you want. Once you've chosen a particular adjustment, the Adjustment tab of the adjustment layer's dialog box is displayed (except in the case of Invert, which has no controls). When you're finished choosing whatever settings you want, click the OK button to return to your image and apply the adjustment.

Editing an Adjustment Layer

An adjustment layer is a greyscale bitmap. When the active layer is an adjustment layer, the only colors available in the Material palette are 256 shades of grey (including black and white). The shade of grey painted on an adjustment layer determines to what extent the adjustment is applied to lower layers beneath the painted area. You edit an adjustment layer by painting it with black, white, or shades of grey (black removing the effect from certain areas, grey lessening the effect, and white for the full effect). However, you can't see the data on an adjustment layer, only the effects on lower layers.

There is a way to see an adjustment layer's data, though. To get a representation of the adjustment layer's data, click the layer's **Overlay** button in the Layer palette. By default, a red overlay is displayed that is 50 percent opaque in areas that are completely affected, is completely transparent where the effect is not applied, and has lowered opacity elsewhere. When you want to turn the overlay off completely, just click the **Overlay** button again.

TIP

Sometimes this overlay makes it hard to see the image, and in that case you can change the color and opacity of the overlay on the Overlay tab of the adjustment layer's property dialog box.

Whenever you want to change the settings of an adjustment layer, call up its property dialog box. Do this just as you would for a raster layer: Double-click the layer's layer button, right-click the layer button, and choose Properties, or choose **L**ayers > **P**roperties from the menu bar.

Limiting the Effects of an Adjustment Layer

By default, an adjustment layer affects an entire layer unless you paint away areas of the layer. However, you can also limit the effects of an adjustment layer to certain areas of a layer by making a selection before adding the adjustment layer. For example, Figure 4.40 shows the effect of adding a Posterize adjustment layer with no selection, while Figure 4.41 shows the effect with a rectangular border selected.

Once you've added the adjustment layer, you can turn the selection off.

Also by default, an adjustment layer affects all layers that are lower in the layer stack. You can limit the effect of the adjustment layer to a single layer or set of layers by creating a layer group and adding the adjustment layer and the layer or set of layers to the group. Figure 4.42 shows an image with an Invert adjustment layer above two raster layers, the lower one containing a pattern and the higher one containing some beveled text. Figure 4.43 shows the same image with the adjustment layer and text layer grouped together, with the pattern layer outside the group.

Figure 4.40
An adjustment layer
affecting an entire layer.

CHAPTER 4

Figure 4.41
An adjustment layer affecting only a selected area of the layer.

Figure 4.42
An image containing an adjustment layer and two raster layers.

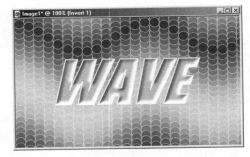

Figure 4.43
The same image with the adjustment layer grouped with only one of the raster layers.

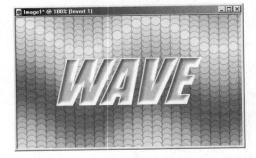

A First Look at Masks

When the goal is to place a figure on a new background, or add a decorative edge to an image, or gradually fade one layer into another, masks are ideal. People new to image editing sometimes shy away from masks, thinking that masks are too complicated. Actually, however, masks are quite simple to understand and use.

What Is a Mask?

A mask is quite similar to an adjustment layer. It seems to affect lower layers in the layer stack. But whereas an adjustment layer affects color, brightness, and contrast, a mask affects opacity.

Think of a mask as a special layer that lets you paint with invisible paint—that is, paint that makes pixels on the layers below the mask layer appear to be invisible. A mask can also partially mask out some areas, as if the invisible paint were diluted, letting the paint of lower layers show through but at a lower opacity. Wash off the paint completely (that is, delete the mask), and the lower layer becomes entirely visible again.

A mask is a greyscale bitmap. In a color image, when you make a mask layer the active layer, the Available Colors panel in the Materials palette changes to show 256 shades of grey (including black and white). Black areas on the mask layer completely mask out paint on affected layers. In contrast, white areas on the mask allow all the paint on affected layers to show, and grey areas on the mask let the paint on affected layers show at reduced opacity. The darker the grey, the lower the opacity of the paint on the affected layers.

A mask seems to both keep new paint off a layer and strip existing paint from the layer. To see what this means, consider a layer with no transparent areas, as shown in Figure 4.44.

NOTE

Masks work only on true layers, so when you add a mask to a Background layer, Paint Shop Pro warns you that the Background is about to be automatically promoted to a layer.

Figure 4.44
A single-layered image.

Now, suppose that on the layer shown in Figure 4.44 you load a mask from one of the sample mask files included with Paint Shop Pro, `Mask002.PspMask` (see Figure 4.45). `Mask002.PspMask` can be found in Paint Shop Pro's Masks folder. (You can load a mask from disk by clicking the **Load Mask From Disk** button on the Layer palette toolbar.) The result of adding this mask to the image in Figure 4.44 is shown in Figure 4.46.

Figure 4.45
`Mask002.PspMask`
sample mask from Paint
Shop Pro.

Figure 4.46
The image with a mask
added.

The mask is added as a new layer above the previously active layer, and those two layers are automatically put together in a layer group. As you see in Figure 4.46, the area covered by the dark part of the mask layer creates transparency on the data layer.

Now, return to the unmasked image of Figure 4.44. Suppose that a new, empty layer is added above the painted layer, and then a mask layer is added above the empty layer. If you then flood fill the empty layer below the mask layer with light-colored paint, the result looks something like Figure 4.47.

Figure 4.47
The flooded masked layer.

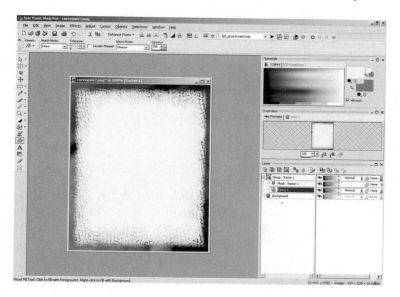

The white area of the mask allows that part of the layer to take on the new paint, whereas the black part of the mask seems to block the paint.

This probably isn't the effect that you normally want from an edge mask, though. Instead, you probably want the solid paint to show around the edge and the central part of the masked layer to be transparent (to let the content of the lower layer show through). You can easily create this effect by inverting the mask. Just make the mask layer the active layer by clicking its layer button and choose **A**djust > Ne**g**ative Image. The result is shown in Figure 4.48.

Figure 4.48
The same image with the mask inverted.

NOTE

A mask *seems* to strip paint away or keep new paint from being applied, but masking is actually a bit different from masking tape or acid. The whole layer really is affected, but you don't see the effect in the masked areas. So for the image in Figures 4.47 and 4.48, the whole top layer is filled with color, but what parts of that colored layer actually show up depends on what parts of the layer are currently masked and unmasked.

Creating and Editing Masks

You can create masks in a variety of ways. One method that you can use to produce quite interesting results is to create a mask from an image. To do so, open both the image that will serve as the basis of the mask and the image that you want to apply the mask to. Then choose **L**ayers > **N**ew Mask Layer > **F**rom Image to open the Add Mask From Image dialog box, shown in Figure 4.49.

In the **Source window** drop-down selection list, select the image that you want to use as the basis of your mask. In the **Create mask from** section of the dialog box, you have three choices:

▶ **Source luminance.** Creates a mask based on the luminance levels in the source image. Dark colors in the source produce transparency on the masked layer—the darker the color in the source, the less opaque the pixels on the masked layer become.

▶ **Any non-zero value.** Black areas in the source image create complete transparency on the masked layer, leaving all other areas fully opaque.

▶ **Source opacity.** Transparent areas in the source produce transparency on the masked layer, opaque areas maintain the opacity of the masked layer, and semitransparent areas produce partial masking.

The last control in the Add Mask From Image dialog box is the **Invert mask data** check box. When this box is checked, the mask is inverted. For example, when you have selected **Source luminance** and have checked the **Invert mask data** check box, lighter colors in the source produce more transparency than darker colors do.

Figure 4.50 shows a high-contrast image that has been added as a mask to the uppermost layer of a two-layered image, converting some of the areas of the upper light-colored layer to transparency, thereby allowing the dark color of the lower layer to show through. (The masked image is shown to the right of the image that was used as the basis for the mask.)

Figure 4.49
The Add Mask From
Image dialog box.

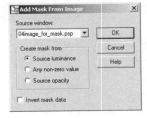

Figure 4.50
Example of a mask
created from an image.

In this example, **Source luminance** is selected and **Invert mask data** is not checked.

You also can create a mask by hand. To do so, choose either **L**ayers > **N**ew Mask Layer > **H**ide All (to start with a mask that completely masks out the paint on the active layer) or **L**ayers > **N**ew Mask Layer > **S**how All (to start with a mask that lets all the paint on the active layer show through).

TIP
You can also click the **Show All** button on the Layer palette to create a new mask layer above the active layer. You won't see any difference on the image until you edit the mask. If you look on the Layer palette, though, you'll see the new mask layer grouped together with the previously active layer.

To edit the mask rather than the image itself, make sure that the mask layer is the active layer and then edit away. When you're editing a mask, it's sometimes helpful to show a representation of the mask. If you click the mask layer's **Mask Overlay** toggle in the Layers palette, the mask displays as a reddish, semitransparent gel covering the active layer. Those parts of the mask that completely mask out the layer's paint appear dark red, whereas those areas that let the paint show through don't show any red at all. Partially masked areas appear as various shades of red, with the degree of semitransparency over the underlying image varying with the level of masking.

Figure 4.51 shows an example of a mask being edited, with **Mask Overlay** on.

You use black, white, and shades of grey to paint on a mask. Black creates total masking, whereas white allows all of the layer's paint to show through. Greys allow various levels of masking—the darker the grey, the higher the degree of masking.

Figure 4.51
Editing a mask with
Mask Overlay on.

You can use just about any of Paint Shop Pro's tools and operations to edit a mask, including the painting tools, the selection tools, most effects, and the color adjustments that affect brightness and contrast.

That just about covers the basics of mask editing. Before you leave this section, though, be sure to try out the **Group Link** toggle for the header of the group that groups together a mask layer and the layer that is masked. A group header's **Group Link** toggle appears at the extreme right in the Layer palette. With the **Group Link** toggled on, if you use the Mover tool to move the mask layer, the layer that is masked moves along (and vice versa). Toggle the **Group Link** toggle off, and the mask layer and the layer that is masked move independently of each other. (That is, of course, unless these two layers are in the same link set.) Toggling the **Group Link** toggle on has the same effect as assigning the layers in the group to the same link set.

Deleting Masks

Masks are saved along with an image (as long as the file format used supports layers, as does the PSPimage format). You can also either permanently remove a mask or permanently merge a mask with the affected layer, however. In either case, you first delete the mask layer, using any of the normal methods for deleting a layer. You're then presented with a prompt that asks whether you want to merge the mask layer into the layer below it. If you just want to get rid of the mask, choose No. If you want to permanently merge the mask with the layer below it, choose Yes.

NOTE
You can also merge mask layers with other layers using the standard Merge operations for layers.

There are several reasons why you might choose to merge a mask with the layer it affects. One is that masks take up space in your image, in terms of both file size and the amount of resources required during editing sessions. So, for example, if you're low on disk space, you should merge masks where you can rather than save them with your images. Another reason for merging a mask is to remove paint permanently. A mask itself doesn't really *remove* paint—it only makes it look like the paint is removed. If you want to remove paint entirely and permanently, merge your mask with the affected layer.

This is just the beginning of what you can do with masks. We'll explore masks in more detail in the next chapter.

The Deform Tool

There are a couple of tools that you can use only on raster layers that support transparency. One of these is the Deform tool. You use the Deform tool to resize, rotate, or deform a figure on a layer.

When you select the Deform tool, a bounding box with handles surrounds the content of the active layer. Drag any of the corner handles to resize the image. (Drag with the right mouse button depressed if you want to maintain the aspect ratio of the original.) Drag inside the bounding box to reposition the content of the layer, and drag with the handle that extends from the center of the bounding box to rotate the layer's contents.

Drag the top or bottom handle to change the vertical dimension without affecting the horizontal. Drag one of the side handles to change the horizontal dimension without affecting the vertical.

Figures 4.52 through 4.54 show how you can deform the contents of a layer in several other ways as well. In each of the examples, a regular five-pointed star is being deformed.

Figure 4.52
Deform in Shear mode.

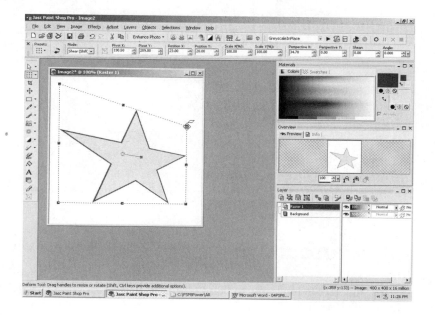

Figure 4.53
Deform in Perspective
mode.

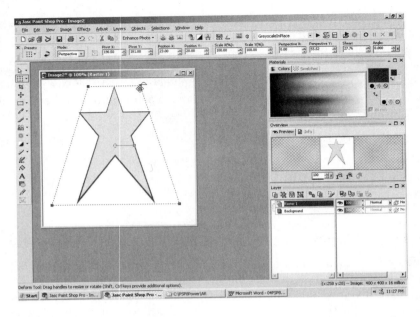

Figure 4.54
Deform in Free mode.

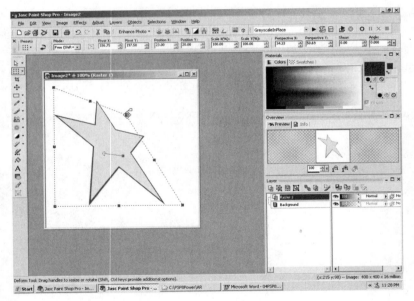

The Background Eraser

The other tool that can be used only on raster layers that support transparency is the Background
Eraser. This remarkable tool, new to Paint Shop Pro 8, enables you to easily eliminate the
background from around a figure.

To use the Background Eraser, set the brush size fairly high. Click with the center of the brush positioned over the background you want to eliminate, with the figure that is to be isolated contained within the edge of the brush, as shown in Figure 4.55.

Figure 4.55
Using the Background
Eraser.

It's almost always best to use the default settings. For more detailed tips on using the Background Eraser, head over to **http://www.campratty.com** and search on "background eraser." This is one incredibly useful tool, so be sure to give it a try.

5

Mastering Selections, Masks, and Channels

To have real control over your images, you need a firm understanding of selections, masks, and channels. Used in combination, selections, masks, and channels can make many image-editing tasks relatively easy, especially those that involve isolating particular areas of an image.

Here's what you'll be exploring in this chapter:

▶ Understanding the relationship between selections, masks, and channels
▶ Using selections, masks, and channels to isolate image areas and produce special effects
▶ Editing, saving, and loading selections and masks

Selections

In Chapter 3, "Being Selective," you already explored how to use the selection tools and how to add to and subtract from a selection. In this section, you'll take a closer look at how a selection is represented in Paint Shop Pro and how you can edit, save, and load selections.

Editing, Saving, and Loading Selections

A selection can be represented as a greyscale bitmap, with fully selected areas represented as white, feathered areas as grey, and unselected areas as black. If you have a selection and choose **S**elections > **E**dit, this becomes clearer: The Available Colors panel in the Materials palette changes to a palette of 256 shades of grey, and the selection data is displayed with an overlay, as in Figure 5.1.

As with an adjustment layer or a mask, a selection in Edit Selection mode can be modified by painting on it or by applying operations that you can normally apply to a greyscale image. For example, Figure 5.2 shows a text selection being modified with the Deform tool.

You can use Edit Selection mode to add to or subtract from the selection, to create special effects, or to warp the selection's shape. You can even paint your selection entirely by hand. Simply choose **S**elections > Select **A**ll followed by **S**elections > **E**dit Selection. You could then paint with black or grey to remove areas from the selection. Or for something a bit more intuitive, eliminate the **S**elections > Select **A**ll step and begin with **S**elections > **E**dit Selection. You could then paint with white and grey to create your selection.

Figure 5.1
Selection data revealed
in Edit Selection mode.

Figure 5.2
Text selection being
modified with the
Deform tool.

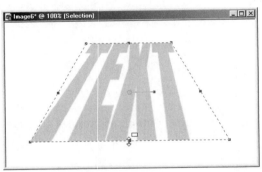

Another consequence of a selection being represented as a greyscale bitmap is that you can save it to a special channel called an alpha channel. The purpose of an alpha channel is to store noncolor information so that you can reuse it or edit it later, either in the original image or in another image. To save a selection to an alpha channel, choose **S**elections > **L**oad/Save Selection > Save Selection To Alpha **C**hannel. The Save Selection To Alpha dialog box appears, as shown in Figure 5.3.

In the dialog box's Preview window, you see a black-and-white representation of the selection. If you have more than one image open, you can select which image to add the selection to. Name the selection, if you want to, or keep the default name that Paint Shop Pro suggests, and then click Save.

A selection can also be saved to disk by choosing **S**elections > **L**oad/Save Selection > **S**ave Selection To Disk. In the Save Selection To Disk dialog box, enter a name for the selection file (which is automatically given an extension of .PspSelection) and click the Save button.

To load a selection from an alpha channel, choose **S**elections > **L**oad/Save Selection > Load Selection From Alpha **C**hannel to access the Load Selection From Alpha dialog box (see Figure 5.4).

Figure 5.3
The Save Selection To
Alpha dialog box.

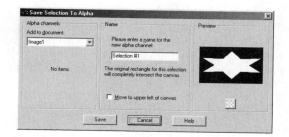

NOTE

Why save a selection to disk? To reuse it later, either in its original source image or in another image.

Paint Shop Pro comes with several saved selections, some in standard video display sizes and some in common Web element sizes.

Figure 5.4
The Load Selection From
Alpha dialog box.

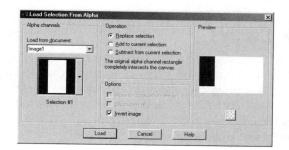

In the Load Selection From Alpha dialog box, you can choose any open image that has an alpha channel as the source image. A black-and-white representation of the alpha channel is displayed in the Preview window. If you want, you can choose to invert the selection. Click the **Load** button, and the alpha channel is loaded in the active image as a selection.

NOTE

When a loaded selection is added to the active image, the loaded selection has the same dimensions as the original selection.

Suppose that you then want to reposition the selection marquee in the active image. Choose the Mover tool, right-click within the selection area, and right-drag until the selection area is where you want it.

To load a selection from disk, choose **S**elections > **L**oad/Save Selection > Load Selection From **D**isk. In the Load Selection From Disk dialog box, select the selection file you want, and then click Load. As with a selection loaded from an alpha channel, the selection is loaded into the active image in the same dimensions as the original selection. If you want to reposition the selection marquee in the active image, just right-drag with the Mover tool.

NOTE

When you load a selection that is larger than the image you're loading to, you'll have the option to clip the selection to the image canvas. If you select this option, portions of the selection that don't fit in the image canvas are clipped off.

TIP

Although you'll usually use a PspSelection file as the source for a selection to load to disk, you can use any greyscale or color image as the source for your selection. The only limitation is that the image must be in one of the selection folders specified in Paint Shop Pro's File Locations.

When you create a selection from an image, you can choose to base the selection on **Source luminance**, **Any non-zero value**, or **Source opacity**. (With **Any non-zero value**, all pixels that are not black are selected.)

Beyond Mask Basics

Recall that a mask is a layer that makes areas of a lower layer or group of layers appear transparent. A mask's data is represented as a greyscale bitmap. You use black, white, and shades of grey to paint on a mask. Black produces total masking, white no masking, and grey partial masking. You can use just about any of Paint Shop Pro's tools and operations to edit a mask, including the drawing and painting tools, the warping tools, selection tools, effects, and the adjustments that affect brightness and contrast.

Loading and Saving Masks

To load a mask from disk, choose **Layers** > Load/**S**ave Mask > Load Mask From Disk (or click the **Load Mask From Disk** button in the Layer palette) and then choose the file name of the mask you want. Click Load and your mask will be loaded onto the current active layer. Figure 5.5 shows Mask002.jpg being loaded from disk.

To save a mask to disk, choose **Layers** > Load/**S**ave Mask > Save **M**ask To Disk and save the mask in whatever folder you select.

You can also save a mask to an alpha channel, an option that offers several advantages. For example, you might want to save a mask to an alpha channel so that you can reuse it in another image. Or maybe you want to end your current editing session, but you also want to be able to edit the mask later. Saving the mask to an alpha channel sometimes is a good thing to do before merging the mask with affected layers. After a merge, you can't get the mask back later on. But if you first save the mask to an alpha channel, you have the option of reloading the mask and modifying it, even in a later editing session. As you'll see later in this chapter, saving to an alpha channel also gives you the option of later loading the saved mask as a selection. (Saving a mask to disk is best when you want to reuse the mask in images other than the one in which the mask was created.) Saving a mask to an alpha channel is similar to saving a selection to an alpha channel.

Figure 5.5
Loading a mask from
disk.

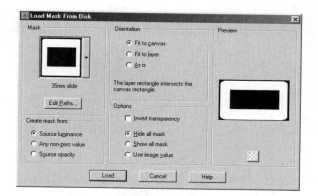

First, choose **L**ayers > Load/**S**ave Mask > Save Mask To Alpha **C**hannel. Then, in the Save To Alpha dialog box, you'll see a black-and-white representation of the mask in the Preview window. Name the mask and click **Save**.

You also load a mask from an alpha channel much as you would load a selection. Choose **L**ayers > Load/**S**ave Mask > Load Mask From **A**lpha Channel, and then choose the alpha channel from the Load Mask From Alpha dialog box.

NOTE

A selection that you load from disk or an alpha channel always has the same dimensions as the original selection. You have some leeway with masks loaded from disk or an alpha channel, though. Choose Fit to canvas to stretch or shrink the mask to conform to the target image's image canvas. Choose Fit to layer to make the mask conform to the size of the target image's active layer. To keep the mask the same size that it was originally, choose As is.

What You Can Do with Masks

Here are a few examples of things you can do with masks:

▶ **Add a decorative edge to your image.** You can also create your own decorative edges by hand using masks. For example, here's how to make the edge shown in Figure 5.6:

1. Open a photo.
2. Add a new raster layer and fill it with white.
3. Add a mask above the white layer.
4. Use the Selection tool set to Ellipse to define a selection on the mask layer.
5. Fill the mask with black and deselect.
6. On the mask layer, apply the Wave effect (**E**ffects > **D**istortion Effects > **W**ave) and then apply a Gaussian Blur (**A**djust > **B**lur > **G**aussian Blur). For each effect, use whatever settings give you the look that you want.

Figure 5.6
A handmade decorative
edge.

▶ **Isolate a figure.** A mask can be used to isolate a figure and place it on a new background. For example, in Figure 5.7 a layer below the portrait layer was filled with a pattern, and then a gradient was added to the pattern layer with the Flood Fill tool with **Blend mode** set to Overlay. A mask was added to the portrait layer to hide the old background.

▶ **Restrict effects.** Duplicate a layer, select the part that you want the effect to be applied to, and then add a mask with **Layers > New Mask Layer > S**how Selection. Deselect with Ctrl+D, and then apply the effect to the duplicated layer. An example is given in Figure 5.8.

In this case, the portrait layer was duplicated, and the duplicate layer was blurred. The figure on the blurred layer was then hidden with a mask, letting the unblurred original version show through. The advantage of using a mask here instead of a selection is that you can modify the boundaries of where the effect shows up and that you can, if you like, adjust the opacity of the duplicated layer to fade the effect.

Figure 5.7
A figure placed on a new
background.

Figure 5.8
An effect applied only to unmasked areas.

▶ **Create a mask from an image.** As you saw in Chapter 4, an image can serve as the basis for a mask. For example, you can open the image you want to use as a mask and open a new image filled with a dark solid color. Add a raster layer above the colored layer and fill it with white or some other light color. Add a new mask with **Layers > New Mask Layer > From Image.** Choose **Source luminance** as the source for creating the mask and click OK. You'll get a result like the one in Figure 5.9. (The final result is also shown in the color plate section.)

▶ **Blend two or more images together.** You can blend images together using masks. For example, you can place one image above another and add a mask layer to the upper layer, filling the mask with a black-and-white gradient. Refine the edges a bit, and you get something like what you see in Figure 5.10, where the portrait is blended together with a landscape.

Figure 5.9
Using a mask created from an image.

CHAPTER 5

Figure 5.10
Blending images together
with a gradient mask.

Color Channels

Like selections and masks, color channels are represented as greyscale bitmaps. White pixels in one of the channels represent full intensity in the channel; for example, a white pixel in the Red channel's bitmap represents full-intensity red. Black pixels represent no intensity—a black pixel in the Red channel's bitmap represents no red at all. Colors in digital images are produced by combining the greyscale bitmaps that make up the separate color channels.

The RGB Color Model

The *Red-Green-Blue* (RGB) color model is the one typically used for images for display on a video screen, such as Web graphics. Under the RGB color model, a 24-bit image is a composite of three channels: one Red channel, one Green channel, and one Blue channel. You can take a look at each of the three channels of an image separately by choosing Image > Split Channel > Split to RGB to split the image into its RGB channels. Figure 5.11 shows an image along with its three RGB channels.

NOTE
A 24-bit image has 8 bits for each of its channels. These 8 bits allow for 256 levels of brightness for each pixel in each channel, from black (0) to white (255). This is why each channel of a 24-bit image can be represented as a 256-shade greyscale image.

When the individual channels are split apart like this, they can be edited separately. You can recombine them later by using Image > Combine Channel > Combine from RGB.

The HSL Color Model

The *Hue-Saturation-Lightness* (HSL) color model is an alternative to RGB and, like RGB, is used primarily for images for display on a video screen. Under the HSL color model, a 24-bit color image is also represented as a composite of three greyscale bitmaps, with one bitmap for the Hue channel, one for the Saturation channel, and another for the Lightness channel.

Figure 5.11
An image and its RGB channels.

You can split an image into its HSL channels by using **I**mage > Split **Ch**annel > **Sp**lit to HSL. You also can edit each of these channels separately and then recombine them with **I**mage > **Co**mbine Channel > **Co**mbine from HSL.

TIP

You can create color images from greyscale images by combining the separate greyscale images as either RGB or HSL channels. This probably isn't a technique you'll use often, but you might have fun trying it out, just to see how it works.

You can make plaid or gingham patterns, for example, by using three greyscale images with differently shaded horizontal and vertical stripes as the three channels of an RGB image.

The CMYK Color Model

One other color model exists that we haven't explored yet: the *Cyan-Magenta-Yellow-Kohl* (CMYK) color model. Cyan, magenta, yellow, and kohl (black) are the basic colors used in printing. Paint Shop Pro provides limited support for CMYK, and part of this support is the capability to split an image into the four color channels for CMYK. You do this by selecting **I**mage > Split **Ch**annel > Split to CMY**K**.

For more information on CMYK, see the *Paint Shop Pro Users Guide*. And be sure to consult your print shop to find out specifically what it needs from you for your print jobs. If you're doing all of your printing on an inkjet printer at your home or office, you don't need to know anything about CMYK, because your printer driver will take care of translating your RGB image for printing.

Advanced Techniques for Isolating Areas

This section shows you how you can really make the most of selections, masks, and channels to isolate areas in an image.

Converting Selections and Masks

As you saw earlier, both selections and masks can be represented as greyscale bitmaps, and both can be saved to alpha channels. Because selections and masks are such close cousins, a selection can be converted to a mask, and a mask can be converted to a selection.

You can create a mask from a selection in the active image by choosing either **Layers** > **New Mask Layer** > **Hide Selection** (to mask out the area of the selection) or **Layers** > **New Mask Layer** > **Show Selection** (to mask out everything except the selection). You can then edit the mask, if you like, or save it to disk or an alpha channel.

To create a selection from a mask, choose **Selections** > **From Mask**. You can then use the selection on the currently active layer or any other layer of the image, or you can save the selection to disk or to an alpha channel.

NOTE

Remember that a selection saved to an alpha channel can be loaded as a mask, and a mask saved to an alpha channel can be loaded as a selection.

TIP

You can convert a vector object to a raster selection, perhaps then converting the selection to a mask. This allows you to define a precise path around a figure or to draw a shape that you can then use for a selection or mask.

To convert a vector object to a selection, click the object's object button in the Layer palette and choose **Selections** > **From Vector Object**, or right-click the object's object button and choose Create Raster Selection.

Combining Selections

In Chapter 3, you saw how to add to or subtract from a selection when using the selection tools. You can also combine saved selections to create complex selections. Here's how:

1. Create the first part of your complex selection, and then save it to disk or to an alpha channel.

2. Create the second part of your complex selection, and then load your saved selection.

3. In the Load Selection From Disk or Load Selection From Alpha dialog box, choose how to combine the saved selection with the current selection. The choices are **Replace selection** (for when you simply want to abandon your new selection and load the old one), **Add to current selection** (to overlay the saved selection onto the current selection), and **Subtract from current selection** (to remove from the selection any areas where the saved selection and the new selection overlap).

Figure 5.12 shows a simple example, where a saved text selection is being subtracted from an arrow-shaped selection.

Figure 5.12
Subtracting a saved selection from the current selection.

Combining Masks

Although Paint Shop Pro provides no *direct* way to combine two masks, some *indirect* ways are available. Here's one that isn't much trouble. You just saw that there is a direct way to combine two selections, and you know that you can create a mask from a selection. Use these two bits of knowledge to combine masks:

1. Save all the individual masks to disk or to alpha channels.
2. Load the first saved mask as a selection.
3. Load the second saved mask as a selection. In the Load Selection From Disk or Load Selection From Alpha dialog box, choose either **Add to current selection** or **Subtract from current selection**, as appropriate.
4. Repeat until you've combined all the saved masks into a single selection. Then choose either **L**ayers > **N**ew Mask Layer > **H**ide Selection or **L**ayers > **N**ew Mask Layer > **S**how Selection.

Admittedly, it would be easier if masks could be combined in the same way that selections can be. But this method involves only a couple extra mouse clicks or keystrokes, and the results can be remarkable.

NOTE
Another way to add masks together is to create a mask layer above an existing mask. You can't mask a mask layer itself, but you can add a mask to the group header of a layer group that includes a mask. Just make the header the active layer, and then add the new mask.

Using Channels to Make Selections

Let's now bring channels into the picture. Sometimes, making a good selection on your image by using the Magic Wand or other selection tools is just about impossible. You might find, though, that making your selection on one of the image's RGB, HSL, or CMYK channels is much easier. A hazy, brown object on a green background might be hard to select in the complete image, for example, but might be a piece of cake to isolate from the Red color channel. And because a split channel is an image, and a selection or mask can be loaded from one image to another, you can save a selection made in one of the image's channels and then load it into the original image itself.

Take a look at a simple example. The rightmost image in Figure 5.13 shows a somewhat complex figure against a speckled, multicolored background. The foreground figure isn't a good candidate for the Magic Wand, and the background would be nearly impossible to select directly. You might be able to do a passable job of selecting the foreground figure with the Freehand Selection tool set to Smart Edge or Edge Seeker, but you have an easier route available here:

1. Split this image into its HSL channels (using **I**mage > Split **C**hannel > S**p**lit to HSL). You'll see that, in the Saturation channel, the glossy figure is quite distinct from the background (see Figure 5.13).

2. Click the Magic Wand on the dark figure in the Saturation channel to make the selection.

3. Save the selection to an alpha channel with **S**elections > Load/**S**ave Selection > Save Selection to Alpha **C**hannel.

4. Make the original image the active image by clicking its title bar, and then load the selection to this image with **S**elections > Load/**S**ave Selection > Load Selection from **A**lpha Channel.

5. In the Load Selection From Alpha dialog box, choose the Saturation channel from the **Load from document** drop-down list and choose your saved selection from the selection list (see Figure 5.14).

TIP
You can use the operations accessed from the Adjust menu to make the contrast in a split channel even sharper.

Figure 5.13
Saturation channel of the example image, with original image behind.

Figure 5.14
Choosing the selection.

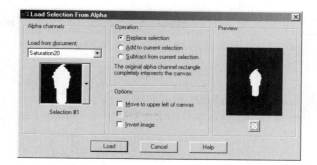

You can then make any adjustments to the selection that you still need to make (such as contracting, expanding, or feathering the selection). You're then ready to use the selection in any way that you wish: Copy the selected area to the Clipboard and paste it as a new image, invert the selection and press the Delete key to delete the background, convert the selection to a mask, or whatever you like. For instance, Figure 5.15 shows the selected figure in the example after it has been copied to the Clipboard and then pasted into an image with a gradient background.

Figure 5.15
Selected figure pasted on
a new background.

NOTE

In real graphics projects, you'll probably need to do more work than in this simple example to get your selection right, but this method can bring seemingly impossible-to-make selections into the realm of the possible.

Editing and Recombining Channels

You just looked at channel splitting as a means of making selections. Earlier in the chapter, you explored splitting an image into its CMYK channels for professional print jobs. Now you are going to see that splitting an image into separate channels also can be useful for color correction and for creating odd effects.

For example, you can reduce a blue cast in an image by splitting the image into its RGB channels and darkening the Blue channel. Then recombine the channels with **Image** > **Combine Channel** > **Combine From RGB**. See the color plate section for the original image and for its modified Blue channel counterpart.

You also can adjust an image by using filters on one or two split channels. For instance, sharpening sometimes introduces unwanted noise. But try one of the Sharpen filters on only one or two channels and then recombine the channels. The result will probably be subtle sharpening without noise.

To create effects, try using other filters on a channel, such as Emboss, Hot Wax Coating, or Mosaic. Also try applying one of the Histogram functions to a channel. Combine the modified channel with the other channels and see what results! Also try shuffling the channels (for instance, using the Red channel as the Blue channel, the Blue channel as the Green, and the Green as the Red) or splitting into RGB channels and then recombining as HSL channels. Much of the time, the result will be positively hideous, but sometimes, you'll be in for a pleasant surprise. (See the color plate section.)

6

Working with Vectors

One of the handiest features of Paint Shop Pro is its ability to create and manipulate vector objects on vector layers. Here's what you'll be exploring in this chapter:

▶ Drawing vector shapes and curves

▶ Deforming and editing vector objects

▶ Using vector text

Vector Basics

Vector objects aren't defined as collections of pixels but instead are defined by instructions to the computer on how to draw the lines and/or shapes that make up an object. To create a vector line, shape, or string of text, select the Create as vector check box in the Tool Options palette of the Pen or Preset Shapes tool, or select Vector in the **Create as** drop-down list in the Tool Options palette of the Text tool.

Vector objects reside on vector layers. Raster layers ("normal" layers) cannot hold vector objects, and if you try to add a vector object to a raster layer, Paint Shop Pro will immediately create a new vector layer above the raster layer, adding the vector object to the vector layer. In the Layer palette shown in Figure 6.1, notice that the icon that identifies vector layers differs from the icon for raster layers.

Figure 6.1
Display for a raster and a vector layer in the Layer palette.

NOTE

You can convert a vector layer to a raster layer, but raster layers can't be converted to vector layers. To convert a vector layer to a raster layer, right-click on the vector layer's layer button and then choose Convert to Raster from the resulting menu.

TIP

Unlike raster layers, vector layers can be used with 8-bit, 256-color images. Keep in mind, however, that antialiasing doesn't work in 256-color images.

Vector Objects

To practice handling vector objects, create a vector shape, as follows:

1. Open a new image with a solid white raster background. (Having a raster layer isn't necessary, but the solid-colored background makes it easier to see your drawing as you're creating it. The raster layer can always be deleted later, if you like.)

2. If the Tool Options palette isn't visible, press F4 to make this palette visible. Then select the Preset Shapes tool. In the Materials palette, set the Stroke to Solid Color mode, setting the color to whatever you want for the stroke, and set Fill to Transparent. In the Tool Options palette, select Star 2 in the drop-down list. **Retain style** is not to be checked, but be sure to check Create as vector (see Figure 6.2.). Set Width to whatever width you want for the stroke.

3. Draw a star in the middle of your new image by dragging from the upper-left to the lower-right corner (or by right-dragging from the center out). When you release the mouse button, you'll see something like Figure 6.3.

    Notice the rectangular border around the star, which indicates that the object is selected. Also notice the control handles on the top, bottom, corners, and sides of this border and the bar radiating from the center of the circle, along with its control handles. You can use the border and control handles to move or deform the object.

4. If the Layer palette isn't visible, press the F8 key to make that palette visible. Notice that there is a plus sign to the left of the vector layer icon, indicating that this layer contains at least one object. Click on the plus sign and the vector layer information will be expanded, showing a button for the new Star 2 object (see Figure 6.4).

Figure 6.2
Tool Options palette for
Preset Shapes.

Figure 6.3
A vector shape.

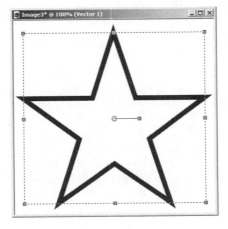

Figure 6.4
Layer palette display for a
vector object.

5. When an object is selected, its name appears in boldface on its object button in the
    Layers palette. To deselect an object, right-click the object button for the selected
    object and choose Select None. The label on the button becomes unbolded, and
    the object becomes deselected. Click the object button of the object again and that
    object becomes selected again.

Deforming a Shape

Now try moving, resizing, rotating, and deforming the vector object. Before beginning, be sure that
the Star 2 object is selected and that you're using either the Preset Shapes tool or the Object
Selection tool.

1. Reposition the object by placing the mouse cursor on the center handle or on any
    edge of the object itself. When the cursor is in the correct position, the shape of the
    cursor changes to the double-headed crossed arrows of the Mover tool. Then drag
    to move the object. Until you release the mouse button, you'll see both the original
    object in its initial position and a thin moving outline of the object.

2. To resize the object, place the mouse cursor on one of the control handles on the
    selection border and drag. Dragging the top or bottom handle alters the height of
    the object, whereas dragging a side handle alters the width. To change both the
    height and width at the same time, drag a corner handle.

3. To rotate the object, position the mouse cursor on the handle at the outer end of the
    bar radiating from the center of the object. When the cursor is in the correct position,
    the shape of the cursor changes to two arrows forming a circle (see Figure 6.5).

4. There are several ways you can deform an object: Drag on a handle with either the
    Shift key, the Ctrl key, or both keys depressed, as shown in Figures 6.6 through 6.8.
    The shape of the cursor when the mouse is positioned over a handle will give you
    a clue about what will happen when you drag with that particular handle. When
    you release the mouse, the object will take on its new shape.

TIP

To maintain the aspect ratio while resizing your object, right-drag on one of the
corner handles.

NOTE

As we saw in Chapter 2, "More Painting Tools," you deform figures on a raster
layer with the Deform tool. The Deform tool is unavailable when the active layer
is a vector layer.

Figure 6.5
Rotating a vector object.

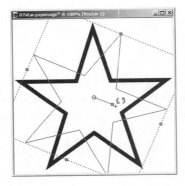

Figure 6.6
Deform with Shift+drag.

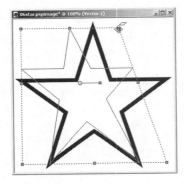

Figure 6.7
Deform with Ctrl+drag.

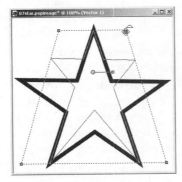

Figure 6.8
Deform with
Shift+Ctrl+drag.

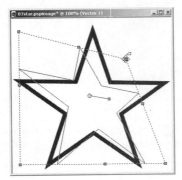

Modifying an Object's Properties

There are three ways to access an object's properties:

▶ Double-click on the object's object button in the Layers palette.

▶ Right-click on the object's object button in the Layers palette, and then select Properties from the resulting menu.

▶ Choose the Object Selection tool, select the object that you're interested in (either by clicking its object button or by dragging the tool around the object), and then right-click anywhere within the object's selection border and select Properties.

The Vector Property box of the Star 2 object looks something like what you see in Figure 6.9.

Figure 6.9
The Vector Property dialog box.

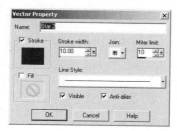

You can modify any of the vector object's properties. To change the stroke or fill colors, click on the appropriate color box in the Vector Property dialog box and then select the material you want, just as you would with the Materials palette. For example, Figure 6.10 shows the settings you'd use to change the stroked star to one with a gradient fill and no stroke.

Figure 6.10
Modifying a vector object's properties.

Object Alignment and Distribution

Sometimes you'll want to position an object in the exact center of the image canvas, align one object with another, or evenly space a group of objects on the image canvas. Commands for all these operations are available as suboptions on the Objects menu:

▶ **Align.** These options enable you to precisely align selected objects with each other or in relation to the image canvas.

▶ **Distribute.** These options enable you to precisely distribute selected objects in the image canvas.

▶ **Make Same Size.** This enables you to make selected objects all the same size as the first object selected, either in height or width or both.

▶ **Arrange.** This enables you to move objects on a vector layer within the layer stack. For example, you could move the object at the top of the stack down in the stack.

Modifying a Shape

To really exploit the power of vectors, try the Pen tool's Edit mode. Any vector object is made up of at least two nodes, with pairs of nodes connected by segments. Entering Edit mode gives you access to an object's nodes, enabling you to reshape and refine the object.

The best way to learn about node editing is to jump right in, so let's try working through an extended example.

Node Editing

With the Pen tool's Edit mode, you can make complex shapes from relatively simple shapes. For example, starting with a five-pointed star, you can make a gingerbread man like the one in Figure 6.11.

Figure 6.11
A vector gingerbread man.

Here's how to get there:

1. With the Preset Shapes tool set to Create as vector, draw a filled five-pointed star using Star 2 as your shape (see Figure 6.12). Be sure that in the Materials palette you have Stroke set to Transparent and Fill set to Solid Color, with a brown shade as the fill color.

Figure 6.12
A five-pointed vector star.

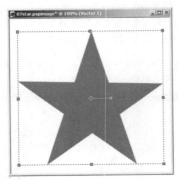

2. Choose the Pen tool, which should automatically be in Edit mode. In the image canvas, you'll see the nodes and segments of the star, as shown in Figure 6.13.

Figure 6.13
The star in Edit mode.

3. Now add a few more nodes to the star. To add a node, hold down the Ctrl key and click on the path of the star wherever you want a new node. Add two nodes for the neck, and add two more nodes for the points where the torso meets the legs, as shown in Figure 6.14.

Figure 6.14
Adding nodes for the neck and torso.

4. At this point, all of the nodes define straight line segments, but what you want instead is for the nodes for the head and the ends of the arms and legs to connect as smooth curves. To convert a node to a different type, select the node by clicking it or dragging a selection box around it with the Pen tool, and then right-click. In the context menu, select **N**ode Type > Symmetric. Notice how the line segments connected to the node then curve at the node. Repeat for each of the other nodes that you want to convert. Figure 6.15 shows how the shape is changed once all the nodes of the star are converted in this way.

5. Now, fine-tune the curves of the head, arms, and legs. Click a node or drag around it to select it. A selected symmetric node displays an arrow-shaped control. Pull on the head or tail of the arrow to adjust the length of the segments connected to the node. Rotate the head or tail of the arrow to adjust the curvature of the path near the node. To move a node, click and drag the node. When you finish adjusting each of the nodes of the head, arms, and legs, the shape will look something like a gingerbread man (see Figure 6.16).

Figure 6.15
Changing some of the
lines to curves.

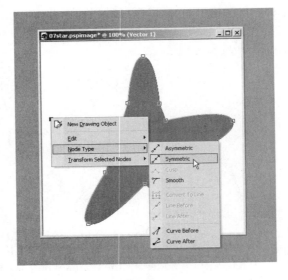

Figure 6.16
The completed
gingerbread man shape.

6.   Now let's add some texture to the gingerbread man:

    a.   Right-click the **Star 2** object button in the Layers palette and choose Copy.

    b.   Right-click the **Star 2** object button again and choose Paste New Vector
Selection. You'll then see an outline of the copied gingerbread man shape. Drag
this shape so that it lines up exactly with the original gingerbread man object.

    c.   Double-click the object button for the copied Star 2 to bring up its Vector
Property dialog box. In the dialog box, click the Fill color box to bring up the
Materials dialog box. In the Color Picker, choose a brown that is slightly lighter
than the original brown. Then select Texture and click the Texture preview to
bring up the Texture Picker. Choose something that will produce a good
texture for gingerbread, such as Asphalt 1. Click OK to exit the Materials
dialog box, and click OK again to exit the Vector Property dialog box. Your
gingerbread man will now look something like what you see in Figure 6.17.

7.   Use the Preset Shapes tool to add stroked, unfilled vector circles for the
gingerbread man's eyes and buttons.

Figure 6.17
Adding texture to the
gingerbread man.

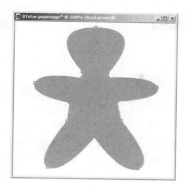

CAUTION

There's a bug in Paint Shop Pro versions 8.0 and 8.01. In these versions, after changing the vector properties of a shape, you won't be able to draw a new shape on top of the existing shape. A workaround is to draw your new shape outside the old shape and then drag the new shape into place.

This bug has been fixed in version 8.10, which is available as a free update.

8. Add a nose and mouth. The nose can be added with the Preset Shapes tool set to Triangle. For the mouth, use the Pen tool. Enter Draw mode by clicking the Draw Mode icon in the Pen tool's Tool Options palette. For **Segment Type**, select **Point to Point**, and then draw like this:

    a. Click where you want the left corner of the mouth. Be sure not to drag.

    b. Click where you want the right corner of the mouth. Again, do not drag. You define straight lines with **Point to Point** by clicking at each endpoint of the line.

    c. Click where you want the middle of the lower part of the mouth and this time drag a little. Dragging with **Point to Point** creates a node that defines a curve before and after it.

    d. Click the **Close selected open contours** icon in the Pen tool's Tool Options palette. The mouth shape is then done.

And that's that. The gingerbread man is now complete. And all from a simple star.

Changing Node Types

In the previous section, node types were mentioned briefly. The nodes for a curve can be any of four basic types: asymmetric, symmetric, cusp, or smooth. An asymmetric node has control arms that control the length of the curves before and after the node independently of each other but that work in concert in determining the orientation of the curve before and after the node. A symmetric node has control arms that influence each other completely—adjust the length or direction of one and the other is adjusted as well. A cusp has control handles that are completely independent of each other; use a cusp node when you want to produce a sharp angle. A smooth node provides a smooth transition from a straight line to a curve.

CHAPTER 6

To change a node's type, use the Pen tool in Edit mode. Select the node that you want to change, right-click in the image canvas, and in the context menu choose Node Type and the specific type that you want.

TIP

You can change several nodes at once to a specific type. Just select all the nodes that you want to change to that type, then right-click in the image canvas, and in the context menu choose the node type that you want.

An easy way to select all the nodes is to double-click one of the object's nodes.

Transforming Selected Nodes

The fifth segment of the Pen tool's Tool Options palette has some useful—but easy to overlook—options for transforming groups of nodes in an object. There's a drop-down list for Transformation Type, two Jasc Numeric Editors (JNEs) whose use is determined by the specific transformation type selected, and an Apply icon.

Here are the various transformation types and their settings:

- ▶ **Duplicate Selected.** All the selected nodes are duplicated as a new contour.
- ▶ **Rotate.** All the selected nodes are rotated.
- ▶ **Skew X.** The shape defined by the selected nodes is skewed horizontally.
- ▶ **Skew Y.** The shape defined by the selected nodes is skewed vertically.
- ▶ **Contract.** Selected nodes are contracted. If only some nodes in the shape are selected, the control arms for those nodes are contracted. If all of the nodes defining a shape are selected, the entire shape shrinks.
- ▶ **Expand.** Selected nodes are expanded. If only some nodes in the shape are selected, the control arms for those nodes are expanded. If all the nodes defining a shape are selected, the entire shape grows in size.

To apply a transformation, select Transformation Type, choose whatever settings you want for that transformation, and click the **Apply** button. You can reapply the same transformation with the same settings by clicking the **Apply** button again.

Experiment with transformations to see just what they can do. We'll be using some transformations in the example at the end of this chapter. You're sure to find many other uses for transformations, too.

TIP

All of the transformations except Duplicate Selected can also be accessed from the Transform Selected Nodes submenu of the Pen tool's context menu. This submenu also provides options for Flip and Mirror.

Making Cutouts with Vectors

Now let's see how to create an object with a cutout (a hole in the object). An example is shown in Figure 6.18.

Figure 6.18
A cutout effect created with vectors.

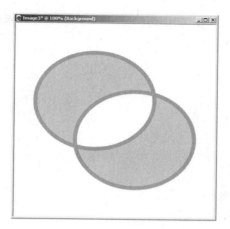

To create this effect, you take advantage of the direction of independent elements (or "contours") of a vector object. A contour is a set of connected nodes, and an object can have one or more contours.

The path of an object made with the Preset Shapes tool has a direction from its Start point to its Close point. For example, if you draw an ellipse by dragging from upper left to lower right, the path will have a clockwise direction. The direction of the path of a shape that you draw by hand depends on how you draw the shape: Proceed clockwise, and the path goes clockwise; proceed counterclockwise, and the path goes counterclockwise. The direction of a path is indicated by the arrow controls on a node—the arrow points in the direction of the path, as shown in Figure 6.19.

Figure 6.19
A vector path has a direction.

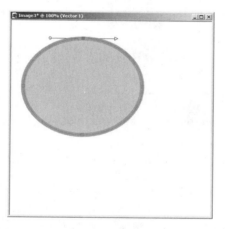

Now consider what happens when you have two independent contours in an object. Figure 6.20 shows an object made of the original shape shown in Figure 6.19 and a copy of that shape. (The copy was made by selecting all the nodes of the first shape with the Pen tool, then using **Duplicate Selected** in the Pen tool's Tool Options palette, with **Duplicate X** and **Duplicate Y** both set to 100.)

Now let's make the cutout. In the Pen tool's **Edit** mode, deselect all the nodes by right-clicking and choosing **E**dit > Select None (or simply click anywhere in the image canvas except on one of the object's nodes or edges). Then select a single node on one of the contours by clicking that node or dragging a selection box around the node with the Pen tool. Right-click to bring up the context menu, and select **E**dit > Reverse Contour (or instead of using the menu, just press Ctrl+R). You'll see that the arrow control has switched to indicate counterclockwise direction for the contour the node is on (see Figure 6.21).

Figure 6.20
An object with two contours.

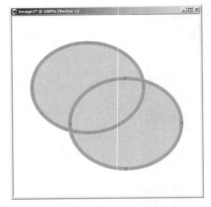

Figure 6.21
Reversing the contour.

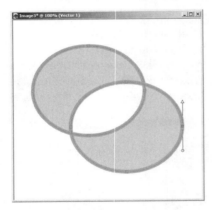

After you deselect the object, you'll see something like what you saw in Figure 6.18.

At the point where the two contours overlap, the intersection is treated as being "outside" the object. In this example, the contours partially overlap, so each contour produces solid areas (where they don't overlap) and a hole (where they do overlap). If one contour is entirely contained in the other, what you get is a continuous object that looks like it has a hole in the middle.

NOTE

If you're trying to make a cutout with vectors but no cutout appears, it may be that you accidentally chose Reverse Path instead of Reverse Contour. Reverse Path reverses the path direction for all contours of an object. Reverse Contour reverses the path direction of only the contour that contains the currently selected node.

To get the cutout, first be sure that you have only one node selected. Then try Reverse Contour again: Right-click to bring up the context menu, and choose **E**dit > Reverse Contour.

Modifying Vector Text

You create vector text by selecting the Text tool, choosing **Create as vector** in the Tool Options palette, clicking in your image to bring up the Text dialog box, and entering your text. Once you've placed your vector text, it can be modified in two ways:

▶ You can modify the standard vector properties by right-clicking the text's object button in the Layer palette and choosing Properties. This brings up the Vector Property dialog box, just as for any vector object.

▶ You can call up the Text box by double-clicking the text's object button or by clicking with the Text tool on the text itself. You can modify any of the settings in the Text tool's dialog box—including the **Font**, **Size**, **Kerning**, and **Leading**—or in the Materials palette.

NOTE

You can't use Paint Shop Pro's effects on vector text—or on any vector object. If you want to add effects to text that you've created as vector, you'll first need to convert the vector layer containing the text to raster. In the Layers palette, right-click the layer button of the vector layer containing the vector text and choose Convert to Raster Layer.

Some raster effects can be simulated with vectors. For example, you can simulate a drop shadow by placing one copy of your vector text on top of another copy, with the top copy slightly displaced. Give the lower copy the color you want for the shadow and give the upper copy whatever materials you want for the text itself.

Creating Text on a Path

Instead of following a straight horizontal line, text can be made to follow a curved path. To make text conform to a path, first define a path by drawing a vector line or preset vector shape and then "attach" the vector text to the path:

1. Begin by creating a path. For this example, we'll draw a horizontal S-shaped curve for the path. Choose the Pen tool in Draw mode, and in the Materials palette set the Stroke style to Solid Color, with the color set to anything other than the image canvas color. In the Tool Options palette, select **Point to Point** as the segment type, and be sure that **Create as vector** is selected.

2. To begin the path, click about halfway down on your image canvas a few pixels to the right of the left edge. Drag straight down until the head of the arrow control is within a few pixels of the bottom edge. Then click near the right edge of the image canvas and drag again straight down until the head of the arrow control is within a few pixels of the bottom edge. (See Figure 6.22.)

3. Choose the Text tool. In the Tool Options palette, set **Create as** to whatever you like—Selection, Floating, or Vector. Choose the font and font size you want. You can also select **Anti-alias** here, if you like. Set the styles and textures in the Materials palette to get the stroke and fill that you want for your text.

Figure 6.22
Defining the path.

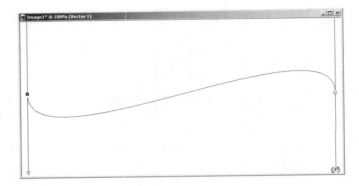

4. Choose the alignment for your text. For text on a path, **Align Left** positions your text so that it begins at the point you click on; **Center** centers the text around the point you click on; and **Right Align** positions the text so that it ends at the point you click on.

5. Click on the vector curve. You'll know that the cursor is positioned so that it will follow the path when it changes to an A with a curve below it. The Text Entry box then appears.

6. Enter the text you want in the Text Entry box and click Apply. You'll then see something like the image shown in Figure 6.23.

Figure 6.23
Text conforming to a path.

If you created your text as vector, both the curve and the text are now selected. You can move, resize, or deform them with the Object Selection tool just as you can any other vector objects. You can also modify the curve with Node Edit.

7. You probably don't want the curve itself to be visible. There are a couple ways to make the path invisible. If you expand the vector layer information in the Layer palette, you can just click the **Visibility** toggle on the curve's object button. Another alternative is to access the curve's Vector Property dialog box and deselect **Visible**.

NOTE

In the preceding example **Warp Text** was selected in the Tool Options palette. With this option, the shape of each text character is warped to better conform to the path. When this option is not selected, each text character retains its normal shape. Compare the two examples in Figure 6.24. (Especially note the differences in the initial "C" and the exclamation point.)

Figure 6.24
Warp Text selected (top) and unselected (bottom).

TIP

Sometimes when **Warp Text** is unselected, the text along the curve is squashed together in places. You can correct problems like this by adjusting the spacing of the whole string of text, or character by character, with **Kerning**.

You can also adjust how close the text on the path is to the path. To move the text below the path, set **Leading** to a negative value. To move the text above the path, set **Leading** to a positive value.

Converting Text to Curves

Text that is created as a vector can be converted to curves. The text can be converted as one multi-path object or as individual objects for each character in the text string. To convert vector text to a curve, select the text and right-click on the image canvas with the Object Selection tool. On the pop-up menu, select either **C**onvert Text to Curves > As **S**ingle Shape or **C**onvert Text to Curves > As C**h**aracter Shapes. (Alternatively, right-click the vector text's object button in the Layers palette, and select Convert Text to Curves in the context menu.)

Figure 6.25 shows a dingbat text character entered as vector text. Once a character is converted to a shape, it can be edited with the Pen tool in Node Edit mode. Figure 6.26 shows the converted character with its nodes revealed, in the middle of being modified with the Pen tool in Node Edit.

Figure 6.25
A dingbat character
converted to a shape.

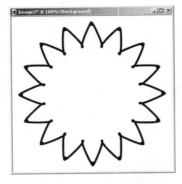

Figure 6.26
The converted dingbat
character edited with the
Pen tool in Node Edit
mode.

NOTE
Immediately after you convert a string of text to a curve as individual character
shapes, the entire vector layer containing the character shapes is selected. If your
converted text has more than one character, all of the characters are selected. To
enter Node Edit mode with the Pen tool, you first need to select only a single
character: Click the character's object button in the Layers palette, or select the
character with the Object Selection tool.

Example: A Simple Vector Drawing

Let's work through a simple example, the butterfly image shown in Figure 6.27. This example
makes use of node transformations and a cutout.

Here are the steps:

1. Open a new image with Vector Background selected.

2. Create the head, thorax, and abdomen of the butterfly with the Preset Shapes tool
   set to Ellipse, Foreground/Stroke set to transparent, and Background/Fill set to
   black, as in Figure 6.28.

3. Draw the antennae with the Pen tool set to **Point to Point**, Foreground/Stroke set
   to black, and Background/Fill set to transparent. Add circles at the ends of the
   antennae with Preset Shapes (with Stroke transparent and Fill black).

Figure 6.27
A butterfly made with vectors.

Figure 6.28
Create the body with Preset Shapes.

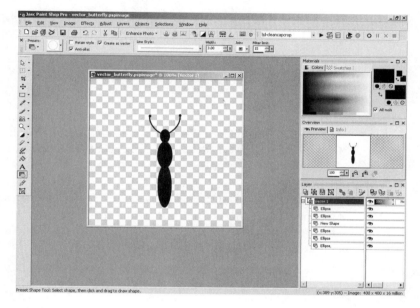

4. Add a new vector layer, and then create the main part of the left wing. Use Preset Shapes set to Triangle, as in Figure 6.29. Have Stroke set to black and Fill set to yellow. Use the object selection handles to modify the size and rotation of the triangle and drag the shape to position it.

5. Select all the nodes of the wing except the one closest to the body: right-click with the Pen tool and choose Edit > Select All in the context menu, and then Shift-click on the one node to deselect it. Right-click and select **N**ode Type > Symmetric. The corners of the triangle become rounded.

6. Right-click the triangle's object button in the Layer palette and select **Copy**. Then right-click the object button again and choose **Paste New Vector Selection**. Drag the new selection so that it overlays the original rounded triangle. Double-click the object button of the triangle that is higher in the layer stack and change its fill to red.

CHAPTER 6

Figure 6.29
Beginning the left wing.

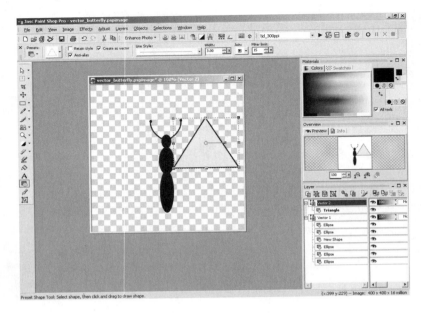

7. Select all of the nodes of the red triangle, and in the Transform panel of the Pen tool's Tool Options palette, choose **Contract** with **Contraction X** and **Contraction Y** set to 10. Click the **Apply** button a couple times, until your image looks something like Figure 6.30.

8. Select all the nodes of the red triangle, and in the Transform panel of the Tool Options palette, choose **Duplicate** with the offsets set to 0, and click **Apply**. Then change the transformation to **Contract** and set the values to 10. Click the **Apply** button a few times, as you did in step 7.

Figure 6.30
Creating the wing pattern with vector transformations.

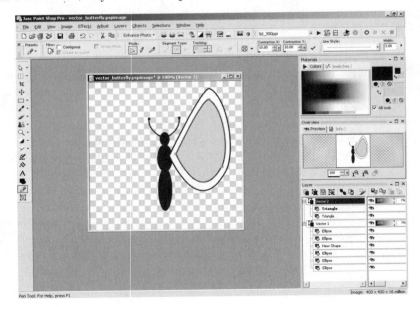

9. Select just one of the nodes of contracted contour, right-click and choose Edit > Reverse Contour to create a cutout. The result will look something like what you see in Figure 6.31.

Figure 6.31
The wing with a cutout added.

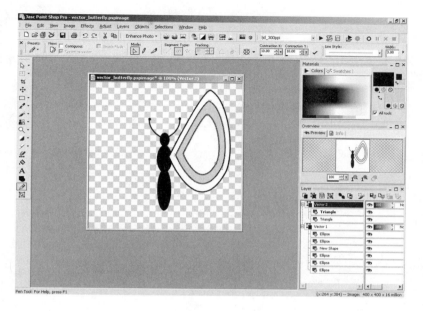

10. Choose the Preset Shapes tool and set the shape to Ellipse. In the Materials palette, set the Fill to a gradient. (The **Button red** gradient set to Linear is used here, with **Angle** and **Repeats** both set to 0.) Create a spot on the wing.

11. With the Pen tool, modify the shape of the spot. You can select all the nodes and use the **Skew X** or **Skew Y** node transformations, or try selecting only two or three of the nodes and using **Expand**, **Contract**, **Skew X,** or **Skew Y**.

12. Repeat steps 10 and 11 to add a second spot to the wing. At this point, your butterfly should look something like what's shown in Figure 6.32.

13. Now to add the lower wing. Right-click the object button of the triangle that is lower in the layer stack and choose **Copy**. Then right-click again and choose **Paste New Vector Selection**. Position the new vector object so that it partially overlaps the upper wing. Then drag the new wing's object button below the layer button of the upper wing. The image will look like Figure 6.33.

14. Double-click the lower wing's object button and change the fill to the same gradient that you used for the spots, setting the gradient style to Sunburst.

15. Now for the last step: adding the left set of wings. Right-click the layer button of the wings (Vector 2) and choose **Duplicate**. Mirror the duplicated layer by choosing Image > Mirror. Position the layer with the Mover tool, and your butterfly is complete.

CHAPTER 6

Figure 6.32
Spots added to the
butterfly's wing.

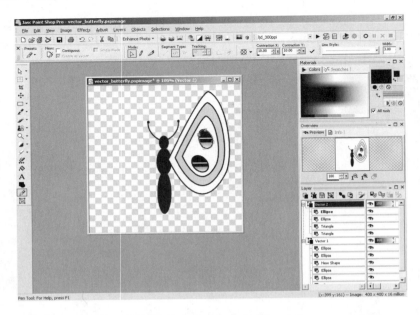

Figure 6.33
The lower wing added.

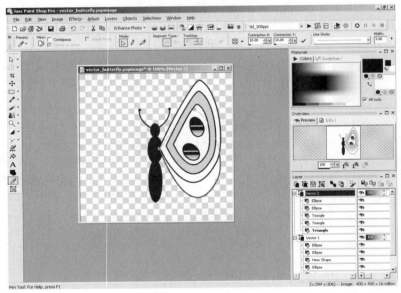

That should get you well on the way to exploring what you can do with vectors. For more
ideas, take a look at Ron Lacey's excellent series on vectors in the archives of *pspPower* at
http://www.psppower.com.

7

Paint Shop Pro 8 Effects

Paint Shop Pro includes many built-in special effects and also enables you to add more effects with both its User Defined Filter function and plug-in filters. This chapter presents extended examples of some of Paint Shop Pro's most useful and powerful effects.

Here's what you'll be exploring in this chapter:

▶ Built-in effects
▶ User Defined Filters
▶ Plug-in filters

NOTE

Paint Shop Pro 7 users should note that the photographic enhancing filters and adjustments (such as Sharpen, Blur, and Automatic Contrast Enhancement) are no longer included in the Effects menu. Instead, they are now found in the various submenus of the Adjust menu.

The photo editing commands are not included in this chapter but are discussed in Chapter 8, "Photo Editing and Enhancement."

All of the built-in effects that have dialog boxes have certain controls in common. Each dialog box has a pair of preview windows, one on the left showing the original image and another on the right showing the result of applying the effect with the current settings.

Above the preview windows is the Presets drop-down list, a **Save Preset** button for when you want to save an effect's settings as a preset, a **Delete Preset** button for when you want to delete a preset from the drop-down list, and a **Reset** button. Use the **Reset** button to return the values to the factory defaults. Hold down the Shift key while clicking the **Reset** button to return the effect's settings to what they were when you opened the effect's dialog box.

Below the preview windows are zoom controls and a control for changing the view area of the preview. Just to the right of those controls is a toggle to hide and display the preview windows, an **Auto Proof** button with a label that looks like an eye and a lock, and a **Proof** button with a label that looks like an eye. Click the **Proof** button if you want to see what the effect with the current settings will look like on the actual image. Click the **Auto Proof** button if you want the effect on your image to change dynamically as you adjust the controls in the dialog box.

To the right of the **Proof** button is a **Randomize** button. Click this button and Paint Shop Pro generates pseudo-random settings for the effect.

Along the bottom of the dialog box are three buttons: **OK**, **Cancel**, and **Help**.

▶ Click **OK** to apply the effect.

▶ Click **Cancel** to exit the dialog box without applying the effect.

▶ Click **Help** to get information about the effect.

Controls specific to the effect appear in the middle of the effect's dialog box, between the preview windows and these three buttons.

Now let's take a look at the individual filters and effects.

Built-In Effects

Built-in effects are operations built into Paint Shop Pro that apply various special effects to your images. Some of them add a 3-D effect, others simulate natural materials or art media, and still others distort your image or add perspective.

You could spend a lifetime experimenting with Paint Shop Pro's built-in effects. Be sure to devote some time to exploring them, both singly and in combination with each other.

TIP

As mentioned earlier, built-in effects allow you to save your favorite settings as presets, which you can load again whenever you want them. When you're first trying out an effect, be sure to try out any presets that are supplied with Paint Shop Pro. That way, you'll get a feel for the various results possible.

You might also want to try out the **Randomize** button for an effect. You won't always get useful results, but sometimes this can help you discover more about an effect.

Let's begin with a brief catalog of the various built-in effects. Later, we'll go through some extended examples of what you can do with them—singly, in combination, and in concert with some of Paint Shop Pro's other facilities. Several of the effects are also featured prominently in Chapter 10, "Tricks and Techniques."

3-D Effects

As the name implies, 3-D effects create various sorts of 3-D looks. Apply these with Effects > 3D Effects > *effect name*.

▶ **Buttonize.** This creates simple rectangular buttons.

Figure 7.1 shows a rectangular image to which Buttonize was applied (with **Transparent Edge** selected, **Height** and **Width** both set to 30, and **Opacity** set to 75).

You also can use Image > Add **B**orders in combination with Buttonize to produce framelike effects. Figure 7.2 shows an example in which a 20-pixel border was added to a rose image, and then Buttonize was applied with **Transparent Edge** selected and **Height** and **Width** set to 15.

Use multiple Buttonized borders to make even fancier frames.

Figure 7.1
Rectangular image after
Buttonize is applied.

Figure 7.2
A Buttonized border
added to an image.

▶ **Chisel.** This creates a chiseled effect outside the edges of a selection.

Figure 7.3 shows some chiseled text with the **Transparent** option selected, and Figure 7.4 shows the same text with **Solid color** selected instead. In each case, **Size** is set to 10.

Figure 7.3
Chisel with **Transparent**
setting.

Figure 7.4
Chisel with **Solid color**
setting.

▶ **Cutout.** This creates a cutout effect inside a selection. You can choose to either fill the interior of the selection with a color, as in Figure 7.5, or not fill the selection with color, as in Figure 7.6. On a layer that supports transparency, this second option "cuts out" the selected area, making it transparent and so letting lower layers show through.

Figure 7.5
Cutout with interior
filled.

Figure 7.6
Cutout with no fill color.

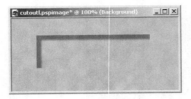

▶ **Drop Shadow.** This creates a drop shadow outside a selection. If you choose to place the shadow on its own layer, you can later reposition the shadow or distort it with the Deform tool to create a perspective shadow.

You can get a nice effect by adding a drop shadow around an empty text selection placed over a patterned background, so that only the shadow defines the text. Something else to try is to make a text selection, invert the selection, and apply Drop Shadow with both offsets set to 0. This produces either a cutout or bas-relief effect, as in Figure 7.7, where this method is used with a character from Astigmatic One Eye's ButtonButton, a dingbat font.

Figure 7.7
Drop Shadow applied to
an inverted selection.

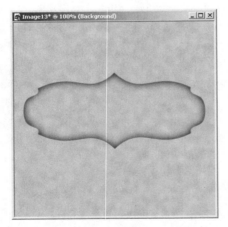

▶ **Inner Bevel.** This creates a beveled effect inside a selection. You can use Inner Bevel to create nonrectangular buttons and 3-D text.

Although the effects produced by Inner Bevel appear quite simple, the controls available are pretty complex. At first, the Inner Bevel dialog box (see Figure 7.8) might seem a little intimidating, but after you've used this effect a few times, it will become second nature to you.

Figure 7.8
The Inner Bevel dialog box.

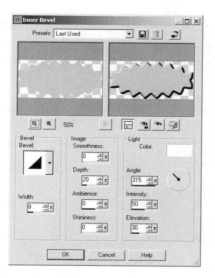

On the left of the dialog box is a section labeled **Bevel**, in which you choose the shape of the bevel and its width. To the right of the **Bevel** section is one labeled **Image**, which contains controls for **Smoothness**, **Depth**, **Ambience**, and **Shininess**, defined as follows:

Smoothness. Determines to what degree the bevel is sharply edged or blends smoothly in with the flat part of the image. The higher the **Smoothness**, the rounder the edges of the bevel.

Depth. Determines how pronounced the edges of the bevel are. The higher the **Depth**, the more pronounced the edges.

Ambience. Determines the overall brightness of the image.

Shininess. Determines how glossy the bevel appears. The higher the **Shininess** value, the more pronounced the highlights on the bevel.

The right section of the dialog box, labeled **Light**, contains controls for setting the light shining on the image. At the top of this section is a color swatch. Click this swatch to call up the Color dialog box, where you can select the color for your light.

Below the color swatch are two controls that you can use to set the angle of the light: a dial and a text box labeled **Angle**. To set the light's angle, you can either drag the hand of the dial or enter a number of degrees in the text box.

Next are two sliders, one labeled **Intensity** and the other labeled **Elevation**. **Intensity** determines the brightness of the light shining on the object. Note that this will be added to the ambient brightness set with **Ambience**, so adjustments to **Intensity** might require you to also adjust **Ambience** in order to maintain a certain overall brightness.

Elevation determines the vertical position of the light source. A setting of 90 places the light source directly overhead. The lower the elevation, the closer the light source is to the "ground."

NOTE

Several of Paint Shop Pro's effects use **Smoothness**, **Depth**, **Ambience**, **Shininess**, and the **Light** controls, including Inner Bevel, Outer Bevel, Sculpture, Texture, and Tiles.

A couple examples of Inner Bevel are shown in Figures 7.9 through 7.11. Figure 7.9 shows an irregularly shaped beveled button, Figure 7.10 shows beveled text, and Figure 7.11 shows a picture frame.

Figure 7.9
An irregularly shaped button made with Inner Bevel.

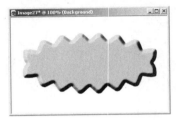

Figure 7.10
Text enhanced with Inner Bevel.

Figure 7.11
A picture frame made with Inner Bevel.

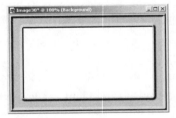

TIP

You can add to a beveled figure's feeling of depth by also applying Drop Shadow to the figure.

After you start experimenting with Inner Bevel, you're sure to find all sorts of uses for it, beyond frames and buttons. You can produce some nice gold text, for example, by filling a text selection with any of the metallic gradients supplied by Jasc and then applying Inner Bevel.

▶ **Outer Bevel.** This creates a beveled effect outside a selection and can be used to make the selected area appear to rise out of the background. (Note that Outer Bevel is unavailable with floating selections.)

TIP

Chisel, Cutout, Drop Shadow, and Inner Bevel can also be applied to a figure surrounded by transparency on a layer, as well as to a selection.

Art Media Effects

Art Media effects create the look of various art media. Apply them with Effects > Art Media Effects > *effect name*.

▶ **Black Pencil** and **Colored Pencil.** These emphasize the edges in your image and lighten other areas, so that the image resembles a pencil drawing.

▶ **Brush Strokes.** Use Brush Stroke to give your image the look of various types of paintings, including oils and watercolor.

▶ **Charcoal** and **Colored Chalk.** These create an effect much like that produced with Black Pencil and Colored Pencil, but with edges that are thicker and rougher.

▶ **Pencil.** This is another effect that can make your image look like a pencil drawing. Good results can usually be achieved with black as the **Color** and a high **Luminance** setting or with white as the **Color** and a low negative **Luminance** setting.

NOTE

While some of these effects—such as Brush Strokes—work quite well with both drawings and photos, you might find that you get the best results from Black Pencil, Colored Pencil, Charcoal, Colored Chalk, and Pencil on drawings.

With photos, you might first want to eliminate a busy background or other unimportant details before applying one of the Art Media effects. Increasing the contrast a bit might also yield the best results.

Artistic Effects

Artistic effects produce quite a few special effects, some of them quite complex. Apply them with Effects > Artistic Effects > *effect name*.

▶ **Aged Newspaper** and **Sepia Toning.** Both of these give a yellowed or sepia tint to your image. In addition, Aged Newspaper slightly blurs the image.

▶ **Balls and Bubbles.** This is an incredibly versatile addition to Paint Shop Pro 8. You can make almost anything that is vaguely sphere-shaped using this effect, from a cloud of bubbles, to snow, to balls, to planets, to eyeballs, and even to various kinds of fruits and vegetables (particularly if you warp the results). Figure 7.12 shows just a few of the things you can make with Balls and Bubbles.

For more information on the basics of Balls and Bubbles, see my tutorial at **http://loriweb.pair.com/8bandb_basics.html**. We'll look more at Balls and Bubbles a bit later in this chapter.

Figure 7.12
A few things made with Balls and Bubbles.

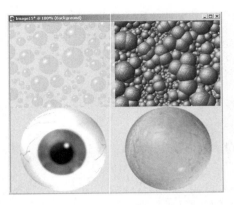

▶ **Chrome.** This gives your image a metallic look.

Because Chrome locates areas of contrast in order to produce a shiny effect, using Chrome on a solid-colored object produces disappointing results. To see Chrome at its best, try it on relatively complex images with areas of contrast.

NOTE

Folks who use Alien Skin Software's Eye Candy filters should note that Eye Candy's Chrome filter works quite differently from Paint Shop Pro's Chrome effect. The Eye Candy filter makes use of selection edges or areas of transparency rather than contrast. It gives pleasing results on solid-colored figures and text but isn't appropriate for use on the more complex images that work best with Paint Shop Pro's Chrome effect.

With Chrome, there are several controls that work together to produce different metal-like effects: **Flaws**, **Brightness**, **Use original color**, and **Color** (see Figure 7.13).

Flaws determines the amount of banding, and **Brightness** is used to adjust brightness. You have the choice of having the filter retain the original color of the image or to change the image to monochrome. To make the image monochrome, click the **Color** box to call up the Color dialog box and then select the color you want.

▶ **Colored Edges.** This enhances the edges in your image.

▶ **Colored Foil** and **Enamel.** These give your image a shiny, 3-D look. Try out the presets to see the different sorts of effects you can create with these.

▶ **Contours.** This gives your image a look that resembles a contour map.

▶ **Glowing Edges** and **Neon Glow.** Both of these emphasize the edges in your image and affect the color. These effects have the same controls that you also find with Black Pencil, Colored Pencil, Charcoal, and Colored Chalk.

▶ **Halftone.** The basic use of this one is to simulate halftone, making your photos resemble photos printed on newsprint. You can also create other effects, such as scan lines or wild abstract patterns, with this effect. We'll look at Halftone again later in this chapter.

Figure 7.13
The Chrome dialog box.

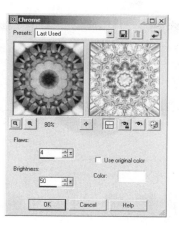

▶ **Hot Wax Coating.** This seems to coat your image with melted wax, the "wax" having the same color as the current Foreground color. This effect can darken your image considerably. For best results, use a light color for the wax.

Hot Wax Coating can be used to create metallic effects. An example of this is shown in Figure 7.14, in which a white Hot Wax Coating was applied to delicate script text filled with a silvery gradient. The results could be colorized to change the look from silver to gold, copper, or bronze.

Figure 7.14
Metallic text created with
Hot Wax Coating.

TIP

Metallic effects created with repeated applications of Hot Wax Coating sometimes benefit from a little sharpening after the colorizing.

▶ **Magnifying Lens.** The basic use for this effect is to produce round or rectangular lenses, with or without a frame. If you set **Opacity**, **Shininess**, and **Gloss** on this effect's Properties tab to 0, you can also create a frame without a lens. Figure 7.15 shows both a framed lens and a lensless doughnut shape created with Magnifying Lens. Doughnut shapes can be used for rings, links of a chain, and even inner tubes.

Be sure to check out the presets for Magnifying Lens. You'll find some effects you probably hadn't imagined you could get with this.

Figure 7.15
A framed lens and a
doughnut shape, both
made with Magnifying
Lens.

▶ **Posterize.** This reduces the gradations of color in your image, giving the image the look of an old-fashioned print poster. You control how much the color gradations are flattened using this effect's **Levels** control.

▶ **Solarize.** This converts the colors in an image or selection to their inverse. You control the range of colors that get inverted using the effect's **Threshold** control. Only colors whose lightness values exceed the threshold are inverted. (The lightness scale ranges from 0 for black to 255 for white.)

▶ **Topography.** This makes your image look a bit like it was made up of hills and valleys, seen from a bird's-eye perspective.

Distortion Effects

As you would expect, each Distortion effect distorts your image. Apply them with Effects > Distortion Effects > *effect name*.

▶ **Curlicues.** This warps your image into a series of rows and columns of curls.

▶ **Lens Distortion.** This simulates three types of lens distortion: barrel distortion, fish-eye distortion, and pincushion distortion. Later in the chapter, we'll look at an example where Lens Distortion and Halftone are used together to simulate an image on a video screen.

▶ **Pinch** and **Punch.** Pinch seems to push your image in; Punch seems to push it out.

▶ **Pixelate.** This paints your image in solid-colored square or rectangular blocks.

▶ **Polar Coordinates.** Use this to change a normal image on a rectangular plane to its polar coordinates equivalent, or to warp a generally circular figure from polar coordinates to rectangular coordinates. We'll look at some examples later in the chapter.

▶ **Ripple.** This makes your image appear as though it's reflected in water that is rippling after a small object has just been dropped into it. Figure 7.16 shows an example.

▶ **Spiky Halo.** This creates a spiky corona around the edge of your image, radiating from a focus point in the image (which is the center of the image when **Horizontal Offset** and **Vertical Offset** are each set to 0). The smaller the **Radius (%)** setting, the closer to the focus point the effect begins.

Figure 7.16
Ripple applied to a photo
of a flower.

▶ **Twirl.** This seems to swirl the colors of your image together, as if the image were a thick liquid being stirred with a circular motion.

▶ **Warp.** This seems to push your image in (somewhat like Pinch) or push it out (somewhat like Punch). For a pushed-in effect, set **Strength** to a negative value. For a pushed-out effect, set **Strength** to a positive value.

▶ **Wave.** This displaces the pixels of your image in vertical and/or horizontal waves.

▶ **Wind.** This produces a directional blurring effect somewhat like a horizontal Motion Blur (which is available under **A**djust > **Bl**ur).

Edge Effects

Edge effects enhance the contrast along the edges of the figures in your images. Apply these with Effects > Edge Effects > *effect name*.

Each of these effects is applied immediately, with no controls.

▶ **Dilate** and **Erode.** Dilate enhances the light areas of the image, while Erode enhances the dark areas. These can be used to good effect in creating digital paintings.

▶ **Enhance** and **Enhance More.** Enhance increases the contrast along the image's edges, with Enhance More providing stronger contrast.

▶ **Find All, Find Horizontal,** and **Find Vertical.** Find All darkens the image and highlights the edges. Find Horizontal does the same thing except that the highlighting is limited to the horizontal edges. And Find Vertical behaves similarly except that the highlighting is limited to the vertical edges.

▶ **Trace Contour.** This traces a line around areas of contrast and turns the rest of the image white. This one can also be used in creating digital drawings and paintings.

Figure 7.17 shows a drawing of a pear, and Figure 7.18 shows the same drawing after Trace Contour and then Erode are applied.

Figure 7.17
An unfiltered image.

Figure 7.18
The same image after
Trace Contour and Erode
are applied.

Geometric Effects

Geometric effects apply simple but useful deformations to your images. Apply them with Effects > Geometric Effects > *effect name*.

> ▶ **Circle** and **Pentagon.** These warp your image into a circle or a pentagon. How the edges of the resulting image appear is dependent on the **Edge mode** setting that you choose. (Note that if Circle is applied to something that is already circular, the result is a diamond shape. Applying Pentagon to something circular produces a shape that resembles a shield.)

> ▶ **Cylinder—Horizontal** and **Cylinder—Vertical.** Each of these seems to wrap your image around a cylinder either horizontally or vertically, as indicated by the particular effect's name.

> ▶ **Perspective—Horizontal** and **Perspective—Vertical.** Perspective—Horizontal adds perspective to your image by narrowing the right or left side of the image. Perspective—Vertical adds perspective by narrowing the top or bottom of the image. How the edges of the resulting image appear is dependent on the **Edge mode** setting that you choose.

You can use either of these effects on a round object—such as the result you get from Balls and Bubbles or Circle—to create an egg-shaped or teardrop-shaped object.

▶ **Skew.** This skews your image either vertically or horizontally. How the edges of the resulting image appear is dependent on the **Edge mode** setting that you choose.

▶ **Spherize.** This seems to wrap your image around the inside or outside of a sphere or elliptical spheroid shape.

Illumination Effects

The two Illumination effects add lighting effects to your images. Apply them with Effects > Illumination Effects > *effect name*.

▶ **Sunburst.** This adds an effect that resembles a lens flare. Set **Brightness** in the **Rays** pane to 0 to add a highlight or glint rather than a lens flare. Be sure to try out the presets for Sunburst to get a feeling for this effect.

▶ **Lights.** This enables you to add all sorts of lighting effects. You have five "lights" to work with, each of which has its own settings. To use a particular light, depress its button on the lower left of the Lights dialog box (Figure 7.19), and then check the **On** check box in the **Settings** pane. You can then select whatever settings you want for that light. Repeat the same procedure for any of the other lights that you want to use. To turn a light off, click its button, and then uncheck the **On** check box.

Figure 7.19
The Lights dialog box.

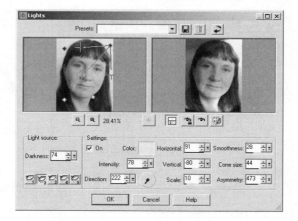

Image Effects

This group is a bit of a grab bag of some useful effects. Apply these with Effects > Image Effects > *effect name*.

▶ **Offset.** This has several uses. One is to swap the quadrants of your image as indicated in Figure 7.20. In this case, **Edge mode** is set to Wrap.

As you'll see later in this chapter, Offset with **Edge mode** set to Wrap is helpful when you want to make a seamless tile by hand: apply Offset, and then cover the seam that appears where the previous edges of your image meet, running horizontally and vertically along the middle of the filtered image.

Figure 7.20
Offset (Wrap) swaps
quadrants of an image.

Another use of Offset, this one with **Edge mode** set to Repeat, is to produce an
effect like the one shown in Figure 7.21.

Figure 7.21
Offset (Repeat) seems to
drag colors from the
image horizontally or
vertically.

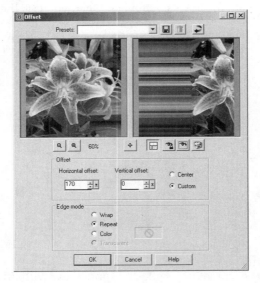

▶ **Page Curl.** This does just as its name implies, adding a page curl effect to any of
the corners of your image.

▶ **Seamless Tiling.** This is a much improved replacement of Paint Shop Pro 7's
Convert to Seamless Pattern. You use Seamless Tiling to create a repeating pattern
that can be tiled with no apparent seam between occurrences of the tiled pattern.
You'll explore Seamless Tiling later in this chapter.

Reflection Effects

Reflection effects repeat elements of your image to produce their results. Most of these effects are useful in creating abstract tiles.

> ▶ **Feedback.** This creates repetitions of your image, laid one on top of the other, with the image shrinking with each repetition. Try it on a layer that contains an object on a transparent background, as shown in Figure 7.22 (where the layer contains a repeated ring on top of a solid-colored layer).

Figure 7.22
Feedback used on an object on a transparent layer.

> ▶ **Kaleidoscope.** This uses your image as the source for creating a kaleidoscopic effect. Figure 7.23 shows the dialog box for Kaleidoscope.

Figure 7.23
The Kaleidoscope dialog box.

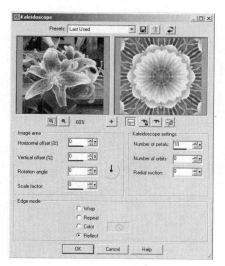

Like several other effects, Kaleidoscope has settings for **Edge mode**. **Edge mode** determines how areas outside the area of the main effect are treated. Kaleidoscope's **Edge mode** settings include Color, Reflect, Repeat, and Wrap, shown in Figure 7.24. Some other effects include Transparent as one of the **Edge mode** options.

Figure 7.24
Results with different
Edge modes: Color (top
left), Reflect (top right),
Repeat (bottom left), and
Wrap (bottom right).

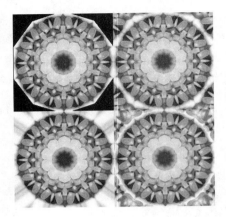

▶ **Pattern.** This can be used to create an abstract seamless tile that is made up of a repeating pattern. You may need to adjust the **Scale** to make your pattern seamless. For your source image, I've found that good results are usually produced when the image's height and width are each evenly divisible by 32. Try a section of a photo or an image canvas that you've filled using the Picture Tube tool.

▶ **Rotating Mirror.** This reflects your image along an axis whose angle you set, as shown in Figure 7.25. This effect can be quite useful when you want to create a symmetrical object from one that is not quite symmetrical.

Figure 7.25
Use Rotating Mirror to
create symmetrical
effects.

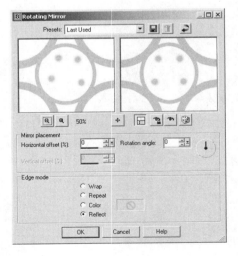

Texture Effects

Texture effects emboss your image, make it appear to be painted on a textured surface, or simulate natural textures such as fur and stone. Apply them with Effects > **T**exture Effects > *effect name*.

▶ **Blinds.** Care to do a little home decorating in your images? Blinds can at least help with the window dressing, as Figure 7.26 shows.

Figure 7.26
The Blinds dialog box.

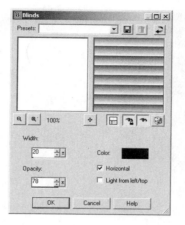

Don't care for horizontal blinds? Uncheck the **Horizontal** control in the Blinds dialog box, and you'll get vertical blinds instead, as shown in Figure 7.27.

Figure 7.27
An example of vertical blinds.

Don't think that window blinds are all you can make with this effect. Figure 7.28 shows a nice log cabin effect made by applying Blinds to a wood-grain pattern.

Figure 7.28
A log cabin effect made with Blinds.

▶ **Emboss.** This makes your image appear to be embossed on the image canvas, as shown in Figure 7.29. Most of the image colors turn to shades of grey, although high-contrast areas will still show a hint of color.

Figure 7.29
Emboss example.

Emboss has no controls, so you have no direct way to specify the direction of the shadows for your embossing. You can easily produce the inverse of the normal Emboss results, though, by choosing **A**djust > Ne**g**ative Image after applying Emboss. Figure 7.30 shows the result of using this method on the example in Figure 7.29.

Figure 7.30
Emboss followed by
Negative Image.

Here's how to produce even more variation in your embossings: *Before* you apply the Emboss filter, use either **I**mage > **Mir**r**o**r or **I**mage > **F**lip or Image > **R**otate on your original image. After that, you can mirror, flip, or rotate the embossed image back to its original position. Consider a few examples of what you can create with these simple techniques. Using the same source image as the one used for the example in Figure 7.29, you can create the image shown in Figure 7.31 by applying Mirror and then Emboss and then Mirror again. Figure 7.32 shows the same image after applying Flip and then Emboss and then Flip again.

Figure 7.31
Applying Mirror, then Emboss,
then Mirror again.

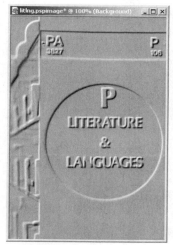

Figure 7.32
Applying Flip, then Emboss,
then Flip again.

▶ **Fine Leather** and **Rough Leather.** Fine Leather makes your image look as though it's dyed into fine-grained leather. Rough Leather makes your image look as though it's embossed on rough-grained leather.

▶ **Fur.** This uses your image as the basis for creating a furry effect. You control the length and density of the "hairs," along with the softness of the hairs (set with **Blur**) and how transparent or opaque the furry effect on the image is (set with **Transparency**).

▶ **Mosaic—Antique.** This gives your image the look of old mosaic tiles.

▶ **Mosaic—Glass.** This makes your image look like it's being viewed through glass blocks.

▶ **Polished Stone.** This makes your image look like it's been carved from hard stone.

▶ **Sandstone.** This makes your image look like it's been carved from soft stone.

▶ **Sculpture.** This seems to carve your image into whatever texture you select.

▶ **Soft Plastic.** This makes your image appear to be molded from plastic.

▶ **Straw-wall.** This gives your image the texture of a straw-plastered wall, with the colors of the image seeming to tint the wall.

▶ **Texture.** This adds a texture to your image, making the image look as though it's painted on a textured surface.

▶ **Tiles.** This makes your image look like it's made from triangular, square, or hexagonal tiles.

Tiles is a versatile effect. You can create anything from simulated crewel work (Figure 7.33) to something like ceramic tile (Figure 7.34) to a leathery look (Figure 7.35).

Figure 7.33
Crewel work made with
Tiles.

Figure 7.34
Ceramic tile made with
Tiles.

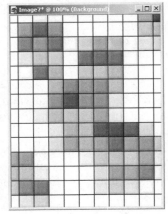

Figure 7.35
Leather made with Tiles.

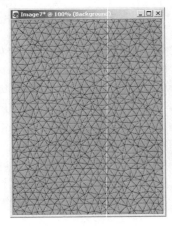

As Figure 7.36 shows, Tiles uses many of the controls familiar to you from Inner Bevel and other effects. The Tile controls, in the leftmost pane of the Tiles dialog box, are the controls unique to Tiles.

Figure 7.36
The Tiles dialog box.

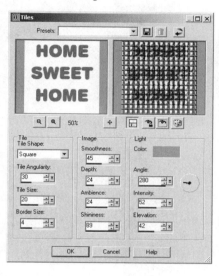

Tile Shape. As its name implies, this control sets the shape of the tiles. For example, you can set the tiles to Hexagon (as in Figure 7.33), Square (as in Figure 7.34), or Triangle (as in Figure 7.35).

Tile Angularity. This control determines whether the tiles are made in a regular, rigid matrix or are made to conform somewhat to the shape of your image; the higher the value, the more the tiles conform to the shape of your image. In Figures 7.33 through 7.35, the crewel work and leather have high values for **Tile Angularity**, while the ceramic tiles have a value of 0.

Tile Size. This control sets the size of the individual tiles.

Border Size. This control sets the size of the spacing between the tiles. This spacing is always filled in with black.

NOTE

Tile Angularity has no effect on solid-colored images. To create the effect in Figure 7.35, fill a layer with a color, and then use the Airbrush to lightly paint a random pattern on the image in a few colors that are slightly different than the original color. Because the colors are different (even if you might not be able to see the differences), **Tile Angularity** will work just fine.

▶ **Weave.** This makes your image look as if it's painted on a woven basket or woven fabric strips.

Let's take a quick look at a few more of the effects you can create with the Texture effects. Figure 7.37 shows an unfiltered image, and Figure 7.38 shows the same image with Fine Leather, Polished Stone, and Straw-wall applied.

Figure 7.37
An unfiltered image.

Figure 7.38
The same image with a few Texture effects applied: Fine Leather (left), Polished Stone (center), and Strawwall (right).

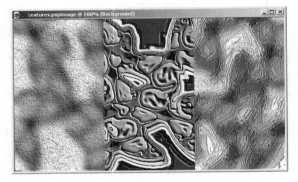

Extended Examples Using Built-In Effects

Now let's take a look at some of the effects you can produce using effects in combination with each other or with other tools and commands.

All Kinds of Seamless Tiles

Paint Shop Pro 8 has three excellent effects that are useful in making seamless tiles: Seamless Tiling, Offset, and Pattern. Use Pattern to create abstract tiles. Use Offset for creating your own natural texture tiles. And Seamless Tiling is good for both abstract and natural tiles.

Pattern is straightforward, and we won't look at it further here. Offset isn't much more complicated. As you saw earlier, with its **Edge mode** set to Wrap, Offset wraps the quadrants of your image so that the outer corners meet in the middle of your image.

When you use an image whose edges aren't uniform, you'll see quite noticeable seams running down and across the middle of your image. To make the image tile seamlessly, you need to get rid of those seams. You can do that by cloning over the seams with the Clone Brush or in some cases blurring the seam with a retouch tool such as Smudge or Soften. If you created the basic tile image by filling an image with Picture Tube elements, you can paint over the seams with the Picture Tube tool. You just need to be careful not to paint outside the boundaries of your image canvas. If you do, the result will be noticeable when you use your image as a tile.

For a nice use of Offset that also pleasantly enhances the result of the Weave effect, see Angela Cable's tutorial at **http://www.fortunecity.com/westwood/alaia/354/tutorials/basketweave**. The resulting Fill pattern produces results like those in Figure 7.39.

Figure 7.39
A Weave-based seamless pattern made with Offset.

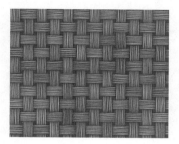

Tile makers will be thrilled when they try out Seamless Tiling. This is a powerful and helpful tool. With Seamless Tiling you have three different tiling methods and can set the effect to adjust the image only horizontally, only vertically, or in both directions. You can protect parts of the image so that they aren't blurred by the effect by selecting those areas that you want protected before applying the effect.

Even if you don't use Seamless Tiling to create your tile, you can use it to check your tile for seams. Prepare your tile by whatever method you like. Then invoke Seamless Tiling. Check the box labeled **Show tiling preview**. In the Seamless Tiling Preview window, shown in Figure 7.40, you can toggle between seeing your original image tiled and the results of Seamless Tiling tiled by checking and unchecking **Show original**.

Figure 7.40
The Seamless Tiling Preview window.

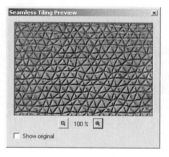

For more information on Seamless Tiling and other seamless tiling methods, see the tiling tutorials listed on my "How To" page at **http://loriweb.pair.com/howto.html**.

You can also make some pretty nice geometric tiles by starting off with a simple grid. To make a grid with 100-pixel cells, open a new image that is 92×92 pixels and is whatever color you want for the center of the grid cells. Next choose **I**mage > Add **B**orders. In the Add Borders dialog box, set the color that you want for the grid outline, check **Symmetric**, and set any of the **Size in pixels** values to 4. Click OK and your basic grid cell should look something like what's shown in Figure 7.41.

Figure 7.41
A simple grid cell.

Use this image itself as a pattern to flood fill an image, and you'll get a straightforward grid, as in Figure 7.42.

Figure 7.42
A grid made with the simple grid cell.

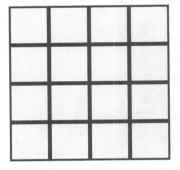

Now for the nifty part. For variations on the grid theme, try adding various Texture effects to your grid cell. Figure 7.43 shows the result of filling an image with our basic grid cell after Polished Stone (at its default settings) has been applied to the cell image.

Figure 7.43
The result of applying Polished Stone to the grid cell.

And if your modified tile isn't quite seamless, just give it a pass through Seamless Tiles. To get the cell used for the fill in Figure 7.44, apply Soft Plastic with **Blur** set to 92, **Detail** set to 18, **Density** set to 42, **Angle** set to 326, and **Color** set to a pale green. Then apply Seamless Tiling with the default settings except for **Tiling method**, which should be set to Mirror.

Figure 7.44
Fill made with Soft Plastic followed by Seamless Tiling.

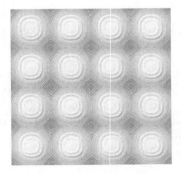

Try out your own variations and see what sorts of interesting tiles you can come up with.

What Can You Do with Polar Coordinates?

Some folks just don't know what to do with Polar Coordinates. With Polar Coordinates set to **Polar to rectangular**, you can go from a more or less circular image into a drapelike effect, as in Figure 7.45.

Figure 7.45
Polar Coordinates (**Polar to rectangular**) applied to a somewhat circular image.

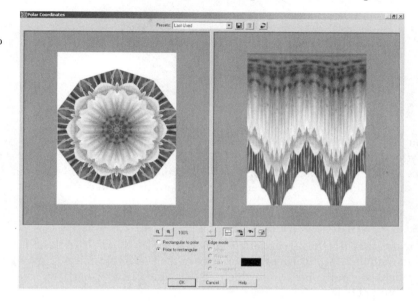

It's a nice enough effect, and you may find uses for it. But what Polar Coordinates is really useful for is taking a line or rectangular shape and warping it into something round. Consider the image in Figure 7.46, where a plaid pattern fills most of the image except for a solid-colored band across the bottom of the image. Apply Polar Coordinates to this image with **Rectangular to polar** selected and **Edge mode** set to Repeat, and you get a sort of dartboard with the solid color surrounding it, as in Figure 7.47.

Figure 7.46
A plaid pattern and white band.

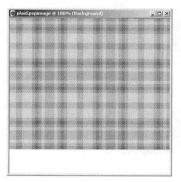

Figure 7.47 demonstrates the basics of Polar Coordinates used with **Rectangular to polar**: The top of the original pattern is pulled into the middle of the circle. The horizontal parts of the pattern become centric circles, while the vertical parts of the pattern become wedges. The white line at the bottom of the original becomes the white background surrounding the circle.

Figure 7.47
Polar Coordinates
(**Rectangular to polar**)
applied to the pattern.

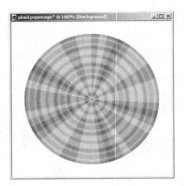

You can use Polar Coordinates to make phonograph records or CDs, rings, wreaths—just about anything circular. Start out with a rectangular figure that spans the width of the image canvas. If necessary, apply Seamless Tiling with **Direction** set to Horizontal so that the two ends of the rectangular image mesh. Then apply Polar Coordinates and see what you get.

Balls, Bubbles, and Beyond

To make something that is not quite spherical, begin with Balls and Bubbles, and then deform the result with the Warp Brush or one or more of the Geometric effects. Figure 7.48 shows a strawberry and the unwarped sphere from which it began, and Figure 7.49 shows a wooden bowl made from the output of Balls and Bubbles.

And to get an idea of the sorts of shapes you can get with the Geometric and Distortion effects, take a look at Figures 7.50 and 7.51, where each shape began as the sphere in Figure 7.52.

Figure 7.48
A strawberry (left)
created from a ball (right).

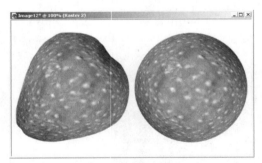

Figure 7.49
A wooden bowl made
from a ball.

Figure 7.50
Geometric effects applied
to a ball: (top, left to
right) Circle, Cylinder—
Horizontal, Cylinder—
Vertical, Pentagon;
(bottom, left to right)
Perspective—Horizontal,
Perspective—Vertical,
Skew.

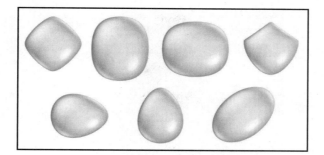

Figure 7.51
Distortion effects applied
to a ball: (top, left to
right) Curlicue, Pinch,
Punch; (middle, left to
right) Polar Coordinates,
Ripple, Twirl; (bottom,
left to right) Warp, Wave,
Wind.

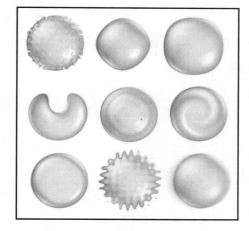

Figure 7.52
The basic ball.

Use Balls and Bubbles along with these effects and the warping tools to make cups, goblets, bowls, spoons, fruits, vegetables, eggs, shields, and faces. You may think of many other uses for Balls and Bubbles, too.

Miscellany

Now for a few other nice effects.

Gradients and Effects

Many of the Texture effects and edge-sensitive Artistic effects can be applied to gradients to produce interesting geometric backgrounds. To give you some ideas, start out with an image filled with a linear gradient such as Paint Shop Pro's own Metallic Silver, as shown in Figure 7.53.

Figure 7.53
An image filled with a
linear gradient.

Now apply Contours with its default settings to get the effect shown in Figure 7.54.

Figure 7.54
The gradient after
applying Contours.

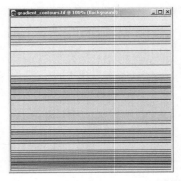

And Figure 7.55 shows an example where Mosaic—Glass is applied to the same gradient. Here the settings are **Number of columns** 36, **Number of rows** 39, **Glass curvature** 38, **Edge curvature** 16, **Grout width** 7, and **Grout diffusion** 71.

Figure 7.55
The gradient after
applying Mosaic—Glass.

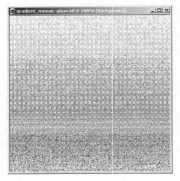

Experiment on your own to see what you can get. Be sure to try out **Rectangular**, **Sunburst**, and **Radial** gradients in addition to **Linear** gradients.

Halftone and More

Sure, Halftone is great for producing simulations of newsprint. But this effect can be used for lots more than just that. One thing it's good for is creating scan lines. Use Halftone set to Line followed by Lens Distortion set to Barrel to simulate a video display, as in Figure 7.56.

Figure 7.56
A video screen made with Halftone and Lens Distortion.

For more ideas about what to do with Halftone, be sure to try out its presets.

Magnifying Lens Isn't Just for Lenses

As mentioned earlier, Magnifying Lens can be used to make lensless frames as well as lenses. To make a circular frame, set **Lens type** to Spherical. To make a rectangular frame, set **Lens type** to either of its other settings. In both cases, set **Opacity**, **Shininess**, and **Gloss** to 0 if you want a lensless frame.

You can define a rectangular frame on a transparent layer, stretched out as far as possible on the image canvas, to create a simple picture frame. Or make a round frame that you flatten into a link of a chain using the Deform tool or Mesh Warp. You can overlay several links one on top of another, each link on its own layer. Then, using the Eraser judiciously where the links overlap, create a piece of chain, as in Figure 7.57.

Figure 7.57
A chain created from a deformed frame made with Magnifying Lens.

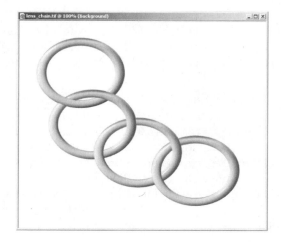

TIP

When making the chain, you don't have to be all that careful in your erasing if you use this trick: Once you've positioned each of the links, hide the Background layer by toggling its **Visibility** toggle off in the Layers palette. Then choose **Edit** > **Copy Merged**, followed by **Edit** > **Paste** > Paste As New Layer. Drag this new layer down in the layer stack so that it's the first layer above the Background layer. Position the merged layer with the Mover tool so that the links align precisely with their analogs on the upper layers. Then when you erase on the links layers, overly enthusiastic erasing isn't a problem, because the parts that shouldn't be erased will still show up on the merged layer.

And that's only the beginning. Explore the effects, singly or in combination, to see what else you can do beyond the obvious with these fun and useful features of Paint Shop Pro.

User Defined Filters

You can create your own simple filters with the User Defined Filter facility. When Paint Shop Pro had limited blur, sharpen, and edge detection functions, User Defined Filters were particularly useful for getting fine-tuned effects of these sorts. Paint Shop Pro now has much more powerful adjustment filters, but that doesn't mean User Defined Filters are passé, and I strongly encourage you to give them a try.

To start a new filter, choose Effects > User Defined. You'll then see the User Defined Filter dialog box, which includes a matrix into which you enter values, and a few other controls. The effect that your filter produces depends on the settings you enter.

There are several useful presets for User Defined Filters, including several excellent embossing effects. Be sure to check out the presets, even if you're not interested in creating your own filters. If you do want to try creating your own User Defined Filters, see Chapter 11, "Adding to Your Toolkit."

Plug-In Filters

There are many plug-in filters available for Paint Shop Pro, some for free and some for sale. Two popular commercial plug-in packages are SuperBladePro from Flaming Pear (**http://www.flamingpear.com**) and Eye Candy 4000 from Alien Skin Software (**http://www.alienskin.com**).

To install commercial plug-in filters, follow the manufacturer's directions. To install free, downloadable filters that have no installer, put the filters in the folder where you want to store them. If you put the filters in your Paint Shop Pro PlugIns folder, there's nothing more you need to do. If you put the filters in some other folder, be sure that that folder is specified in your file location preferences: In Paint Shop Pro, choose File > Preferences > File Locations. In the File Locations dialog box (shown in Figure 7.58), choose Plug-ins in the selection list. Click the **Add** button and then the **Browse** button. Choose the folder in which you've placed your filters. Click OK after choosing the folder. Repeat for any other folders where you want Paint Shop Pro to look for plug-ins, and then click OK again to return to Paint Shop Pro.

Figure 7.58
The Plug-in Filters
display on the File
Locations dialog box.

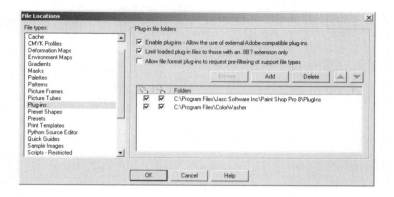

To apply a plug-in filter, choose Effects > Plugins > *filter family* > *filter name*. For example, to apply the Eye Candy 4000 filter called Wood, you'd choose Effects > Plugins > Eye Candy 4000 > Wood.

NOTE

Plug-ins require that MSVCRT10.DLL be in your Windows\System folder. If you don't have this file, you can download it from nearly any filter download site or from the Jasc FTP site at **ftp://ftp.jasc.com**. You can access the Jasc site via anonymous FTP.

Some Filter Factory plug-ins also require that PLUGIN.DLL be in your Windows\System folder. If you have one of Adobe's graphics products, you probably already have this file and simply need to copy it to Windows\System. If you don't have this file, don't despair. Just head over to The Plugin Site (**http://www.thepluginsite.com**) and download a free copy of Harry Heim's Plugin Commander Light or purchase Plugin Commander Pro. PiCo (as it's called by its fans) lets you translate the old plug-ins to a form that Paint Shop Pro can use. PiCo also has several other handy functions, including some specifically for Paint Shop Pro, so you might want to check it out even if you have a copy of PLUGIN.DLL.

8

Photo Editing and Enhancement

Paint Shop Pro has numerous tools and commands that any digital photographer will find handy. Here's what you'll be exploring in this chapter:

▶ Correcting lens distortion, distorted perspective, contrast, and color

▶ Rotating, straightening, resizing, and cropping your photos

▶ Eliminating dust spots, scratches, and other imperfections

Quick Fixes

If you don't know a lot about digital photography—or sometimes even if you do—you'll find some of Paint Shop Pro's automatic photo correction tools quite useful. For a really quick fix, try zapping your photo with One Step Photo Fix, available on the Photo toolbar or the Script palette. In most cases, your photo will be improved.

For a little more control, try this sequence of commands (all available from the Photo toolbar or the Adjust menu):

1. Automatic Color Balance
2. Automatic Contrast Enhancement
3. Clarify
4. Automatic Saturation Enhancement
5. Edge Preserving Smooth
6. Unsharp Mask

Automatic Color Balance, available under **A**djust > **C**olor Balance, corrects the color of your photo. Automatic Contrast Enhancement and Clarify, both available under **A**djust > **B**rightness and Contrast, correct contrast, with Clarify oftentimes bringing out the detail in shadow and highlight areas. After correcting the contrast, you'll usually find that the colors have become washed out. Automatic Saturation Enhancement, available under **A**djust > **H**ue and Saturation, will put some verve back in those colors.

Digital photos usually have some noise (that is, tiny specks of random color). To get rid of excess noise, you can use a smoothing command. Edge Preserving Smooth, available under **A**djust > Add/Remove **N**oise, is an excellent choice here, because it smoothes out the noise without blurring edges. Still, smoothing of any kind will probably require you to sharpen the photo a bit. The best choice for sharpening is Unsharp Mask, available under **A**djust > **S**harpness.

If you use these commands in the order just listed and with their default settings, the results will be pretty much what you'd get with One Step Photo Fix. The reason you'd want to use the commands separately is so you can tweak the settings to best suit your specific photo. For example, if you have a low-resolution image, you might want to turn down the strength of Edge Preserving Smooth so you don't get too much smoothing. Or you might want to increase the strength of Clarify or apply it two or three times in a row to bring out hidden detail in your photo. Or if your photo is a portrait, you'll want to check the **Skintones present** check box in Automatic Saturation Enhancement.

But what if you want something other than what the automatic correction tools can offer? For that, let's turn to Paint Shop Pro's more advanced and more specialized photo correction tools.

Correcting Lens Distortion

There are a few things you might want to address before you begin adjusting the color or contrast of your images. One of these things is lens distortion.

A camera's lens can produce distortion. This is particularly true of zoom lenses zoomed to their wide-angle and telephoto extremes and of ultra wide-angle lenses. With telephoto lenses you can get barrel distortion, which makes your image look like it's bowed around the edges. With wide-angle lenses, you can get pincushion distortion, which makes your image look like it's pushed in in the middle. And fisheye distortion, which you get with ultra wide-angle lenses, makes your image look as if it's being reflected on a sphere: Areas in the middle are enlarged while areas at the edges are compressed. Fortunately, all three kinds of distortion can be corrected with **A**djust > Lens Correction.

Figure 8.1 shows the dialog box for Barrel Distortion Correction.

Note that although the **Preserve central scale** setting isn't very important for Barrel Distortion Correction or Pincushion Distortion Correction, it is very important for Fisheye Distortion Correction, because in fisheye distortion the difference in scale between the center of the image and the edges is extreme.

Figure 8.1
Barrel Distortion
Correction.

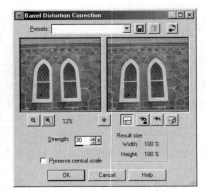

CAUTION

Always correct lens distortion before you crop or rotate your photo. The Lens Correction commands make assumptions about your image that do not hold once the image is cropped or rotated.

Rotating and Straightening

A couple other things you might need to adjust with your photos are the rotation and the horizontal or vertical alignment.

You might need to rotate your photo for one of several reasons. The photo might be in landscape orientation when it really should be in portrait orientation (or vice versa). Or you may not have been holding the camera level when you took the shot. Or the photo may be one that you scanned and the original wasn't exactly square with the scanner bed, giving you an image that is slightly off-kilter.

To take care of the first of these problems, you can use Image > **R**otate > Rotate **C**lockwise 90 or Image > **R**otate > Rotate Counter-clock**w**ise 90. There's also a Free Rotate option under **I**mage > **R**otate, but if you want to straighten out a crooked photo, a much better bet is to use the Straighten tool.

Figure 8.2 shows the Straighten tool in action, and Figure 8.3 shows the result. Straighten couldn't be easier to use: Just position the level line along the intended horizontal or vertical, and then click the **Apply** button in the Tool Options palette.

Figure 8.2
Using the Straighten tool.

Figure 8.3
The straightened photo.

Correcting Perspective

When you photograph a tall object, such as a building or large monument, the top of the object can seem to lean back and grow smaller than the base. Sometimes you'll purposely try to achieve this effect, but in the cases where you'd prefer that the photo look like it was taken head-on at the object's midpoint, try the Perspective Correction tool.

Figure 8.4 shows the Perspective Correction tool being put to use. What you do is place the tool's bounding box nodes on the corners of the figure that should be rectangular. When you click the **Apply** button in the Tool Options palette, the result should be something like what's shown in Figure 8.5.

Figure 8.4
Using the Perspective
Correction tool.

Figure 8.5
The result of Perspective Correction.

NOTE

Sometimes you'll get some odd distortion when you use the Perspective Correction tool. For example, consider the result shown in Figure 8.5. Notice how the frieze at the top of the building is much taller than you'd expect it to be.

A distortion like this is easy to fix, however. Just use the Mesh Warp tool to squash that extra tall frieze down to its proper size, as shown in Figure 8.6.

Figure 8.6
Adjusting the results with Mesh Warp.

CHAPTER 8

Improving Brightness and Contrast

You might think that when your photo needs some adjustment to its brightness or contrast, you should head right to **A**djust> **B**rightness and Contrast > **B**rightness/Contrast. Nothing could be further from the truth. Stay far, far away from Brightness/Contrast when editing your photos. Brightness/Contrast affects the whole image uniformly, when what you really want is to be able to adjust different parts of the tonal range separately. The commands of choice here are Levels, Histogram Adjustment, and Curves (with perhaps a touch of Clarify afterward).

Levels

Levels is one of the best operations for adjusting brightness and contrast, especially for black-and-white photos. It enables you to make separate adjustments in the shadow, midtone, and highlight areas of your photo.

Figure 8.7 shows the dialog box for Levels.

Figure 8.7
The Levels dialog box.

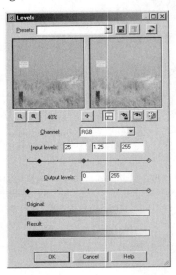

The left and right **Input levels** sliders adjust the contrast, making shadows darker when you move the left slider to the right and making highlights brighter when you move the right slider to the left. The middle **Input levels** slider adjusts the brightness of the midtones. In general, after pulling the left and right sliders in toward the middle to adjust the contrast, you'll need to lighten the midtones by moving the middle slider to the left.

Histogram Adjustment

Histogram Adjustment is also great for adjusting brightness and contrast. In fact, some folks swear there's nothing better. Take a look at the Histogram Adjustment dialog box, in Figure 8.8.

Don't let all those controls and that graph confuse you. The graph is a histogram, a representation of the brightness values in your image. The left side represents the dark pixels (at the shadow end of the image's tonal range), and the right side represents the light pixels (at the highlights end of the range). The middle represents the midtones.

The only controls you'll probably ever need to use in Histogram Adjustment are **Low** (for the low clip limit) and **High** (for the high clip limit), **Gamma**, and sometimes **Midtones: expand** or **Midtones: compress**. In general, you should move the **Low Clip** to where the graph starts on the left and move the **High Clip** to where the graph starts on the right, as shown in Figure 8.9.

Figure 8.8
Histogram Adjustment.

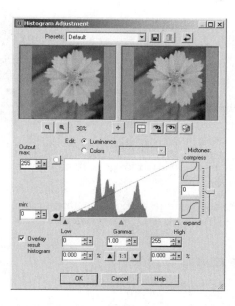

Figure 8.9
Adjusting the **Low** and **High Clip**.

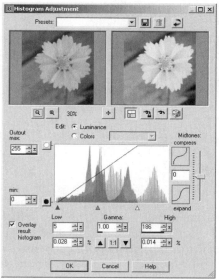

Adjusting the **High** in this way makes the brightest highlights pure white, and adjusting the **Low** in this way makes the darkest shadows pure black. What this does is ensure that the brightness of the image spans the whole tonal range from black to white.

CAUTION

Try to limit the **Low** and **High** adjustments to values of 0.1 or lower. Too high a value for the **Low** and you'll lose detail at the shadow end. Too high a value for the **High** and you'll lose detail at the highlight end.

After adjusting the **Low** and **High**, which affect the contrast of your photo, adjust the **Gamma**, which affects brightness. Be careful here—small adjustments are usually best.

Once you've adjusted the **Gamma**, you may also want to adjust the Midtones slider. **Midtones: compress** lessens the contrast in the midtone range, while **Midtones: expand** heightens the contrast in the midtone range. Be careful here—too much compression can cause loss of detail, and too much expansion can introduce noise (random specks of color).

Curves

Curves is also touted by some as the best operation for adjusting brightness and contrast, vying with Histogram Adjustment for that honor.

Curves lets you fine-tune brightness and contrast along the whole tonal range, from shadows to highlights, adjusting any number of subranges. To see how, take a look at the Curves dialog box, shown in Figure 8.10.

Figure 8.10
The Curves dialog box.

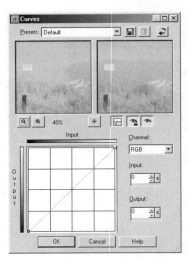

The graph in Figure 8.10 represents the input and output brightness values along the whole tonal range, with shadows represented at the left side and highlights on the right, with black at the bottom and white at the top. When you open Curves, the graph is a straight line from the lower left to the upper right, because the input and output values match up 1-to-1 before you make any adjustments.

You make adjustments by dragging any node on the curve. When you begin, there are only two nodes, one at the far left (for black) and one at the far right (for white). To add new nodes along the curve, just click on the curve. To lighten pixels at any point, click a node and drag upward. To darken pixels at any point, click a node and drag downward. Figures 8.11 and 8.12 show examples of each.

You can even produce a negative version of your photo with Curves. Just drag the leftmost node to the top and the rightmost node to the bottom, completely inverting the original curve. An example is shown in Figure 8.13.

Figure 8.11
Lightening areas of an
image with Curves.

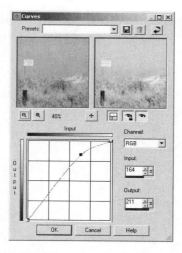

Figure 8.12
Darkening areas of an
image with Curves.

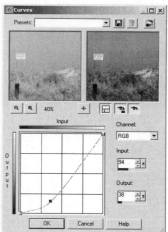

Figure 8.13
Creating a negative
version with Curves.

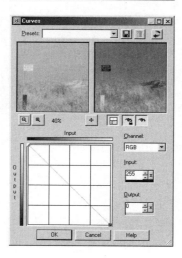

Contrast in any area is affected by the steepness of the graph in that area. The steeper the curve, the higher the contrast. Figures 8.14 and 8.15 show examples of increasing the contrast in the midtone region.

Figure 8.14
Increasing the contrast in an area by increasing the graph's steepness.

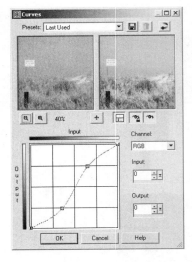

Figure 8.15
Increasing contrast even further.

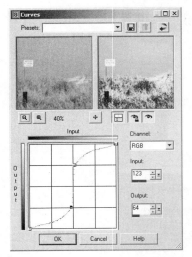

A commonly used rule of thumb is that a photo benefits by having a slightly S-shaped curve, as in Figure 8.16.

There are many exceptions to this rule, though, so don't be a slave to it. Especially keep in mind that what this curve does is increase the contrast for the midtones by sacrificing detail in the shadow and highlight ranges.

Figure 8.16
An S-curve can benefit
many photos.

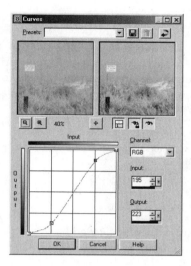

One problem with Curves is that it can produce unintended changes to your image's color. To avoid this problem, try the following technique:

1. Duplicate the Background layer of your photo.
2. On the duplicate layer, apply Curves.
3. Set the **Blend Mode** of the duplicate layer to Luminance.
4. Adjust the duplicate layer's **Opacity** until you get the effect you want.

A variation on this technique is to use a Curves adjustment layer. Make your adjustments to the curve on the adjustment layer. Then set the adjustment layer's **Blend Mode** to Luminance and adjust the adjustment layer's **Opacity** until you get the desired effect.

NOTE

For adjusting brightness and contrast, the **Channel** control for Curves should be set to RGB. Curves can also be used to adjust the Red, Green, and Blue color channels separately to make color adjustments. For example, you can set Curves to Red and pull down the node at the highlight end to lessen the amount of red in the highlight and upper midtone range.

TIP

Curves isn't just for straightforward adjustments of contrast, brightness, and color. As you'll see in Chapter 10, "Tricks and Techniques," you can also use it for special effects, including producing some rather realistic metallic effects.

Color Adjusting

Most color photos could do with a little color adjustment. Your photo may have a color cast, perhaps because it was shot with the camera's white balance set inappropriately for the lighting conditions or maybe your camera or scanner is sensitive to some colors more than others. Whatever the case, Paint Shop Pro provides a number of tools for correcting problems with color.

NOTE
Several examples of corrected photos can be found in the color plate section. Be sure to give these a look as you go through this chapter.

Fade Correction

If you have a scan of an old color photo whose dyes have faded because of exposure to light or simply because of age, the first thing you should try is **A**djust > **C**olor Balance > **F**ade Correction, as shown in Figure 8.17. In many cases, that might be all the color correction your old photo needs.

Figure 8.17
Fade Correction.

Don't make the mistake, though, of using this command on overexposed photos or other images where the overall brightness is rather high and the contrast rather low. Instead, if the photo is extremely light or extremely dark, correct the contrast with one of the operations already discussed in this chapter, and then correct the color with one of the operations described in the next few subsections. If the overall brightness of your photo is more or less fine but the contrast needs adjusting, do the color correction first followed by brightness/contrast adjustment.

Red/Green/Blue, Color Balance, and Channel Mixer

If your photo has an obvious color cast, Red/Green/Blue (Figure 8.18), Color Balance (Figure 8.19), or Channel Mixer (Figure 8.20) can be used to eliminate the cast.

We won't go through these in any detail. However, we'll take a look at Channel Mixer in Chapter 10, where we'll use it for a totally different purpose: converting a color photo to black and white.

For general color correction, some of the other options available under **A**djust > **C**olor Balance are your best bets. Let's turn to those now.

Figure 8.18
Red/Green/Blue.

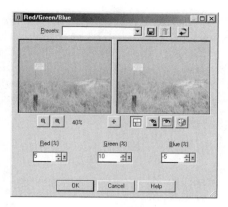

Figure 8.19
Color Balance.

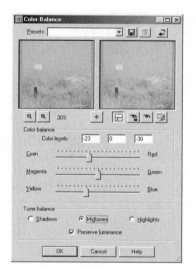

Figure 8.20
Channel Mixer.

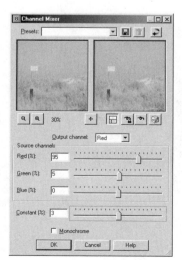

Grey World Color Balance

This is probably my favorite color adjustment command. It's easy to use, and the results are usually quite good, especially for outdoor shots. If you take a look at the dialog box for Grey World Color Balance, shown in Figure 8.21, you'll probably be reminded of the dialog box for Automatic Color Balance. This isn't surprising, because both commands are basic color balancing operations (differing only in their assumptions about how to make their color adjustments).

Figure 8.21
Grey World Color Balance.

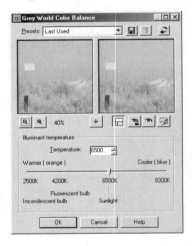

Grey World Color Balance relies on the assumption that in nature colors average out to neutral grey, and it adjusts your photo in accordance with this assumption. The Paint Shop Pro Grey World Color Balance command in fact goes a little farther than this, because it also lets you adjust the output appropriately for different lighting conditions.

Black and White Points

This is my next favorite color correction command after Grey World Color Balance, and it's only slightly harder to use. Take a look at its dialog box, shown in Figure 8.22.

Figure 8.22
Black and White Points.

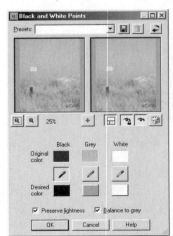

When you first begin exploring this command, try it with **Preserve lightness** and **Balance to grey** both checked. You can then use the droppers to sample areas of your photo that should be pure black, or pure white, or a neutral grey. For example, click on the **Black** dropper and then click in the left preview window on an area that should be pure black. You can also use the **Grey** dropper to sample an area that should be neutral medium grey or the **White** dropper to sample an area that should be pure white. Use any one of the three droppers alone or in combination with either or both of the others. If you make a mistake, just right-click the appropriate dropper button to reset that dropper.

NOTE

The dropper used in Black and White Points uses whatever the current Eye Dropper tool's setting for sample size is. For Black and White Points, a 1×1-pixel sample size is usually best. An exception would be when the image you're editing contains a lot of noise.

NOTE

When **Preserve lightness** and **Balance to grey** are both selected, it doesn't matter what shade of grey you click on with the Grey dropper. Whatever pixel you sample, it will be changed to a neutral grey with the same lightness the pixel had before it was desaturated.

TIP

If you leave **Balance to grey** unchecked, Black and White Points can also be used to tint your photos. Click a dropper's lower color box and set the color to what you want for your target color. Then use the dropper to sample the color that you want to change.

Some of the presets for Black and White Points provide examples. For instance, on a black-and-white photo try Black and White Points' Gold tone, Selenium tone, or Sepia tone preset. (If the photo is a greyscale image, be sure to increase the color depth to 16 million colors first.)

Manual Color Correction

Manual Color Correction probably has the most complicated dialog box of all the color correction commands, but it's worth taking the time to explore its different options. Take a look at Figure 8.23.

To use Manual Color Correction, first click a source pixel in the left preview window, or drag to select a group of pixels to average. Then set the target color in any of the following ways:

▶ Choose a preset color from the selection list.

▶ Set the target color manually (providing values for the color's hue, saturation, and lightness).

▶ Click the **Target** color box and choose a color from the Color dialog box.

Figure 8.23
Manual Color Correction.

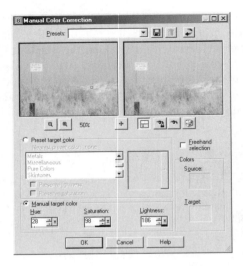

Saturation Adjustment

Saturation determines the vividness of a color, from neutral grey to fully saturated. You may need to adjust the saturation of your photo, especially if you've increased the brightness, which can result in washed-out colors.

Automatic Saturation Enhancement is always a good choice for this purpose. If you'd like a little more control, try **A**djust > **H**ue and Saturation > Hue/**S**aturation/Lightness, adjusting its Saturation slider.

Noise Reduction

After you've corrected the brightness, contrast, color, and saturation of your photo, you may need to reduce noise. There are several noise reduction filters, but probably the best choice for most photo work is Edge Preserving Smooth.

There are a few other commands available under **A**djust > Add/Remove **N**oise that you might want to try in specialized situations. For single-pixel specks that are mostly black and white, try Despeckle. For larger black-and-white specks, try Salt and Pepper. And for removing the regular pattern that often appears when a printed image is scanned, try Moiré Pattern Removal.

Blurring and Sharpening

The noise reduction commands all work by blurring your image to some extent. But in addition to the noise reductions commands, Paint Shop Pro includes some dedicated blur commands. Of these, only Gaussian Blur is really useful for photo work. With Guassian Blur, you set a Radius to determine the amount of blurring, as shown in Figure 8.24.

Figure 8.24
Gaussian Blur.

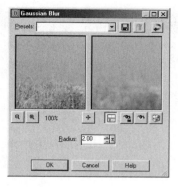

You can use Gaussian Blur to simulate out-of-focus areas in your photo (for example, to blur an overly distinct background in a portrait). In Chapter 10, we'll also use Gaussian Blur to help create drawings from photos.

Blurring has its occasional uses. Sharpening, on the other hand, is something you'll use on nearly all your photos. Once you've finished with other corrections and enhancements, particularly if you've reduced noise in your photo, you'll want to end with a little sharpening.

There are three sharpening commands available under **A**djust > **S**harpness. Of these, the only one you'll want to use for photo work is Unsharp Mask. Unsharp Mask's name might seem rather confusing, because you want to sharpen your image, not make it unsharp. This seemingly odd name comes from the process's origins in the physical darkroom, where a blurred version of a negative was used to create sharpening.

In the digital darkroom, all you need to know about are Unsharp Mask's three controls, shown in Figure 8.25.

Figure 8.25
Unsharp Mask.

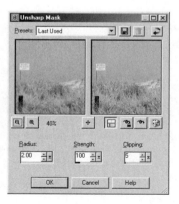

Strength affects contrast. For grainy images, use a low setting here (15–20). For other photos, you can have a **Strength** setting as high as 200. Increase **Strength** until the sharpening is a bit too strong, then turn it back down gradually until the sharpening looks rather good. (If you see obvious haloing along areas of contrast, the **Strength** is too high.) Next, adjust **Radius**. With high values for **Strength**, use a low **Radius** (0.5–1.5). With low **Strength** values, you'll need higher **Radius** settings (5 or more). Typically, you'll get good results with **Strength** set to 100–150 and **Radius** set to 0.5–1.5.

Lastly, adjust the **Clipping**, which determines how different two areas need to be before sharpening takes place. When **Clipping** is set to 0, everything is sharpened. The higher the value for **Clipping**, the more different two areas must be before sharpening kicks in. For portraits and other photos where areas of smoothness are important, you'll need a relatively high setting for **Clipping**. In general, it's best to start at 0 and gradually increase the **Clipping** until you get the result you want.

TIP

Images that you intend to display on a video monitor should be sharpened so that they appear appropriately sharp when you view them in Paint Shop Pro. Images that you intend to print should be slightly oversharpened.

Photo Enhancement

Do you have scratches in your photos or an imperfection that you'd like to remove? The Scratch Remover tool or the Clone Brush can help you out. Do you have areas of your photo that are too dark or too light? The Dodge Brush and the Burn Brush could help you out. Are there areas where you'd like to make localized adjustments to the lightness or saturation? The Change To Target Brush might be what you want. Let's take a look at these and other photo enhancement tools.

Using the Scratch Remover

The Scratch Remover can be used to get rid of a scratch or a hair on the scan of a photo. Scratch Remover can also be used to eliminate other imperfections as well. For example, if the subject of a portrait has wrinkles that you'd like to remove, try the Scratch Remover with its **Width** set to the width of a wrinkle. For something wider, like a mole, just set the **Width** to a larger value and drag over the mole. The Scratch Remover blends the area you drag across with the background at the edges of the tool's bounding box. It works best where the background is relatively smooth. (For more complex backgrounds, the Clone Brush is a better choice of tool.)

TIP

Remember that the Scratch Remover tool can only be used on a Background layer. If you want to make subtle changes by fading an edited duplicate layer into the original, try this: Duplicate the Background layer, then toggle the visibility of the duplicate off. Make the Background layer the active layer and edit with the Scratch Remover. Promote the Background layer to a true layer, and then move it above the duplicate layer. Toggle the visibility of the duplicate layer back on, and then adjust the opacity of the edited layer to get the effect you want.

Using the Clone Brush

We looked at the Clone Brush in Chapter 2. In its Aligned mode, the Clone Brush is handy for eliminating objects that you don't want in your image or for correcting imperfections like facial blemishes in portraits. Here are a few pointers for using the Clone Brush to correct photos:

▶ Set the **Hardness** of the brush rather low so that the edges of your corrections blend in well with the rest of the image.

▶ When correcting blemishes, set the **Opacity** rather low and click the blemish several times, sampling from slightly different areas of your photos. This, too, will help blend the correction in with the rest of the image.

▶ In almost all cases, you'll get better results with multiple clicking rather than dragging. In situations where you do want to drag, be sure that **Step** is set to a low value.

Using the Dodge and Burn Brushes

The Dodge and Burn retouch brushes can be used to lighten overly dark areas (Dodge) or darken overly light areas (Burn). The opacity of the brushes should be kept quite low so the effect isn't overdone. And, if you like, you can restrict the effect to only the shadows, only the midtones, or only the highlights.

I find the effect of these tools less than ideal. An alternative, which I myself prefer, is to use layers for dodging and burning, as in Figure 8.26.

Figure 8.26
Using Blend Modes and
Blend Ranges to Dodge
and Burn.

In this method, you add a new raster layer above your image, setting **Blend Mode** to Dodge or Burn as appropriate, lowering the opacity significantly, and then painting on the layer. For Dodge, paint with white. For Burn, paint with black. If you want to limit the application to shadows, midtones, or highlights, you can use blend ranges to get just what you want. (See Chapter 4, "Mastering Layers and Blend Modes," for discussion of blend ranges.)

Using the Change To Target Brush

Change To Target has settings for **Color**, **Hue**, **Saturation**, and **Lightness**. When you paint with one of these tools, the painted pixels take on the chosen attribute of the Foreground color set in the Materials palette. You can use this tool to colorize areas of a black-and-white photo or to adjust saturation or lightness in localized areas.

NOTE
Other related retouch tools to try out are Lighten/Darken, Saturation Up/Down, and Hue Up/Down.

Red-Eye Correction and JPEG Artifact Removal

Two more problems the digital photographer will occasionally meet are red-eye and JPEG artifacts. Red-eye is that pesky discoloration you find in the eyes of people or pets in your portraits taken with a digital flash. JPEG artifacts are areas of murkiness that you find in JPEG images that have been overcompressed. Paint Shop Pro provides you with the means for dealing with each of these problems.

You could correct red-eye by hand by making a selection, adjusting the color of the selection, deselecting, and adding a glint with the Paint Brush or Airbrush. Red-eye Removal makes your work a bit easier, though. Take a look at the Red-eye Removal dialog box, shown in Figure 8.27.

Figure 8.27
Red-eye Removal.

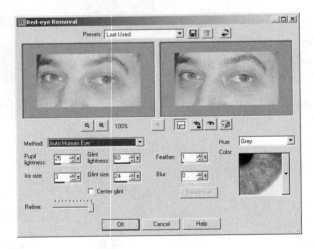

To apply Red-eye Removal, select either Auto Human Eye or Auto Animal Eye and then click in the left window on a pupil. A selection box appears around the pupil, and the results are shown in the preview window on the right. You can move the selection box by clicking inside the selection and dragging. You can resize the selection by dragging any of the handles along the selection boundary.

If more than one pupil needs correction, click on the next pupil in the left preview window and make whatever adjustments you need. Continue in this way until you've corrected all the pupils showing red-eye. Then click OK and you're done.

Figure 8.28 shows an example with Auto Human Eye chosen. Figure 8.29 shows an example with Auto Animal Eye.

Figure 8.28
Red-eye Removal using
Auto Human Eye.

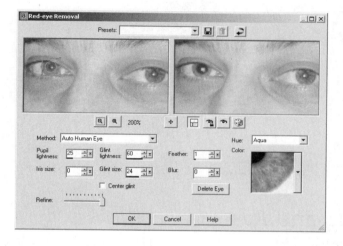

Figure 8.29
Red-eye Removal using
Auto Animal Eye.

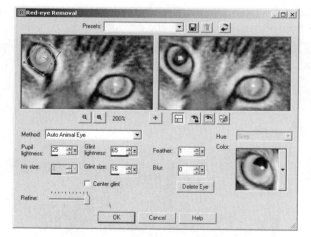

NOTE
With Auto Human Eye, you can change the size of the selection but not its shape. With Auto Animal Eye, you can change the height and width of the selection independently. (For even more control over the shape of the pupil, try Freehand Pupil Outline or Point-to-point Pupil Outline.)

JPEG Artifact Removal is easy to use, as you can tell by looking at its dialog box, shown in Figure 8.30. Try out the different **Strength** settings to see what removes the artifacts without eliminating too much actual image detail. Then adjust **Crispness** to restore lost detail.

Figure 8.30
JPEG Artifact Removal.

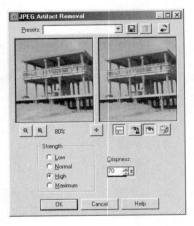

Cropping and Resizing

For a finishing touch, you may want to crop or resize your photo. There are two ways to change the size of your photo: cropping and resizing. Cropping cuts away some of the original photo. You lose some of the data, but the quality of the image doesn't change. Resizing keeps all of the areas that appeared in the original photo, but quality can be noticeably degraded.

Cropping

The most common reason for cropping a photo is to improve its composition. Take, for example, the photo in Figure 8.31.

Figure 8.31
A photo in need of cropping.

This is a nice enough casual portrait, but the busy background pulls attention away from the subject. Crop the photo to center on the subject, as in Figure 8.32, and the viewer's attention is now drawn to the subject.

Figure 8.32
Cropping improves the composition.

In Paint Shop Pro, you crop with the Crop tool or by making a selection and then cropping to the selection. To crop with the Crop tool, drag it to define a bounding box for the crop area, and then click the **Apply** button in the Tool Options palette. You can also tweak the dimensions and placement of the crop box using the controls on the Tool Options palette.

To crop to a selection, make your selection (which doesn't have to be rectangular), and then choose Image > Crop to Selection. Alternatively, you can make your selection, and then choose the Crop tool. In the Tool Options palette, click the **Snap crop rectangle: Current Selection** button. The selection is then replaced with a crop box that defines the smallest possible rectangular area that includes all of the selection. You can then click the **Apply** button to make the crop.

Resizing

To resize your image, choose Image > Resize, which opens the Resize dialog box (shown in Figure 8.33).

With **Resample using** checked, the image can be resized in terms of exact pixels or percentage of original dimensions. With **Resample using** unchecked, the resolution of the image can be changed with no change in number of pixels.

Keep in mind that you'll get best results if the aspect ratio of the original image is maintained. Also, you'll almost always get better results when decreasing the image's size than when increasing the size. In either case, it's best to use **Smart Size**, letting Paint Shop Pro choose the proper resampling method for the situation. (For more discussion of Resize, see Appendix D, "Printing.")

Figure 8.33
The Resize dialog box.

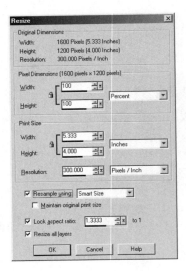

Things to Do with Your Photos

Now that you know how to improve the quality of your photos and get them to the size you want, you might ask yourself what sorts of things you can do with those photos. Sure, you can print them or make JPEG versions that you can post on the Web, but what else can you do with your photos?

You can add a digital Picture Frame to your photo with **I**mage > **P**icture Frame. Or, as you saw in Chapter 5, "Mastering Selections, Masks, and Channels," you can add a decorative edge. Other interesting twists are to give your photo a sepia, a cyanotype, or some other old-fashioned tone. Or transform your color photos into high-quality black-and-white photos, perhaps simulating the style of Ansel Adams or the effect of infrared film. Or maybe you want to combine several photos into a panorama or a collage. We'll look at some of these in Chapter 10.

9

Web Tools

Images are used on Web sites for a variety of purposes—as Background tiles, buttons, bars, banners, and other accents. To be effective, however, Web graphics must both be well designed and have file sizes that are compact enough to load quickly.

Here's what you'll be exploring in this chapter:

▶ File formats for the Web
▶ Optimizing Web graphics
▶ Slicing large images, creating image maps, and making rollovers

NOTE
The topic of Web graphics is more than enough to fill a book of its own, and there are quite a few good books on Web graphics. For more information on Web graphics issues, you might want to head out to the Basics section of Lori's Web Graphics at **http://loriweb.pair.com/basics.html**.

GIF, JPEG, and PNG

Three file formats generally are supported for display in Web browsers: *Graphics Interchange Format* (GIF), *Joint Photographic Experts Group* (JPEG), and *Portable Network Graphics* (PNG). (Even now, however, you might find that your browser or Web host supports only GIF and JPEG.)

▶ GIF images are 8 bit and have a palette of colors from a minimum of 2 to a maximum of 256. The compression method used for GIF is lossless, which means that GIF compression does not involve loss of data. GIF compression favors solid blocks of colors (especially horizontal blocks) and therefore is best for images with sharp edges and few colors, such as line art and other simple drawings.

▶ JPEG images are 24 bit and thus can have up to 16.7 million colors. JPEG compression is lossy—when you compress a JPEG, you lose data. JPEG compression is best for images with many colors and subtle color shifts, such as photorealistic images.

▶ PNG is many people's idea of an ideal format for digital images. PNGs can have up to 16.7 million colors, and the PNG compression method is lossless. However, universal support for all features of PNGs is still not entirely established.

NOTE

Some folks make the mistake of thinking that JPEG is always the best format for any Web graphic. But the JPEG versions of images that are best suited for GIF compression usually have larger file sizes and generally show degraded image quality when compared to their GIF counterparts.

If you're unsure which format to use to save a particular Web graphic, begin by saving the image in PSP format. Then you can use File > Export to save both a JPEG version and a GIF version of your image, allowing you to compare the two to see which is best in terms of file size and/or quality.

Interlaced GIFs and Progressive JPEGs

You should, of course, try to keep the file sizes of your Web graphics as compact as you can (while maintaining acceptable image quality). If you have a relatively large image that you just must use on your site, however, consider saving your image as an interlaced GIF or as a progressive JPEG.

Interlaced GIFs and progressive JPEGs load in stages. Using such an image won't decrease download time—in fact, download time is likely to increase—but many visitors to your site will find that having something to look at makes the wait seem shorter. (Be warned, though, that some folks find the gradual display annoying.)

To save a file as a progressive GIF, click the **Options** button on the Save As or Save Copy As dialog box, and then select **Version 89a** and **Interlaced**. To save a file as an interlaced JPEG, click the **Options** button on the Save As or Save Copy As dialog box, and then select **Progressive Encoding**.

Transparent GIFs and PNGs

One of the reasons that GIFs and PNGs are so useful for Web graphics is that they allow transparency in your images. GIF lets you translate a single color to transparency. The PNG specification allows you to translate more than one color to transparency, and semitransparency is also allowed. In this section, we'll look at some do-it-yourself methods of creating palette transparency. Later in the chapter, we'll look at the GIF Optimizer and PNG Optimizer, which make it especially easy to optimize your Web images and produce palette transparency.

Reducing Color Depth

When you start working on a transparent GIF, you'll likely begin with a 24-bit color depth, because this makes all of Paint Shop Pro's filters and other operations available to you. When it comes time to set your transparent color, however, you need to reduce your color depth to 256 colors. To reduce the color depth by hand, choose Image > **D**ecrease Color Depth > 256 Colors (8 bit). When the Decrease Color Depth - 256 Colors dialog box opens, choose the **Palette** and **Reduction method** (and other relevant options, if any).

CAUTION

Although PNGs normally have 24-bit color depth, Paint Shop Pro reduces the color depth to 8 bit if you set a transparent color with Image > Set Palette Transparency. And, as with GIFs, you can set only a single, completely transparent color in an 8-bit PNG.

You can maintain 24-bit color and still get transparency (and semitransparency) with PNG by adding an alpha channel. Be aware, though, that not all browsers properly display PNGs that have an alpha channel. For now, the safest way to get transparency with PNGs is to use 8-bit paletted color.

Eliminating Dithering

If you use Decrease Color Depth and choose one of the reduction methods that produces dithering, you should check whether the color that you want to translate to transparency has become dithered. Keep in mind that only a single color can be translated to transparency, so if you have dithering where you want transparency, you need to eliminate the dithering. Use the Zoom tool (the magnifying glass) to zoom in on your image to look for dithering. Figure 9.1 shows an example of an image with a dithered background.

NOTE

Dithering is the process of mixing together two or more different colors that occur in a Materials palette in order to approximate another color that doesn't occur in that palette.

Figure 9.1
Image with a dithered background (magnified 250 percent).

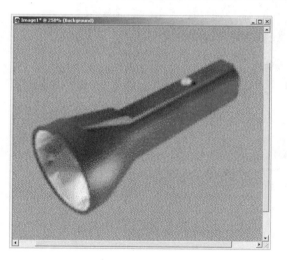

If you want to eliminate dithering, use the Color Replacer tool (discussed in Chapter 2, "More Painting Tools"). For the image in Figure 9.1, most of the dithered background is a medium blue, which is sprinkled with dots of two different shades of light blue.

CHAPTER 9

To eliminate the dithering, take the following steps:

1. Choose the Color Replacer. Set the Foreground color in the Materials palette to the color that you want to translate to transparency by clicking with the Eye Dropper on a pixel of that color in the image.

2. Right-click a pixel of the color you want to eliminate from the background to set the Background color in the Materials palette.

3. If the Background color set in the Materials palette isn't present in the image except where you want to eliminate that color, just double-click in the image.

4. If, however, the color that you want to eliminate from some areas in your image also appears in other areas where you'd like to keep the color, you need to carefully paint with the Color Replacer to eliminate only the dithering in the area that you want to translate to transparency. If the dithering in your image includes more than two colors, repeat this process with the other dithering colors until you've cleaned up the whole area so that it is only a single, solid color.

Figure 9.2 shows a cleaned-up version of the image shown in Figure 9.1.

Figure 9.2
Cleaned-up version of the
dithered image
(magnified 250 percent).

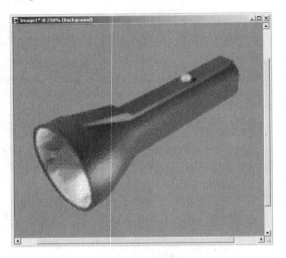

NOTE
Of course, it's even easier if from the beginning you don't have any dithering in the area that you want to translate to transparency. One way to achieve this is to use the GIF Optimizer and on the Colors tab set the amount of dither to a very small value, preferably 0. If you use a color selection method other than Standard / Web-safe, you're quite likely to get the results you want without compromising image quality.

Setting Transparency

After you have a version of your image with a single, solid color in the area that you want to make transparent, you're ready to set transparency.

CAUTION

Be sure that the color used for transparency occurs in your image *only* where you want transparency. *All* occurrences of the color will be translated to transparency, so you need to be careful.

Paint Shop Pro provides three ways to set transparency. One method makes use of the GIF Optimizer, discussed later in this chapter. The other two methods—setting the Background color and setting the palette index—make use of the Image > Palette > Set Palette Transparency operation.

The first method that makes use of Image > Palette > Set Palette Transparency enables you to set transparency based on the current Background color as set in the Materials palette.

1. Set the Materials palette's Background color to the color that you want to translate to transparency by choosing the Eye Dropper tool and right-clicking the appropriate color in your image.

2. Choose Image > Palette > Set Palette Transparency. You'll then see the Set Palette Transparency dialog box, shown in Figure 9.3.

Figure 9.3
The Set Palette Transparency dialog box, with transparency set to the current Background color.

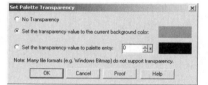

3. Select **Set the transparency value to the current background color**.

4. If you like, you can proof the result before actually setting the transparent color by clicking the **Proof** button. To set the transparent color, click OK.

The second method that makes use of Image > Palette > Set Palette Transparency enables you to set transparency by entering the palette index.

1. Choose Image > Palette > Set Palette Transparency to open the Set Palette Transparency dialog box, shown in Figure 9.4.

2. Select **Set the transparency value to palette entry** and fill in the appropriate palette index.

   If you don't already know what the index is, move the cursor to your image. The cursor changes to the Eye Dropper tool, and you can click the color you want for the transparent color. This enters the palette index for you automatically.

   Alternatively, you can click the color box on the right to call up the image's palette, displayed in a dialog box titled Select Color From Palette. Then click on the appropriate color swatch in the displayed palette. As shown in Figure 9.5, the color's swatch in the palette is then highlighted, with the palette index displayed at the bottom portion of the palette, along with the RGB values and HTML specification for the color.

   Click OK in the Select Color From Palette dialog box, and the palette index will be inserted in the Set Palette Transparency dialog box.

Figure 9.4
The Set Palette
Transparency dialog box
set to palette entry.

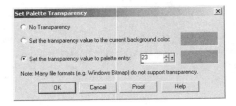

Figure 9.5
Palette index is indicated
in the image's palette.

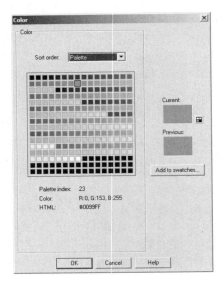

3. Proof the result, if you like, by clicking the **Proof** button. Click OK to set the
    transparent color to the color with the palette index that you specified.

No matter which method you use, you can proof the result after you set the transparent color by
choosing Image > Palette > View Palette Transparency. You can toggle off View Palette
Transparency by selecting this menu option again. If something looks wrong, you can undo the
setting by choosing Edit > Undo or by pressing Ctrl+Z. You also can undo the transparency setting
at any point (even in a later editing session) by choosing Image > Palette > Set Palette
Transparency and selecting **No Transparency**.

When you're satisfied that the transparent color has been set correctly, save your image as either a
GIF or PNG. Remember that only these file formats support Web transparency.

Optimizing and Previewing Web Graphics

Now let's see how easy it is to optimize Web graphics and create palette transparency using Paint
Shop Pro's Web image optimizers. We'll work through some examples using a button on a
transparent background, as shown in Figure 9.6.

TIP

Because the edges of a figure are typically antialiased, some fringe of residual color almost always appears around the edges of the opaque figure in a transparent GIF or PNG. To lessen this effect, it's best to use as your transparent color a color that matches the color of the Web page on which the image will be displayed.

If there's a possibility that you'll be using the same image on different pages with different Background colors, place the figure on its own layer, with real transparency surrounding the figure, and save as a PspImage file. You can then alter the color of a layer below the figure's layer, as needed, and use Save Copy As to save a GIF or PNG with that Background color. Change the lower layer's color whenever you need to, and use Save Copy As again to save another copy with another Background color. (Alternatively, as you'll soon see, you can use the GIF Optimizer to translate layer transparency to GIF transparency.)

Figure 9.6
A button for a Web page.

JPEG Optimizer

Keeping file size small while maintaining good image quality is the central challenge for any Web graphics designer. Paint Shop Pro helps you out in this regard with the file format optimizers for JPEG, GIF, and PNG available under **F**ile > Export.

To export an image as a JPEG, choose **F**ile > Export > JPEG Optimizer. This opens the JPEG Optimizer dialog box on its Quality tab, shown in Figure 9.7.

Figure 9.7
The Quality tab of the JPEG Optimizer.

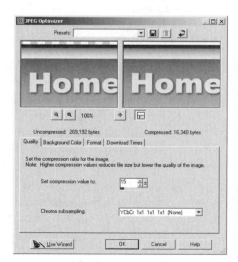

Here, the original image is shown in the image window on the left, with a preview of the image's optimized version shown on the right. In general, it's best to leave **Chroma subsampling** at its default setting. But if your image contains a lot of red, as the button example does, you might get better results with **Chroma subsampling** set to None. To adjust the compression level for your image, set the value in the box labeled **Set compression value to**. When the compression level gives you a small enough file size that still shows acceptable image quality, you're ready to go on to the other tabs in the dialog box.

If your image contains a figure surrounded by transparency, you should click on the Background Color tab, shown in Figure 9.8. (This tab does not appear if there is no layer transparency in your image.)

Figure 9.8
The Background Color tab of the JPEG Optimizer.

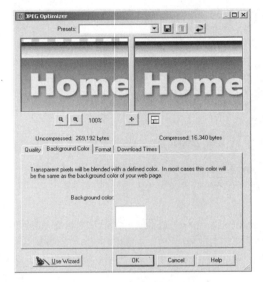

The JPEG file format does not support any kind of transparency, so you'll need to tell Paint Shop Pro what color to use in place of transparency for your JPEG. Click the color box labeled **Background color** to call up the Color dialog box, and select the color that matches the color of your Web page. Click **OK** to set the color and exit the Color dialog box.

Now, click the Format tab, shown in Figure 9.9.

On this tab, you choose whether you want to save your JPEG with **Standard encoding** or **Progressive encoding**. For most images, you'll choose **Standard encoding**, but for large images that download slowly, you'll probably want to choose **Progressive encoding**. With **Progressive encoding**, your image will load in stages, with the image becoming more and more distinct. (You might be surprised to learn that for many images, the progressive JPEG version has a smaller file size than the standard version.)

The last tab in the JPEG Optimizer is the Download Times tab, shown in Figure 9.10. Click this tab to see estimates of the download times of your image at various connection speeds. If the estimated download times aren't acceptable, you can click on the Quality tab again and try increasing the compression level.

Figure 9.9
The Format tab of the
JPEG Optimizer.

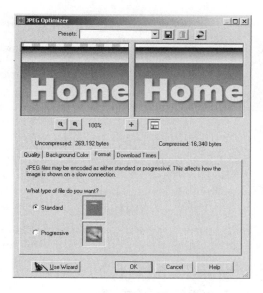

Figure 9.10
The Download Times tab
of the JPEG Optimizer.

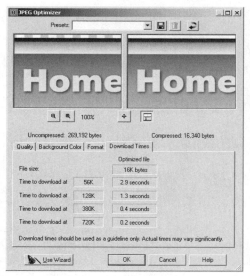

If you'd prefer to be stepped through the optimization process, you can bypass the controls on the JPEG Optimizer's tabs by pressing the **Use Wizard** button at the bottom left of the JPEG Optimizer window. Whether you use the wizard or not, when you're finished optimizing, you're prompted to save your image. You then have an optimized JPEG version of your image on disk, as well as the original version of the image open in Paint Shop Pro.

NOTE
In Paint Shop Pro 8.10, the dialog box for the JPEG Optimizer changed a bit. The Background Color tab is eliminated, and on the Quality tab, there's a check box that allows you to choose whether or not to save any EXIF data that might have been recorded if the image originated as a digital photo.

GIF Optimizer

You can also export your image as a GIF, optionally choosing one color to translate to transparency. To export your image as a GIF, choose **F**ile > Export > **G**IF Optimizer. The first tab you'll see in the GIF Optimizer window is the Transparency tab. GIF Transparency deserves a section of its own, so for now just select None and skip over the Transparency and Partial Transparency tabs.

The tab that you'll use most often, because it's where you'll do your GIF optimizing whether your GIF is to have a transparent background or not, is the Colors tab. (See Figure 9.11.)

Figure 9.11
The Colors tab of the GIF Optimizer.

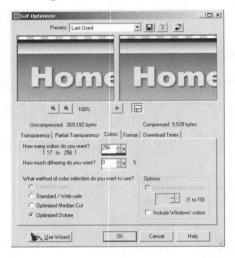

On the Colors tab, you choose what palette creation method to use for your GIF, how many colors to use, and whether to use dithering. In general, you'll get the best image quality with Optimized Octree as the creation method. And you'll get the smallest file sizes with a low number of colors and no dithering. What gives you the best image quality might give you an unacceptable file size, and what gives you the file size you'd prefer might give you unacceptable image quality, so be prepared to make compromises. You might be surprised, though, at how small your file size can be while still maintaining good quality.

The Format tab (shown in Figure 9.12) enables you to choose whether to save your GIF in Non-interlaced format or Interlaced format. An interlaced GIF loads on a Web page in stages, one set of lines loading before the next set until the image is loaded completely. This doesn't decrease the load time of your GIF—in fact, an interlaced GIF typically loads more slowly than a non-interlaced version would, and its file size is larger—but most visitors to your Web page will feel as if the image is loading at an acceptable rate, because they have some of the image to look at while they're waiting.

Figure 9.12
The Format tab of the GIF
Optimizer.

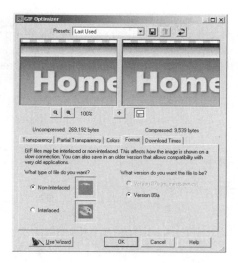

In addition, the GIF Optimizer also has a Download Times tab. And if you'd prefer some help rather than making all the settings on your own, you can forgo all these tabs and click the **Use Wizard** button to call up the GIF Optimizer wizard instead.

Creating Transparent GIFs with the GIF Optimizer

If you want to save your image as a transparent GIF, you can do so from within the GIF Optimizer. Begin by clicking the Transparency tab, shown in Figure 9.13.

Figure 9.13
The Transparency tab of
the GIF Optimizer.

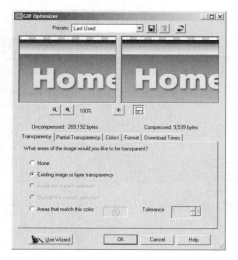

If you don't want any transparency, select **None**. If your image has layer transparency that you'd like to translate to GIF transparency, or if your image already is a transparent GIF and you'd like to retain its transparency, select **Existing image or layer transparency**. If you have a selection, you can choose either **Inside the current selection** or **Outside the current selection**, whichever defines the area where you want transparency. Another alternative is to select **Areas that match this color**.

For this option, either accept the current Background color, which is shown in the color box to the right of this option, or change the color by clicking the color box to call up the Color dialog box or by right-clicking the color box to call up the Recent Colors dialog box. You can also set the **Tolerance**, telling Paint Shop Pro whether you want to match the color exactly or within some tolerance level.

In addition to being able to translate a color to transparency, you can tell Paint Shop Pro how to handle pixels that are partially transparent. Controls for this are located on the Partial Transparency tab, shown in Figure 9.14.

Figure 9.14
The Partial Transparency tab of the GIF Optimizer.

GIF doesn't support partial transparency, so if you have any partially transparent pixels in your image, you need to decide which of these pixels should be translated to full transparency and which should be made fully opaque. You also need to decide whether to blend the partially transparent pixels with a Background color. If you choose to blend with a Background color, be sure to set that color to the color of your Web page.

PNG Optimizer

The third available optimizer is the PNG Optimizer, which you open with **File** > Export > PNG Optimizer. You then see the PNG Optimizer dialog box open on its Colors tab, shown in Figure 9.15.

On the Colors tab, you choose whether to save your PNG with paletted color (like a GIF), as a greyscale (with 256 shades of grey), or with 16.7 million colors (like a JPEG). If you choose **Palette-Based**, the controls for choosing a palette and setting the number of colors and amount of dithering become active.

The Transparency tab, shown in Figure 9.16, lets you choose whether to translate areas of your image to transparency. Be careful here: Although PNG allows you to create transparent areas using alpha channels, most Web browsers do not support alpha channel transparency. Your safest bet if you want transparency is to use paletted color and set a single color as a fully transparent color, just as you would with GIFs.

Figure 9.15
The Colors tab of the
PNG Optimizer.

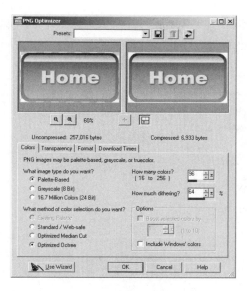

Figure 9.16
The Transparency tab of
the PNG Optimizer.

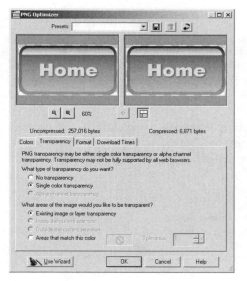

In addition, the PNG Optimizer also has a Format tab (like the one for the GIF Optimizer) and a Download Times tab. And if you'd prefer to forgo all these tabs, click the **Use Wizard** button to call up the PNG Optimizer wizard instead.

NOTE

In Paint Shop Pro 8.10, there's also a tab for Gamma in the PNG Optimizer. This tab is for expert users only. Most users should simply leave the Gamma setting at its default.

CHAPTER 9

Preview in Web Browser

A handy feature for Web designers is the ability to preview your image in your Web browser without leaving Paint Shop Pro. To preview your image, choose **View** > Preview In **W**eb Browser, which opens the dialog box shown in Figure 9.17.

Figure 9.17
The Preview in Web
Browser dialog box.

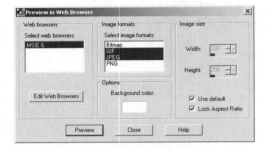

Here you choose the format(s) in which you want your image to be displayed, the dimensions at which to display the image, the Background color of the Web page, and what Web browser to use.

NOTE

The first time you use Preview In Web Browser, you'll need to click the **Edit Web Browsers** button and then choose whatever Web browser(s) you have available. You can choose up to three different browsers to appear in the Preview in Web Browser list.

When you click the **Preview** button, Paint Shop Pro will run the appropriate optimizer(s) and then display your image. Each version of the image, along with information on the file format and file size, is displayed in the Web browser(s) you selected.

NOTE

The Image Mapper and Image Slicer, discussed in the next sections, also allow you to preview your image map or sliced image in your Web browser. Just click the **Preview** button in the Image Mapper or Image Slicer dialog box. The **Preview** button is labeled with an image that looks like an eye.

Using the Image Mapper

Paint Shop Pro has a built-in image-mapping utility, the Image Mapper (Figure 9.18).

To run the Image Mapper, choose **F**ile > Export > Image **M**apper. You then see the Image Mapper dialog box, which has several tools. Three are area-defining tools (Polygon, Rectangle, Circle), enabling you to define clickable areas for the image. Three others (Mover, Eraser, Arrow) allow you to modify and/or select your clickable areas. Following are descriptions of the seven tools you can use for image mapping:

Figure 9.18
Using the Image Mapper.

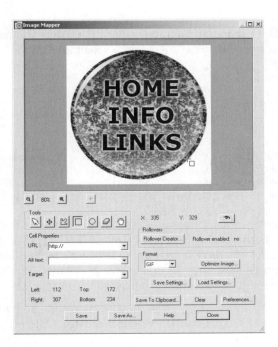

▶ **Arrow tool.** Use the Arrow tool to resize the areas you've defined (and, in the case of polygons, to reshape the areas). The Arrow tool is also used to select a clickable area that you've defined. Once you select an area, you can enter the appropriate URL for that area, along with a value for the ALT attribute and a value for TARGET, if you like.

▶ **Mover tool.** Use the Mover tool to move an area by dragging the area in the preview window.

▶ **Polygon tool.** With the Polygon tool, define a clickable area by clicking with the tool in the preview window and dragging to form a straight line. Click again when you reach the end of the line segment you want to make, and then continue clicking and dragging to make the other line segments for your polygonal area. To close the polygon, click on the starting point or simply right-click anywhere in the preview window.

▶ **Rectangle tool.** Define a rectangular area by dragging in the preview window with the Rectangle tool. The Rectangle tool draws from one corner of the rectangle to the diagonally opposite corner.

▶ **Circle tool.** Define a circular area by dragging with the Circle tool. The Circle tool draws from the center of the circle out.

▶ **Eraser.** Click an area with the Eraser to remove that area. (To remove all of the clickable areas you've defined, just click the **Clear** button.)

CHAPTER 9

▶ **Pan tool.** The Pan tool, which looks like a hand, lets you move the preview image around in the preview window. Simply select the Pan tool and drag in the preview window.

To optimize your image map, choose a file format in the Format section of the dialog box and then click the **Optimize Image** button.

TIP

If you want to save your settings for later use on the same image or on another image, press the **Save Settings** button. To load previously saved settings, press the **Load Settings** button.

To save the HTML code for your image map, press the **Save** or **Save As** button to call up the HTML Save As dialog box. In that dialog box, enter a name for the HTML file that contains the code for your image map. Click the **Save** button in the HTML Save As dialog box, which saves the HTML file and opens the Image Map Save As dialog box. Navigate to the file folder that you want, and enter the name for the optimized image map image.

To include the image map on your own Web page, copy the map code from the HTML file that Image Mapper created and paste it into the HTML file for your Web page. (Alternatively, instead of **Save** or **Save As**, you can choose **Save To Clipboard** and then just paste your saved code into your HTML file from the Clipboard.) After adding your new code, upload your newly edited HTML file for your page, along with the optimized image map image, to the proper folder(s) on your Web server.

NOTE

In addition to creating simple image maps, you can create JavaScript rollovers for your image map. Rollovers, which can also be created for sliced images, are discussed later in this chapter.

Using the Image Slicer

Use the Image Slicer to slice a large image into pieces that can then be reassembled on your Web page in an HTML table. To open the Image Slicer, choose File > Export > Image Slicer. You'll then see the dialog box for the Image Slicer, with its various tools.

As with the Image Mapper, you can use the Pan tool to move the preview around in the preview window.

To slice your image into evenly spaced rows and columns, choose the Grid tool and click in the preview window. In the Grid Size dialog box, enter the number of rows and columns. After you click OK, you'll see grid lines showing the cells into which your image will be sliced, as shown in Figure 9.19.

You can readjust the position of the grid lines by dragging on them with the Arrow tool or the Slicer tool. The Slicer can also be used to add cells. In the preview window, drag up or down with the Slicer to make a vertical slice or drag right or left to make a horizontal slice.

Figure 9.19
Slicing an image with
Image Slicer.

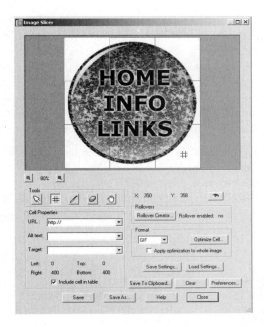

You can delete cells with the Eraser tool. Just click on a slice segment with the Eraser to delete a particular segment. (To erase all the grid lines, click the **Clear** button.)

To make a particular cell clickable, click in the cell with the Arrow tool and then set a URL in the Cell Properties pane. You can also set ALT text and/or a TARGET, if you like.

TIP

If you want to save your settings for later use on the same image or on another image, click the **Save Settings** button. To load previously saved settings, click the **Load Settings** button.

You can optimize the entire set of slices in a single file format or optimize individual slices separately. To optimize the entire set of slices at once, choose the file format that you want in the Format pane and check the **Apply optimization to whole image** box, and then click the **Optimize Cell** button, which starts the appropriate optimizer. To optimize an individual cell, select the cell with the Arrow tool, then set the format as you like, and click the **Optimize Cell** button, being sure that **Apply optimization to whole image** is not checked.

TIP

Image Slicer is handy for large images that contain some areas that are best optimized as GIFs and other areas that are best optimized as JPEGs, such as an image that fades from a landscape on the left to a solid color on the right. Slice the image so that one section contains the landscape, and then optimize this slice as a JPEG. Optimize the solid-colored slice as a GIF.

To save your slices and the HTML file containing the code for the table used to reassemble the slices, click the **Save As** button. Navigate to the appropriate folder, and enter the name you want for the table's HTML file. By default, each of your slices will have a name that begins with the name of your original image file and that ends with a string of the form _nxm, where n is the row number and m is the column number of the table in which your sliced image is reassembled. If you've previously checked the **Prompt for image folder on Save or Save As** check box in the Slicer Preferences dialog box (accessed with the **Preferences** button), you can specify a string different from the name of the original image to use in the names of your slices.

To include the sliced image on your own Web page, copy the table code from the HTML file that Image Slicer created and paste it into the HTML file for your Web page. Or, if your HTML file already exists and you don't want to save a separate HTML file for your sliced image, choose **Save To Clipboard**, and then paste the HTML code from the clipboard directly into your HTML file. Upload your newly edited HTML file for your page, along with all of the sliced images, to the proper folder(s) on your Web server.

CAUTION

Contrary to what many people believe, slicing your image usually will not decrease download time. In fact, download time is quite likely to increase. For many folks, though, there is a psychological effect: Because they can see parts of the image as the whole thing is loading, it seems like the download time is shorter.

Creating Rollovers

You're sure to have seen rollovers all over the Web. Move your cursor over a button or other image, and the image's appearance changes. Move the cursor away from the image, and the image reverts back to its original state. Using Paint Shop Pro's Rollover Creator, available from the Image Mapper or Image Slicer, you, too, can create fancy rollovers.

As an example, let's create a navigation bar and add rollovers to it. Begin by creating two versions of the bar, one that shows the hot spots in their neutral state, as in Figure 9.20, and another that shows the hot spots in their "on" state, as in Figure 9.21.

Figure 9.20
A navigation bar with hot spots in their neutral state.

Figure 9.21
A navigation bar with hot spots in their "on" state.

Make the "on" version the active image or visible layer (depending on whether you made your two versions as separate images or as two layers in the same image file). Then start up the Image Slicer with **File > Export > Image Slicer**. In the Image Slicer, click the **Preferences** button, and in the Slice Preferences dialog box, shown in Figure 9.22, choose **Prompt for image folder on Save or Save As,** and then click **OK.** With this preference set, Paint Shop Pro will prompt you for a folder and the initial portion of file names for your slices.

Figure 9.22
Setting slice preferences.

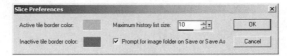

Next, slice the bar into cells for each of the hot spots, as in Figure 9.23. Optimize the cells and make any other settings you need. Then click the **Save To Clipboard** button. If you're prompted for a folder, navigate to the folder where you want your images stored, and then click **OK.** When you're prompted for a file name in the Image Slice Save As dialog box, enter a meaningful name (such as "rollover_on"), and then click **Save**.

Figure 9.23
Slicing the "on" version
of the navigation bar.

Back in the Image Slicer dialog box, click the **Save Settings** button. Give your settings a name, and then click **Save.** You'll use the saved settings in just a bit, when you slice the navigation bar in its neutral state.

Close the Image Slicer by clicking its **Close** button. Then make the neutral version of the navigation bar the active image or visible layer. Start the Image Slicer again, and in the Image Slicer dialog box click the **Load Settings** button. Choose the settings file you just saved, and then click the **Open** button. The settings you used for the "on" version are now loaded onto the neutral version, as shown in Figure 9.24.

Figure 9.24
The saved settings applied to the neutral version of the navigation bar.

Now to create the rollovers. With the first cell selected, click the **Rollover Creator** button. In the Rollover Creator dialog box, select **Mouse over** and **Mouse out**. Then click the folder button to the far right of the **Mouse over** check box, as shown in Figure 9.25.

Figure 9.25
Setting the states for your rollover.

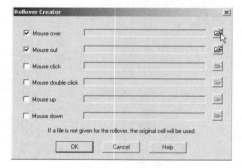

You'll then see the Select Rollover dialog box, shown in Figure 9.26. Navigate to the folder where you saved your "on" slices. Then choose the first of these slices. (Here, that's the file called `rollover_on_1x1.gif`.) Click the **Open** button. You're then returned to the Rollover Creator dialog box, where the file ID of the image you just selected is now displayed in the text box to the right of the **Mouse over** check box, as shown in Figure 9.27.

NOTE

If a rollover state is selected but no file is chosen for that state, then the original image is loaded for that state. In the example here, on mouse over (when the mouse cursor is positioned over the slice), the original image is replaced by the image indicated in the text box. On mouse out (when the mouse cursor is moved away from the image), there is no image file indicated, so the original image is restored.

Figure 9.26
Select the image to load
in the **Mouse over** state.

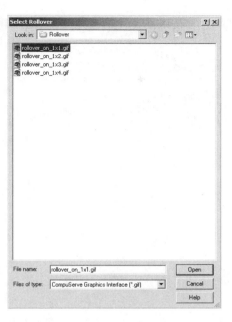

Figure 9.27
The selected file's ID is
now displayed in the
Mouse over text box.

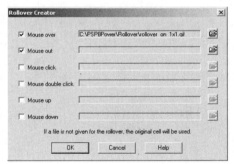

You're now just about done. Click the **OK** button in the Rollover Creator dialog box. Then in the Image Slicer, optimize the cells for your neutral state version of the navigation bar. Next, click the **Save As** button. In the HTML Save As dialog box, navigate to the folder where you want your HTML code saved, and enter a name for your HTML file. Click **Save**. Then in the Image Slice Save As dialog box, enter a name (such as "rollover") for your slices. When you're returned to the Image Slicer dialog box, click the **Close** button.

You can then edit the HTML file you created or copy and paste the code into an existing HTML file. The code puts your image slices in a table, to make the navigation bar appear to be a single image, and it also provides instructions for the rollover. Figure 9.28 shows the example rollover in action, with the mouse cursor over the Links slice.

Figure 9.28
The rollover in action.

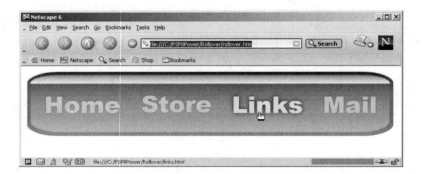

10
Tricks and Techniques

You've already come across quite a few tricks and techniques throughout this book. In this chapter, we'll look at several more, some of them expansions on previous examples and some of them new.

Here's what you'll be exploring in this chapter:

▶ Adding effects to text
▶ Modifying photos and clip art

Text Effects

In Chapter 7, "Paint Shop Pro 8 Effects," you looked at a few effects you can add to text. In this section, you'll try out a few more text effect techniques.

Shaky Text

For starters, let's try creating shaky text like what's shown in Figure 10.1.

1. Open a new raster image with a dark Background color. Then add a new raster layer above Background by clicking the **New Raster Layer** button in the Layer palette.

2. Choose the Text tool and select Floating in the Tool Options palette. Choose the font and size that you want and set **Stroke** to 0. In the Materials palette, set Background/Fill to a light solid color.

3. Be sure that **Alignment** is set to Align Center, and then click in the image canvas where you want your text to appear. The text will be center aligned at the point you click. In the Text Entry box, enter your text and click the **Apply** button. Deselect the selection to drop the floating text selection onto the empty layer. You'll then have something like what you see in Figure 10.2.

Figure 10.1
Shaky text.

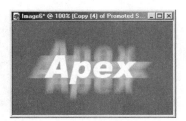

Figure 10.2
Placing the initial text.

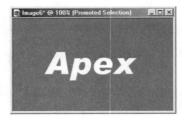

4. Duplicate the text layer four times. On the lowest text layer, choose **A**djust > Bl**u**r > **M**otion Blur. Set **Angle** to 270 and **Strength** to 100. After clicking **OK**, the result looks like Figure 10.3.

Figure 10.3
Applying Motion Blur.

5. On the next layer up, apply Motion Blur again, but this time set **Angle** to 90 to get the result shown in Figure 10.4.

Figure 10.4
A second motion blur.

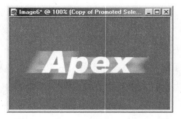

6. Apply Motion Blur to the next layer with **Angle** set to 0, and apply Motion Blur to the layer above that with **Angle** set to 180.

7. On the uppermost layer, add a drop shadow. For the shadow's color, use the same color as the Background color. Set both offsets to 0 and use **Opacity** and **Blur** settings that make the text stand out from the blurred layers. Your shaky text is then complete.

Metallic Text

Now for some nice metallic text, as shown in Figure 10.5.

1. Open a new raster image with whatever color you want for Background.

2. Add a new raster layer by clicking the **New Raster Layer** button in the Layer palette.

3. Choose the Text tool set to **Floating** and **Center Align**. Use whatever font and size you want. In the Materials palette, set Foreground/Stroke to a medium grey and set Background/Fill to a light grey. Click in the image canvas where you want your text to appear, set **Stroke width (pixels)** to 1, and enter your text, as shown in Figure 10.6.

Figure 10.5
Easy metallic text.

Figure 10.6
Placing the basic text.

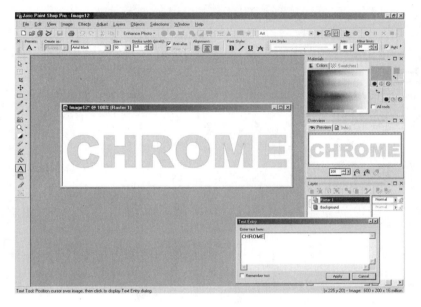

4. After clicking **Apply** in the Text Entry box, deselect the text with Ctrl+D to drop the text onto the empty layer. Then choose Effects > 3D Effects > Inner Bevel. Because the text on the layer is surrounded by transparency, the effect behaves as it would if the text were selected. Use the default settings, except for **Smoothness** and **Intensity**. Set **Smoothness** to 35 and **Intensity** to 30, as shown in Figure 10.7.

5. After clicking **OK**, choose Adjust > Brightness and Contrast > Curves. Create a curve shaped like a W or an M, as shown in Figure 10.8, and then click **OK**. If you like, add a drop shadow, as I did in the example.

Your metallic text is done. You can leave it as is for a silver or chrome look, or colorize it to give it a gold, brass, or copper look.

Figure 10.7
Adding a bevel to the
text.

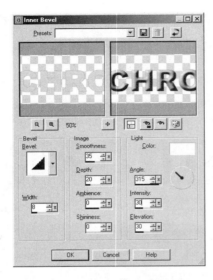

Figure 10.8
Using Curves to produce
a metallic effect.

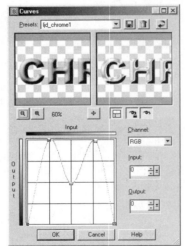

Cracked Text

Sometimes you might want to give your text a distressed look, such as the effect in Figure 10.9.

Figure 10.9
Cracked text.

1. Open a new image canvas with a light Background color, and then add a new raster layer.

2. Choose the Text tool and this time choose **Selection** as the **Create as** setting. Click in the image canvas where you want your text to appear, and then enter the text, as shown in Figure 10.10.

Figure 10.10
Creating a text selection.

3. With your text selection active, choose **S**elections > **E**dit Selection. Choose the Paint Brush tool and set the Foreground color in the Materials palette to white. If the Brush Variance palette isn't visible, press F11. In the Brush Variance palette, set **Jitter (%)** for **Thickness** to a rather high value. Then paint some vertical lines through the text selection, as shown in Figure 10.11. If the amount of variation in the brush thickness is too little or too great, then undo your brush stroke, reset **Jitter (%)**, and try again.

Figure 10.11
Adding the distress cracks.

4. Choose the Warp Brush and click the **Noise** button in the Tool Options palette. Paint over the text selection to randomly warp the text a bit, as shown in Figure 10.12. If you get too much warping, use **Iron Out**.

Figure 10.12
Warping the selection.

5. Next, choose Effects > Edge Effects > **D**ilate. Apply Dilate two or three more times by pressing Ctrl+Y to get the effect in Figure 10.13.

Figure 10.13
Partially fill in the cracks with Dilate.

6. Choose **S**elections > **E**dit Selection to exit edit selection mode. Then choose the Flood Fill tool with **Match mode** set to None. Set the Foreground color to the color you want for your text and click in the selection, as shown in Figure 10.14.

Figure 10.14
Filling the selection with color.

7. Deselect the text selection with Ctrl+D. Your distressed text is then complete.

Glassy Text

Now for one more text effect. This time, let's add transparent glassy text to a photo, as in Figure 10.15.

1. Open your photo and add a new raster layer.
2. Create a text selection by using Selection as the **Create as** setting for the Text tool, as shown in Figure 10.16.
3. Invert the text selection with **S**elections > **I**nvert. Then choose Effects > 3D Effects > **D**rop Shadow with both offsets set to 6, **Opacity** set to 65, **Blur** set to 7, and **Color** set to white, as shown in Figure 10.17. (Here and in the next step, you might need to use larger settings for the offsets and the blur if your text is quite large.)
4. Add a narrower drop shadow, this time with the offsets each set to 3, **Opacity** set to 50, **Blur** set to 4, and **Color** set to black, as shown in Figure 10.18.

Figure 10.15
Glassy text added to a
photo.

Figure 10.16
Creating the text
selection.

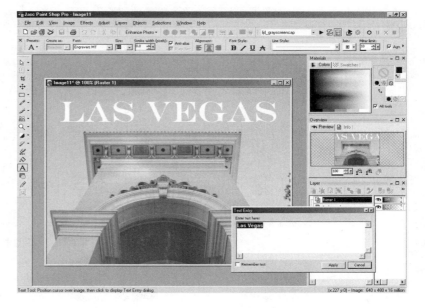

5. Invert the text selection with **S**elections > **I**nvert. Add another drop shadow, with the offsets each set to 0, **Opacity** increased to 70, **Blur** still set to 4, and **Color** still set to black, as shown in Figure 10.19.

6. Deselect with Ctrl+D. Set the text layer's **Blend Mode** to Luminance and set its **Opacity** to 70. Your glassy text is then complete.

TIP
Other Blend Modes to try out with this technique are Overlay and Hard Light.

Figure 10.17
Adding a white drop
shadow inside the text.

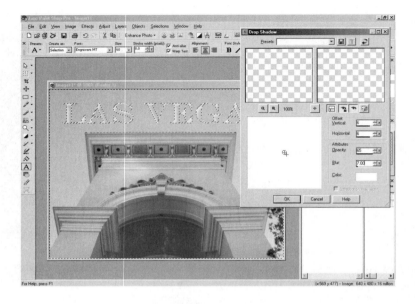

Figure 10.18
Adding a narrower, black
shadow.

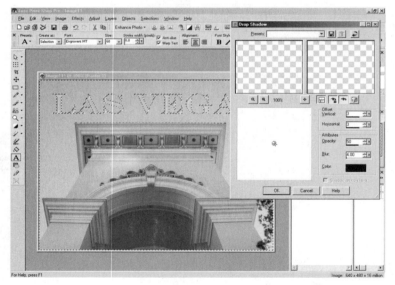

Better Black-and-White Photos

There are several ways to create a black-and-white digital photo. Your digital camera might have a black-and-white setting. Your scanner probably has an option for producing a greyscale scan. Or you can change a color image to greyscale with Paint Shop Pro's **I**mage > **G**reyscale. You can get better, more sophisticated black-and-white versions of color images, though, using other methods in Paint Shop Pro. In this section, we'll look at a couple methods of creating and tinting black-and-white photos.

Figure 10.19
Adding a dark shadow
outside the text.

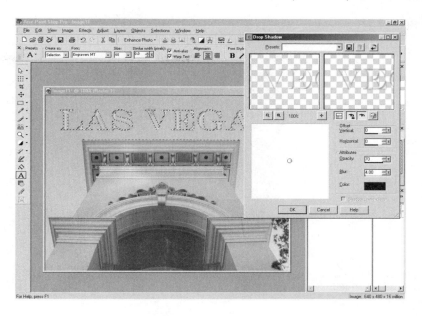

Black-and-White from Channel Mixer

Remember that you can split any color image into its basic color channels and that each color channel is a greyscale bitmap. When you convert a color image to greyscale, Paint Shop Pro blends together the brightness data from the separate color channels. Depending on the particular image, the formula Paint Shop Pro uses can give good, passable, or unsatisfactory results.

Let's look at an example. Figure 10.20 shows the result of applying **I**mage > **G**reyscale to a color photo. Compare this to Figure 10.21 (the Red channel), Figure 10.22 (the Green channel), and Figure 10.23 (the Blue channel).

Figure 10.20
The result when the
photo is converted to
greyscale.

Figure 10.21
The Red channel.

Figure 10.22
The Green channel.

Figure 10.23
The Blue channel.

As you can see, the brightness information in each of the separate channels is quite different from the others, revealing different amounts of detail in the different color regions. Wouldn't it be nice if you could combine the brightness information in the different channels, weighting them as you please? Well, you can: Use Channel Mixer with **Monochrome** selected.

Figure 10.24 shows the results of adding a Channel Mixer adjustment layer above the original flower photo (**Layers** > New Adjustment Layer > Channel **Mixer**). In this case, **Red (%)** is set to 53, **Green (%)** to 46, and **Blue (%)** to 8, with the **Monochrome** check box checked. This version shows more detailed veining in the flower than the greyscale version or any of the separate color channels except the Red channel. And the Red channel alone isn't the best choice here because with it the flower is too bright, making it less distinct from the background.

Figure 10.24
Version produced using
Channel Mixer.

Which settings you use for your own photos will depend on the colors and brightness levels in each particular photo. One thing to keep in mind, though, is that the Blue channel normally contains a lot of noise and thus should generally be the channel with the lowest value. Another general rule of thumb is that the Green channel normally contains much detail. Emphasizing the Green channel is usually a good path to follow for landscapes but generally not for portraits, where minor facial blemishes could be made to look like serious skin problems.

NOTE

The Channel Mixer method yields the biggest improvement over converting to greyscale when the photo has significantly different hues but similar levels of brightness. Greyscale eliminates the differences, losing detail. But Channel Mixer enables you to retain the detail, mixing together the information provided by the differences in hue.

Simulating Infrared Photos

You can also use Channel Mixer to simulate special black-and-white film effects. For example, you could simulate the effect of orthochromatic black-and-white film by de-emphasizing the Red channel, thus making red objects appear darker than they normally would. You can also simulate the effect of infrared black-and-white film. Here's how:

1. If your photo includes the sky, then select the sky and promote the selection to a layer (**S**elections > **P**romote Selection to Layer).

2. On the original photo layer, add a Channel Mixer adjustment layer. Select **Monochrome** and set **Green (%)** to 200, lowering **Red (%)** to somewhere between −70 and −90. The reason for emphasizing the Green channel is that infrared light is absorbed by surfaces that normally look green in a color photo. In an infrared photo, green areas such as trees and grass look much brighter than they do in normal black-and-white.

3. If you added a sky layer, make that layer the active layer. Put this layer into a layer group by clicking the **New Layer Group** button in the Layer palette. Make the sky layer the active layer again, and then add a Channel Mixer adjustment layer. Select **Monochrome**, and set **Red (%)** to about 90. This darkens the sky and emphasizes any clouds.

Photos That Never Were

You've already seen some examples in earlier chapters of how layers, masks, opacity, and blend modes can help you blend together (or composite) separate images into one. And you've seen how the Warp Brush can be used to modify a photo. In this section, we'll look at a couple extended examples of compositing and warping.

Compositing Photos

For this example, we'll take the photos shown in Figure 10.25, placing the woman in the forest.

Figure 10.25
The components of the composite.

Here are the steps:

1. Use your favorite method of isolating a figure to select the woman. The Freehand Selection tool in Point to Point mode is one possibility here. Don't hesitate, too, to use **S**elections > **E**dit Selection to refine your selection. Feather the selection a bit, as shown in Figure 10.26.

Figure 10.26
Feathered selection around figure.

2. Copy the selection by pressing Ctrl+C, and then paste it as a new layer into the forest image with **E**dit > **P**aste > Paste As New **L**ayer (or press Ctrl+L).

3. The woman needs to be resized and repositioned. With the new layer the active layer, choose the Deform tool. Drag inside the bounding box to reposition the woman. With the right mouse button depressed, drag one of the corner handles to resize the figure while maintaining its original aspect ratio. Adjust the positioning if you need to. The result should look something like what's shown in Figure 10.27.

Figure 10.27
Resizing and repositioning the figure.

4. Now to adjust the lighting on the woman. Using the Freehand Selection tool set to Freehand, define a rough selection around the woman's feet and left arm and the lower part of her dress, as shown in Figure 10.28. Feather the selection a bit, and then promote the selection to a layer with **S**elections > **P**romote Selection to Layer and deselect with Ctrl+D.

Figure 10.28
Selecting the lower part of the figure.

5. Choose **A**djust > **B**rightness and Contrast > Cur**v**es. To create a shadow, define a curve like the one shown in Figure 10.29.

Figure 10.29
Creating a shadow.

6. Now to lighten the upper part of the woman. Choose the Selection tool and set the to Ellipse. Select around the upper part of the woman. Feather the selection a bit. The result should look something like what you see in Figure 10.30.

Figure 10.30
Selecting the upper part of the figure.

7. Make the original woman layer the active layer, and then promote the selection to a layer and deselect. Set the **Blend Mode** of the new layer to Dodge and set the **Opacity** to 10. Deselect. The image as it looks now, along with the layer structure so far, is shown in Figure 10.31.

Figure 10.31
The image and its structure so far.

8. As a final touch, let's make the woman look like she's actually standing on the forest floor. Make the uppermost layer the active layer, and then click the **New Raster Layer** button in the Layer palette. Choose the Clone Brush, selecting **Aligned mode** and **Sample merged** in the Tool Options palette. Click the rocky area close to the woman's feet, and then paint over her feet so that some parts are hidden behind rock. The final result should look like what you see in Figure 10.32.

Figure 10.32
The woman's feet planted
firmly on the ground.

Digital Face-Lift

In this section, we'll use the Warp Brush and Clone Brush to return a middle-aged woman to her youth, beginning with a photo like the one in Figure 10.33. (You can use any similar photo to work through this example.)

Figure 10.33
The original photo.

All right, now for the fountain of youth.

1. Begin by choosing the Warp Brush. Click the **Push** button in the Tool Options palette, and set the brush size rather large. Then use the large brush to lift the woman's sagging cheeks, as shown in Figure 10.34.

Figure 10.34
Raising the cheeks.

2. Again using a large brush, push the droopy jowls up, as in Figure 10.35.

Figure 10.35
Eliminating the jowls.

3. Reduce the brush size, and then gently pull up the corners of the mouth just a little, as in Figure 10.36.

4. Now for a step many folks forget about: fixing the neck. Go back to a large brush, and then push the neck in a little, as in Figure 10.37.

5. Switch to the Clone Brush, to clone away the wrinkles. Set the **Opacity** of the brush quite low—about 30 or less is fine. Right-click in an area close to the wrinkle, and then click on the wrinkle itself. Click multiple times, resampling as you need to, to gradually soften the wrinkle. Do the same with other wrinkles. And as Figure 10.38 shows, you should remember the neck as well as the face.

Figure 10.36
Lifting the corners of the mouth.

Figure 10.37
Slimming the neck.

Figure 10.38
Smoothing the wrinkles.

6. As you're working, change the brush size as needed, and dab rather than drag. Keep in mind that the idea here isn't to totally eliminate every line and crease. Even young people have a few lines, and you want to be sure that your edited image looks like a real person, not like a circus clown or a store mannequin. Figure 10.39 shows a side-by-side comparison of the original photo and the completed face-lifted version.

Figure 10.39
Before (left) and after (right).

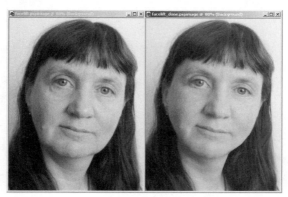

TIP

You can use something like this method in reverse to age a young person, too. Use the Warp Brush to create sags instead of eliminating them, and clone some wrinkles from one photo onto your target photo.

Creating a Panorama

There are software applications such as Jasc's Paint Shop Photo Album that have a built-in facility for creating a panorama from a series of photos. But you can also create a panorama from scratch with Paint Shop Pro without too much extra effort.

You need to start out with two or more photos that you've taken. First take a photo at one end of the scene, then pivot to take the next shot, then pivot to take the next shot, and so on. The photos should be shot so that there's about a 50 percent overlap between adjacent shots. For this example, I'll use the three shots of a desert scene shown in Figure 10.40. (See the color plate section for color versions of these photos.)

Here's how to put the photos together to create a seamless panorama:

1. Open a new image canvas that's large enough to hold all three photos side by side. It's a good idea to have some extra vertical space, because the photos probably won't line up exactly.

2. Copy the first photo and paste it as a new layer in your new image canvas. Position it as needed. See Figure 10.41, where the leftmost desert photo is pasted in as a layer over a transparent image canvas.

Figure 10.40
Beginning with three
separate photos.

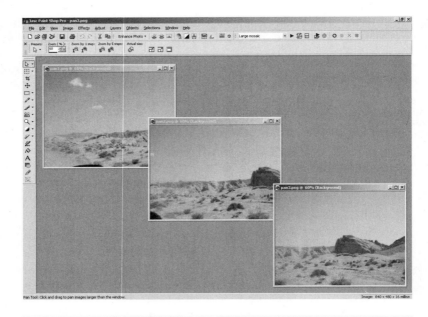

Figure 10.41
Pasting in the first photo.

3. Copy the next photo and paste it as a new layer. Position it as needed. If you need to line the layer up with the previous layer, use **I**mage > **R**otate > **F**ree Rotate or the Straighten tool to do so. The result should look something like what you see in Figure 10.42.

4. Repeat step 3 with the third photo. You'll then have something like what you see in Figure 10.43.

Figure 10.42
Positioning the second photo.

TIP

To help position the pasted-in layer correctly, temporarily reduce the layer's **Opacity** so you can see the layer below. When you're finished positioning the layer, reset the layer's **Opacity** to 100.

Figure 10.43
Positioning the third photo.

5. Use the Eraser with a soft brush setting to make the seams between the three image layers less sharp. You can also use the Clone Brush to edit the seams and to add content where the background of the image canvas shows through along the edges of the image.

6. If necessary, adjust the color, brightness, and contrast of the layers so that they match one another. Then crop your panorama image so that none of the canvas background is left. The final result should look something like what's shown in Figure 10.44. (See the color plate section for a color version.)

Figure 10.44
The completed
panorama.

Drawings and Paintings from Photos

It's fun and satisfying to create drawings and paintings from photos. The easiest way to create a digital painting in Paint Shop Pro is to use the Brush Strokes effect (**Effects** > Art **M**edia Effects > Brush Str**o**kes). There are plenty of ways of getting drawings and paintings by hand, too.

Digital Drawings

You can, of course, create digital drawings purely by hand. With Paint Shop Pro's Paint Brush, you can adjust the brush settings to get a brush that simulates a pencil, chalk, pastels, or charcoal. And it's easy to make a tracing from a photo, too, especially if you have a graphics tablet and stylus. Just add a new layer above your photo, fill the new layer with white, lower the white layer's **Opacity** so you can see the photo beneath, and trace away.

You can also create digital drawings without touching a brush. There are plenty of variations on this technique, but here's one I rather like:

1. Begin with a color or black-and-white photo that has a simple, light-colored background, like the one in Figure 10.45. If it's a color photo, convert it to greyscale or use Channel Mixer set to **Monochrome** to make a black-and-white version. You'll usually get the best results if you increase the contrast, as in Figure 10.46.

2. Duplicate the Background layer. Choose **A**djust > Ne**g**ative Image, and then set the layer's **Blend Mode** to Dodge. The image then looks completely white or nearly so.

3. Choose **A**djust > Bl**u**r > **G**aussian Blur and set **Radius** to a value somewhere between 3 and 10. Use the Preview window to see what value gives you the result you want. The image will then look something like Figure 10.47. If you like this look as is, skip to step 6.

Figure 10.45
The original photo.

Figure 10.46
A higher-contrast version.

Figure 10.47
Blurring the negative
brings out the edges.

4. To add some pencil markings to your sketch, duplicate the Background layer again. On your new middle layer, add some noise with **A**djust > Add / Remove **N**oise > **A**dd Noise. Select **Gaussian**, set **Noise** to 20, and select **Monochrome**. Click **OK**.

5. Set the layer's **Blend Mode** to Darken. Then choose **A**djust > **B**lur > **M**otion Blur. Set **Angle** somewhere between 45 and 55, and set **Strength** to whatever value gives you the effect you want. Click **OK**. The result will look something like Figure 10.48.

Figure 10.48
Pencil marks added.

6. Optional: Merge the layers with **L**ayers > **M**erge > **M**erge All (Flatten). Then adjust the brightness and contrast with Levels, Curves, or Histogram Adjustment.

Digital Paintings

Effects and adjustments that are helpful in creating digital paintings from photos include several of the Edge effects (Dilate, Erode, and Trace Contour), some of the Add/Remove Noise adjustments (Add Noise, Median, and Edge Preserving Smooth), and some of the Blur adjustments (Median, Motion Blur, and Gaussian Blur). Following is an example, starting with the photo in Figure 10.49.

Figure 10.49
The original photo.

1. Open your photo image. Even improperly exposed or blurry photos can work with this technique.

2. Apply **E**ffects > **E**dge Effects > **E**rode. Apply the effect two or three more times by pressing Ctrl+Y. In the result, dark areas of the image are expanded, as shown in Figure 10.50.

Figure 10.50
Emphasizing dark areas
with Erode.

3. Now apply Edge Preserving Smooth (**A**djust > Add / Remove **N**oise > **E**dge Preserving Smooth). Set **Amount of smoothing** quite high. For the example in Figure 10.51, **Amount of smoothing** was set at 20. If you like the effect you have at this point, you're done. Alternatively, you can emphasize the paintinglike effect by reapplying Edge Preserving Smooth by pressing Ctrl+Y, as I did for the example shown in Figure 10.52.

Figure 10.51
Extreme smoothing
produces a painterly
effect.

Figure 10.52
More smoothing gives a
watercolor-like effect.

4. Optional: Add a texture to your painting with Effects > Texture Effects > Texture.

Try out other combinations of Edge effects and Add/Remove Noise and Blur adjustments to create your own digital painting effects.

And you're not limited to modifying photos in order to create digital paintings, of course. You can also create your digital artwork completely by hand. For a couple nice examples of this, head over to JP Kabala's Paranormal PSP8 Tutorials (**http://jpkabala.com/paranormal/tutindex.html**) and take a look at her methods for painting marigolds and lilacs.

Colorizing Clip Art

Clip art is simple ready-made images that you can incorporate into your own graphics projects. Most clip art is line art: two-color black-and-white line drawings. Some clip art also includes areas of colors. In this section, you'll see how to colorize black-and-white clip art and to change colors in color clip art.

Let's start with adding some color to raster clip art, beginning with the two-color black-and-white image from J. O. D.'s Old Fashioned B & W Clip Art (**http://www.oldfashionedclipart.com**), shown in Figure 10.53.

Figure 10.53
Simple black-and-white
raster clip art.

If the piece of clip art is a GIF, as this example image was, you must first increase the color depth of the image using Image > Increase Color Depth > 16 Million Colors (24 bit). And if the image started out as a transparent GIF, change the image's background color to white with the Color Replacer. You're then ready to colorize the piece:

1. Add a layer above the Background layer and set the **Blend Mode** of the new layer to Darken. Choose the Paint Brush, set the Foreground color in the Materials palette to the color that you want, and then paint where you want that color applied. You don't have to be very careful about staying within the lines, because with Darken no color paints over black areas of the lower layer.

2. Add another layer for your next color and set the **Blend Mode** of that layer to Darken. Paint with the new color.

3. Repeat until you have all your colors painted in. Adjust the opacity of your layers, if you like. The result for my example is shown in Figure 10.54.

Figure 10.54
The Colorized version and its layer structure.

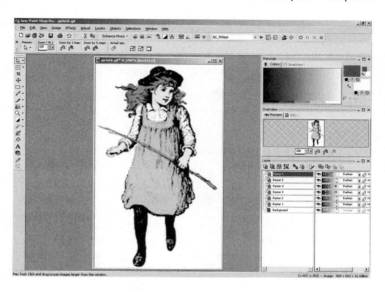

NOTE

You can use a similar method to recolor areas of a 16-million color image, too. Add a new layer, set its **Blend Mode** to Color, and then paint the new color on the layer. With the Color blend mode, paint on the layer affects areas on lower layers where the brightness values are darker than white and lighter than black.

Vector clip art is even easier to colorize. Let's begin with a piece of clip art that comes with Microsoft Word, shown in Figure 10.55. If you don't have this particular image, you can use any other vector image that has more than one color.

Figure 10.55
Original vector clip art.

1. Open the image. You'll see in the Layer palette that it's made of a single vector layer. If you like, you can click the plus sign on the left of the vector layer's layer button to reveal the individual vector objects on the layer.

2. Choose the Object Selector tool and click on the first area whose color you want to change. Then choose **O**bjects > **P**roperties or right-click the selected object and choose Properties. In the Vector Property dialog box, shown in Figure 10.56, click the **Fill** color box and choose the color that you want in the Material dialog box.

Figure 10.56
Vector Property dialog box.

3. If there are several objects whose color you'd like to change at once to the same color, do this: Click the first object with the Vector Selector, then Shift-click with the Vector Selector on the next object, and so on. When all of the objects that you want are selected, choose **O**bjects > **P**roperties or right-click on any one of the selected objects and choose Properties. Then choose a fill color and all of the selected objects change color at once.

4. Continue in this way until you're done. Figure 10.57 shows a recolorized version of the example clip art image used here. (The original and the recolorized version can also be seen in the color plate section.)

Figure 10.57
Recolorized version.

You can do more with clip art than just modify its colors. Also try editing your vector clip art with the Pen tool or modifying the shape of your raster clip art with the Deform tool, Warp Brush, or Mesh Warp tool.

Just the Beginning

These examples only touch the surface of what you can do with Paint Shop Pro. Be sure to check out the tutorials listed in Appendix E, "Resources," for more tricks and techniques. And don't be afraid to try out new things on your own, perhaps using tools and operations in ways quite different from their intended uses. You won't always succeed, but the successes will be well worth the time and effort.

11
Adding to Your Toolkit

The standard Paint Shop Pro tools can take you far, but you're not limited to these tools. Paint Shop Pro 8 lets you expand your toolkit by enabling you to create your own textures, patterns, brushes, preset shapes, Picture Tubes, picture frames, and filters. In this chapter, you'll learn how to add to your toolkit and what kinds of effects you can achieve.

Here's what you'll be exploring in this chapter:

▶ Making your own textures and patterns

▶ Making your own shapes and styled lines

▶ Creating your own gradients

▶ Creating your own brushes and Picture Tubes and exploring how the two differ

▶ Making your own picture frames

▶ Rules of thumb for creating your own User Defined Filters

Making Your Own Textures

In Paint Shop Pro, Textures are used with many painting tools and with the Texture effect.

Any greyscale or 16-million color image can be saved for use as a texture. For best results, the image should be a seamless tile and should have dark areas and relatively high contrast. The image must be placed in one of the Texture folders specified in your file locations (accessed with Files > Preferences > File Locations).

TIP

To create a seamless tile in Paint Shop Pro, you can use the Offset or Seamless Tiling effects. (These are both discussed in Chapter 7, "Paint Shop Pro 8 Effects.")

After you create your new texture file and save it to one of your Texture folders, the new texture will be available in the **Texture** drop-down list in the Material dialog box the next time you use a painting tool. Figure 11.1 shows this list with a few of my custom patterns displayed.

You use the new texture just as you would use one of Paint Shop Pro's own textures. Figure 11.2 shows the result of painting with blue on a solid-white background with one of the custom textures shown in Figure 11.1.

Figure 11.1
The new texture appears
in the **Texture** drop-down
list in the Material dialog
box.

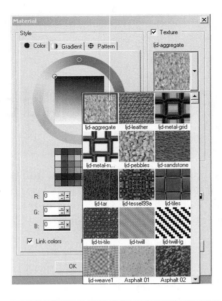

Figure 11.2
Using the new texture.

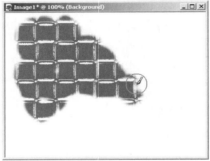

Any image located in one of your Texture folders can also be used with the Texture effect. Figure 11.3 shows the same example texture in use with the Texture effect.

Keep in mind that not all images that make good textures for painting also make good Texture effect textures (and vice versa). You need to use your discretion when selecting a texture.

NOTE

Any seamlessly tiling greyscale or 16-million color image can also be made available as a bump map for use with the Balls and Bubbles effect. In this case, you need to save your image to one of the Bump Map folders designated in your file locations.

A bump map simulates bumps and indentations (as the Texture effect example in Figure 11.3 shows). By default, light areas look raised and dark areas look indented. Set **Depth** on the Map tab of the Balls and Bubbles dialog box to a negative value to reverse this behavior.

Figure 11.3
Using the new texture
with the Texture effect.

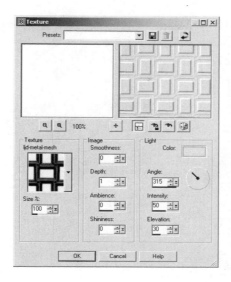

Making Your Own Patterns

Patterns are used as material you can paint with, as a material for Balls and Bubbles, as fill for vector objects, and as a material you can use with the Sculpture effect.

Just as you can make your own textures, you can make your own patterns. Any 16-million color image can be used as a pattern, but for best results, the image should be a seamless tile.

To make a basic tile available for use in Paint Shop Pro, try this:

1. Create a seamless pattern with Paint Shop Pro's Seamless Tiling effect or another effect that can produce a seamless tile. (See Chapter 7 for discussion of Paint Shop Pro's effects.)

2. Save the pattern file to one of your Patterns folders (as specified in your file preferences). Any image in one of the Patterns folders will be recognized as a pattern.

Figure 11.4 shows an example of painting with a pattern made using the Kaleidoscope effect, and Figure 11.5 shows an example of the Sculpture effect with a seamless pattern made with Seamless Tiling.

Figure 11.4
Painting with a
kaleidoscope pattern.

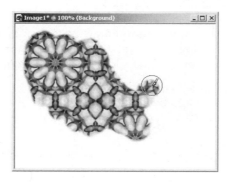

Figure 11.5
The Sculpture effect
using a seamless pattern
made with Seamless
Tiling.

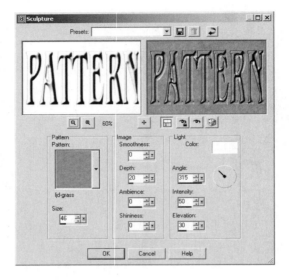

Making Your Own Shapes Library

You can add new preset shapes by creating an image that contains groups of vector objects and then exporting the file with **F**ile > Expor**t** > **S**hape to create a new shapes library. Figure 11.6 shows the structure of the shapes library file for Shapes01.PspShape, an extra shapes library supplied by Jasc.

Figure 11.6
The structure of a shapes
library.

To create your own shapes library, begin by choosing a drawing tool and creating your new shape or the first part of your new shape. (Be sure that the tool is set to its vector mode.) For complex shapes, continue adding vector objects until your shape is complete. Group all of the objects of a complex shape together as follows:

1. Select the objects that should be included in the shape, either by dragging around them with the Object Selector tool or by shift-clicking their layer buttons in the Layer palette.

2. Right-click on one of the selected objects and choose **Group**. (Alternatively, choose **O**bjects > **G**roup.)

Continue in this way until you have created all of the shapes that you want in your new library. Each shape is either an independent object or a set of objects that are grouped together.

Give each shape a meaningful name. For a single-object shape, rename the object. For a multi-object shape, name the group. To rename an object or a group, double-click its object button in the Layer palette and in the Vector Property dialog box, enter the new name in the **Name** text box.

To save your library of shapes, be sure that none of the objects or groups is selected, then choose **F**ile > Expor**t** > **S**hape. When prompted to, enter a name for your shapes library. Your new shapes are then available for use when you next select the Preset Shapes tool.

NOTE

If your image contains non-vector layers, you must make one of the vector layers the active layer in order for **F**ile > Expor**t** > **S**hape to be available. Keep in mind, too, that only objects on the current vector layer will be exported as shapes.

Making Your Own Styled Lines

The stroke of any of the drawing tools—the Pen, Preset Shapes, and Text tools—can be drawn with styled lines rather than solid lines. To choose a line style, click the arrow for the **Line Style** drop-down list in a drawing tool's Tool Options palette and select the line style that you want.

You can also create your own custom styled lines. To create a styled line, choose a drawing tool and then click the arrow or preview window for **Line Style** in the Tool Options palette. Click the **Custom** button at the bottom of the **Line Style** drop-down list. (See Figure 11.7.)

Figure 11.7
To begin creating a line style, click the **Custom** button on the **Line Style** drop-down list of the Pen, Preset Shapes, or Text tool.

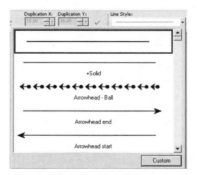

Clicking the Custom button opens the Styled Lines dialog box, shown in Figure 11.8. Here, you can manipulate several line properties, including start and end caps for the entire line, segment start and end caps, and dashes and gaps.

To set one of the caps, click the arrow button near the cap's preview window to get the selection box shown in Figure 11.9. Choose the cap you want by clicking it. You can then set the size of the cap relative to the line width by clicking the cap's **Size** button and then setting the Height and Width for the cap, as shown in Figure 11.10.

Figure 11.8
Create your new line
style with the Styled
Lines dialog box.

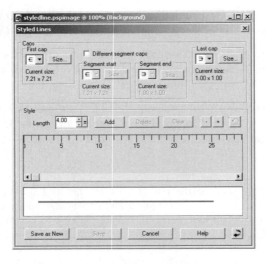

Figure 11.9
Choosing a cap.

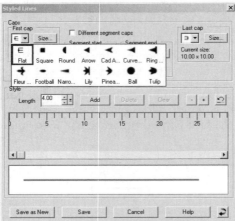

Figure 11.10
Setting the cap's size.

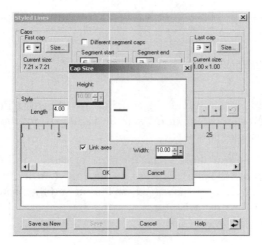

You add dashes and gaps in the Style pane of the Styled Lines dialog box. (See Figure 11.11.) Click Add and adjust the length of the dash or gap by entering a value in the text box or by dragging the arrow marker in the control box. You can keep adding dashes and gaps. To resize a particular dash or gap, click its marker and then make your adjustment, or set a value directly in the **Length** control.

Figure 11.11
Adding dashes and gaps to the line.

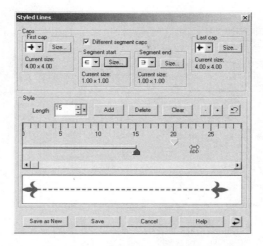

Figure 11.12 shows an example of the Styled Lines dialog box with the following settings:

> **First cap** and **Last cap** set to Tulip, each with **Size** set to 5.00 x 5.00
>
> **Different segment caps** checked, with **Segment start** and **Segment end** both set to Pineapple, each with **Size** set to 2.00 x 2.00
>
> **Dash** set to 40 and **Gap** set to 25

A preview of the resulting line is shown in the preview window at the bottom of the dialog box (refer to Figure 11.11).

Figure 11.12
Example of a fancy styled line.

To save your styled line, click **Save as New** and enter a name when prompted to enter a **Styled Line Name**. If you want to overwrite an existing styled line, enter the same name as the existing line. If you want to create a new styled line without overwriting any existing line, be sure to enter a unique name for your new styled line. (Paint Shop Pro will warn you if you try to give the new styled line the same name as an existing styled line.)

You can create all sorts of styled lines for all sorts of purposes, including navigation buttons for a Web site and separator lines for newsletters.

CHAPTER 11

Editing Gradients

You can create and edit multicolored gradients. To create a new gradient, go to the Gradient tab on the Material dialog box that you access by clicking a color box in the Materials palette. Then click the **Edit** button below the Gradient preview window to open the Gradient Editor dialog box, shown in Figure 11.13.

Figure 11.13
Gradient Editor dialog
box.

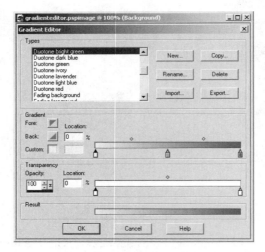

When you want to create a whole new gradient from scratch, click the **New** button. When you'd rather start by editing an existing gradient, highlight the existing gradient's name in the list and then click the **Copy** button. In either case, you'll be prompted to give your gradient a name. You'll then be returned to the Gradient Editor dialog box, where you do the actual editing.

CAUTION

When you edit a gradient and then click **OK** to close the Gradient Editor, the gradient will be permanently changed. So remember to edit and save a *copy* of any existing gradient rather than the original gradient itself, unless you really do want to lose the original gradient!

Notice that there are three bars in the Gradient Editor: the **Gradient** bar, the **Transparency** bar, and the **Result** bar. You use the controls for the **Gradient** bar to set the colors and color blending for your gradient. On the **Transparency** bar, you set the transparency/opacity of the gradient. The **Result** bar gives you a preview of your gradient as you edit it.

Try creating a new gradient step-by-step:

1. Click the **New** button and name your gradient; the Gradient Editor will look something like Figure 11.14.

   Notice that below the **Gradient** bar there are two pointed controls, called markers. You use the marker on the right to set the color for that end of the gradient pattern. You use the marker on the left to set the color for that end of the gradient pattern.

Figure 11.14
Gradient Editor when
you start a new gradient.

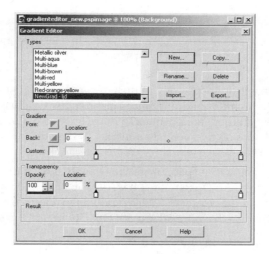

Above the **Gradient** bar is a diamond-shaped control, called a midpoint. Between
any two markers, there's a midpoint. A midpoint controls the blending of the two
colors of the gradient between two markers. Drag a midpoint to the left, and the
colors blend at 50/50 at a location closer to the left marker. Drag a midpoint to the
right, and the colors blend at 50/50 closer to the right marker.

2. To add a marker to the gradient, click beneath the **Gradient** bar anywhere where
    there currently is no marker (see Figure 11.15).

Figure 11.15
Adding a Gradient
marker.

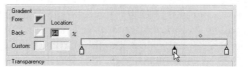

3. To change the color of a marker (thus altering the color of the gradient at the
    marker's location), click the marker to activate it and then click one of the color
    buttons: **Fore**, **Back**, or **Custom**. Choosing **Fore** sets the color to whatever the
    Foreground color in the Materials palette is when the gradient is used, while
    Back sets the color to whatever the Background color is when the gradient is used.
    To choose a fixed color, click the **Custom** button instead. Then, to select a new
    Custom color, click the color box to the right of the **Custom** button to bring up the
    Color dialog box. (Alternatively, you can access the Recent Colors dialog box by
    right-clicking the color box instead.) In this example, activate the new marker and
    change its color to a darker shade. Then drag the midpoints to adjust the blending
    as you like (see Figure 11.16). At this point, the Result bar will look something like
    Figure 11.17.

Figure 11.16
Changing the marker
color and adjusting the
midpoints.

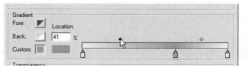

CHAPTER 11

Figure 11.17
Preview of the gradient so
far, shown on the Result
bar.

4. Adjust the opacity/transparency of the new gradient by using the **Transparency** bar, which has markers and midpoints just like the **Gradient** bar. By default, all areas of a new gradient are opaque. To make an area of the gradient transparent or semitransparent, you first activate a marker at the point where you want the adjustment to be made.

Next, set the opacity/transparency in the **Opacity** box on the far left of the **Transparency** bar. An **Opacity** of 100 is fully opaque, and **Opacity** of 0 is fully transparent, with intermediate values producing various levels of semitransparency. Figure 11.18 shows the left marker with **Opacity** set to 75 percent.

Figure 11.18
Adjusting the gradient's
transparency.

5. As with the **Gradient** bar, you can adjust a midpoint between two markers on the **Transparency** bar. This adjusts the blending of the opacity/transparency as set by the markers surrounding that midpoint. For this example, drag the midpoint so that **Location** is set to 60%.

You also can adjust the position of the markers on the Transparency bar. Figure 11.19 shows the left marker dragged to **Location** 35%. This gives all the area to the left of the marker 75 percent **Opacity**, just like the marker itself. (And if you drag the right marker away from **Location** 100%, everything to the right of that marker will have 100 percent **Opacity**, just like the marker itself.)

Figure 11.19
Adjusting a marker on
the Transparency bar.

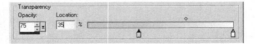

Figure 11.20 shows the finished gradient applied as a Linear gradient to a textured image. The Flood Fill tool was used with **Match mode** set to None, **Blend mode** set to Normal, and **Opacity** set to 100, and with the following gradient settings:

> **Texture**: None
>
> **Angle**: 90
>
> **Repeats**: 0

Before leaving the topic of the Gradient Editor, take a look at the buttons in addition to **New** and **Copy**:

▶ **Rename.** To rename a gradient, highlight its name, click **Rename**, and then enter the new name.

▶ **Delete.** To delete a gradient, highlight the gradient's name and then click the **Delete** button.

Figure 11.20
New gradient applied to a textured image.

▶ **Import.** The **Import** button enables you to import Adobe Photoshop gradients for use in Paint Shop Pro.

▶ **Export.** The **Export** button enables you to export a Paint Shop Pro gradient for use in Photoshop.

One final thing to note is that gradients you create are stored on disk and can be shared with other Paint Shop Pro users. New gradients are stored in Paint Shop Pro's Gradients folder, with an extension of PspGradient. You also can use Paint Shop Pro 7 gradient files (with an extension of JGD); just place these files in your Gradients folder. For Photoshop gradients (which have an extension of GRD), you need to import the gradient in order to use it. On the Web, you can find many sources of downloadable Paint Shop Pro and Photoshop gradients.

NOTE

A gradient file isn't an image but a set of instructions on how Paint Shop Pro should render the gradient. This is why you can't see a thumbnail of a gradient in Paint Shop Pro's Browser.

Creating Your Own Brushes

As was mentioned in Chapter 1, you can create your own brushes for use in Paint Shop Pro. To use a custom brush, select one of the painting tools, such as the Paint Brush or Airbrush. Then go to the Tool Options palette and click the brush preview window or the arrow next to it to access a drop-down list of brushes, shown in Figure 11.21.

The easiest sort of brush you can save is a generated brush tip—one whose characteristics are determined solely by the settings in the Tool Options palette. To create such a brush, choose the Paint Brush or Airbrush, select the settings you want, and then click the preview window for the brush tip (or the arrow adjacent to the preview window). Click the **Create brush tip** button, which is the uppermost button on the right of the **Brush Tip** drop-down list. If you want the current brush variance settings to be saved along with your new brush tip, check the **Save Variance** check box. When you click **OK**, your brush tip is added to the brushes in the drop-down list.

Figure 11.21
The **Custom Brush**
drop-down list.

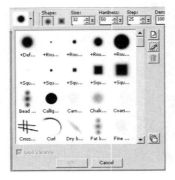

You can also create your own custom brush from any selection or figure. As an example, choose the Picture Tube tool and create a brush out of one of the Picture Tube elements like this:

1. Apply one of the coins from the Coins tube file to a new image with either a white or a transparent background. Crop the image to just a bit larger than the coin.

2. Choose one of the painting tools (to have access to the proper Tool Options palette).

3. Open the **Custom Brush** drop-down list and click the second button on the right, called **Create brush tip from selection**. This opens the Create Brush Tip dialog box.

4. In the Create Brush Tip dialog box, shown in Figure 11.22, give your brush a name and, if you like, enter author, copyright, and description information. If you want the current brush variance settings to be saved along with your new brush tip, check the **Save Variance** check box. You can also set a default step for your brush. When you click OK, the current selection or figure is then added immediately to the available custom brushes.

Figure 11.22
Create Brush Tip dialog
box.

5. To use a custom brush, select the brush from the drop-down list in the Tool Options palette.

Notice that you did not actually have to select the coin. A figure surrounded by white or transparency is all that you need.

NOTE

When you use a custom brush with a custom shape, the **Hardness** and **Thickness** controls in the Tool Options palette are greyed out. These controls modify a brush's shape, and you can't modify the shape of a brush created from a selection.

Now compare the difference between the results produced with the custom brush created from a tube element and the results produced with the tube itself. The custom brush paints with a material color—either the current Foreground material, if you paint with the left mouse button depressed, or the current Background material, if you paint with the right mouse button depressed. The opacity of the paint is determined by the **Opacity** setting selected in the Tool Options palette.

Figure 11.23 shows an example of the coin custom brush in use, with **Opacity** set to 75. (Notice that the parts of the brush that correspond to the dark areas of the figure paint more opaquely than the lighter areas, with white areas being completely transparent.)

Figure 11.23
The coin brush in use.

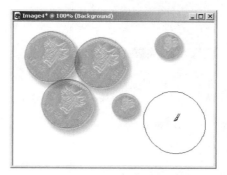

Compare the results shown in Figure 11.23 with the results that you get when you use the tube. With a tube, you paint with a fully opaque, full-color image. Which to choose—the brush or the tube—will depend on what effect you want to achieve.

Now let's try creating another brush, this time using a dingbat character as the selection:

1. Set the Foreground color to black, and then select the Text tool and choose **Floating**. Then click inside an empty image.

2. In the Text tool's Tool Options palette box, select the dingbat font you want to use, in the style and size you want. (Astigmatic One Eye's ButtonButton font is used in the example here.)

3. In the text box, add the dingbat character you want to use for your brush and click OK.

4. Choose one of the painting tools. Click the brush preview button in the tool's Tool Options palette, and in the selection list click the **Create brush tip from selection** button. When the Create Brush Tip dialog box appears, enter a name and choose whether to save the variance settings. The dingbat character is now added to your available custom brushes.

Figure 11.24 shows an example of the dingbat character in use, with **Opacity** set to 15.

NOTE
You aren't restricted to using only one character when you create a custom brush from a text selection. If you want to use a word or phrase or other string of characters as a brush, that works just as well as a single character. Figure 11.25 shows an example.

Keep in mind, though, that the maximum size for a brush is 500×500 pixels.

Figure 11.24
The dingbat brush in use.

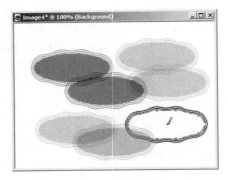

Figure 11.25
A brush made from a text
string.

In similar fashion, you can create a brush from a preset shape or from the output of an effect.
Figure 11.26, for example, shows a brush created from the output of the Kaleidoscope effect.
In short, any figure at all can be used as the basis of a brush.

Figure 11.26
A brush made from the
output of the
Kaleidoscope effect.

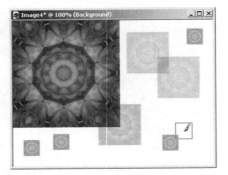

Creating Your Own Picture Tubes

Using Paint Shop Pro's **F**ile > Expor**t** > **P**icture Tube command, you can easily add a new tube that
you've created. To create your own tube, start by opening a new image and selecting Transparent
as the image's Background color. The dimensions of this tube canvas should be large enough to
hold all of your Picture Tube elements in a series of regularly spaced columns and rows.

As an example, suppose that you want to make a tube based on the viola images shown in Figure
11.27, where each of the flowers has been isolated from a photograph.

Figure 11.27
Images used to create the example tube.

To create the tube, I used these images and mirrored versions of the originals.

Each of the four images for this tube is 270×264 pixels, so to accommodate the four tube elements, the tube canvas in this case needs to be either 1080×264 (four columns and one row) or 266×1080 (one column and four rows) or 540×528 (two columns and two rows). For this example, a 540×528 canvas is used, as shown in Figure 11.28.

Figure 11.28
Open a new canvas for positioning your tube elements.

TIP

Although the size of Picture Tube elements can be scaled either up or down when you select a particular tube to paint with, the results are much better when you scale down than when you scale up. For this reason, it's best to make your tube elements as large as you're likely to want to use them.

For example, suppose that you'll usually want to paint with the elements in your tube displayed at about 50×50 pixels, but occasionally you'll want them to be about 100×100 pixels. In that case, create the tube with elements that are 100×100 pixels.

CHAPTER 11

Before you place the Picture Tube elements on your newly opened canvas, turn on Paint Shop Pro's grid—which makes aligning objects easier—by selecting **View > Grid**. You can adjust the spacing of the grid lines by selecting **File > Preferences > General Program Preferences** and going to the Rulers and Units tab, or by right-clicking your image canvas's title bar and choosing **Change Grid, Guide, & Snap Properties**.

Follow these steps to place the Picture Tube elements on the tube canvas:

1. Copy a selection from a source image to the Clipboard, and then paste the copied selection to the tube canvas as a new selection.

2. Position the selection, centering it within the first cell area of your tube canvas. In this example, the first pasted-in selection is positioned in the upper-left area of the tube canvas, as shown in Figure 11.29. After you position the selection correctly, click with the right mouse button outside the selection to anchor the selection and turn off the selection marquee.

Figure 11.29
Position each tube element.

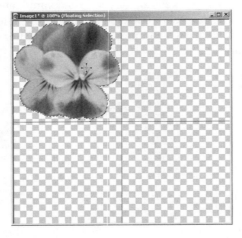

CAUTION

All opaque areas on the tube canvas will appear as opaque paint when you use your tube. You normally will want each tube element to be a figure surrounded by transparency. When the figure that you want for your tube element is only part of an opaque area of the source image, be sure to select only the part of the image that you want for your tube before using **Edit > Copy**.

3. Continue in the same way to copy, paste, and position the next tube element. Do the same with all the tube elements, positioning each in an appropriate area of the tube canvas.

4. When all of your tube elements are positioned correctly, you're ready to export the image as a tube. Make sure that the tube canvas image is the active image by clicking its title bar. Then choose **File > Export > Picture Tube**. The Export Picture Tube dialog box, shown in Figure 11.30, is displayed.

TIP

If you want to add a drop shadow to each of your tube elements, you don't need to make a selection before you apply the effect, nor do you have to add a shadow to each element individually. Drop Shadow (available under Effects > 3D Effects) works without a selection on a layer anytime the layer contains transparency. Just apply Drop Shadow to the layer, and drop shadows will be added around each opaque figure on the layer.

Figure 11.30
Exporting a Picture Tube.

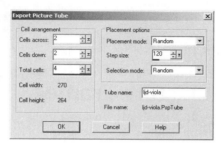

CAUTION

Before you export your image as a Picture Tube, be sure that it has exactly one layer and no floating selections. If it has more than one layer, you've flattened the image, or a floating selection is active, Paint Shop Pro will refuse to export the image as a tube. Instead, you'll receive this rather confusing error message: "To save the image as a Picture Tube, the image must be 24-bit and have only one layer with a transparency."

5. In the Export Picture Tube dialog box, fill in the number of **Cells across** and the number of **Cells down**. The field for **Total cells** updates automatically. This example has two cells across and two cells down, for a total of four cells.

6. Fill in the settings you want for the **Placement mode** (Random or Continuous), **Step size**, and **Selection mode**. Here's a summary of the **Selection mode** options:

   ▶ **Random.** Tube selection is random.

   ▶ **Incremental.** Each tube element is selected sequentially, and then the sequence is repeated.

   ▶ **Angular.** Tube selection is determined by the direction in which you drag the mouse as you paint.

   ▶ **Pressure.** This is effective only if you're painting with a pressure-sensitive graphics tablet and have Paint Shop Pro set up to recognize different pen pressures.

   ▶ **Velocity.** Tube selection is dependent on the speed of your mouse drag.

   In the **Tube name** field, enter the name of the new tube as you want it to appear in the **Tube** drop-down list in the Picture Tube tool's Tool Options palette. (The name of the example tube was entered as "ljd-viola.") After you choose all the settings and enter the name of the tube, click OK.

CHAPTER 11

After you click **OK** in the Export Picture Tube dialog box, Paint Shop Pro creates the new tube file and adds its name to the list of available tubes.

The new tube is ready to use. Choose the Picture Tube tool and select the new tube from the **Tube** drop-down list in the Tool Options palette. Then paint away with your new creation!

TIP
Most tubes have more than one tube element. After all, why have a tube when you can just cut, paste, and resize a single figure? But there's at least one case where it makes sense to have a single tube element: where the tube has a **Step** of 1 and is used as a 3-D brush, like the 3D gold, 3D green, and 3D orange tubes.

Creating Your Own Picture Frames

You can enhance an image by adding a Picture Frame. To add a frame to your image, choose Image > Picture Frame to start the Picture Frame wizard (see Figure 11.31).

Figure 11.31
The Picture Frame wizard.

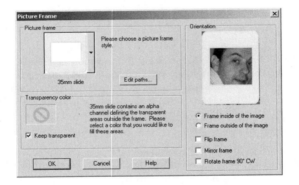

In the wizard, select the frame you want to use. You can choose to apply the frame either inside the existing canvas or outside, and you can flip, mirror, or rotate the frame. If you select a rectangular frame with no transparent areas outside the frame, you then just click OK to apply the frame. If there are transparent areas around the edges of the frame (as there are for any nonrectangular frame), either check **Keep transparent** or uncheck this check box and choose a color to replace the transparency by clicking in the dialog's color box and then choosing the color you want. Figure 11.32 shows an example where transparency outside the frame is replaced with a color.

To apply the frame, click **OK.**

It's easy to make your own rectangular Picture Frames. Create a new 24-bit image on a transparent layer, as in Figure 11.33. Here, the Texture and Inner Bevel effects are applied to a frame-shaped selection, and then the selection is turned off.

Export this file as a Picture Frame with **File** > Export > Picture **Frame.** This saves your new frame with the PspFrame extension and places it in the Picture Frames folder specified in your File Locations preferences (**File** > **Preferences** > File **Locations**). The next time you use the Picture Frame wizard, you'll see your new frame in the list.

Figure 11.32
Replacing transparency
with a color.

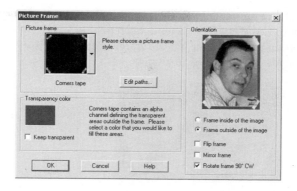

Figure 11.33
Creating a new Picture
Frame.

Creating a nonrectangular frame is almost as easy as creating a rectangular one. Before saving the file, select the picture frame and the internal "hole," as shown in Figure 11.34. (An easy way to make such a selection is to select the outer transparent areas and then choose **S**elections > **I**nvert.)

Figure 11.34
Selecting the frame of a
new nonrectangular
Picture Frame.

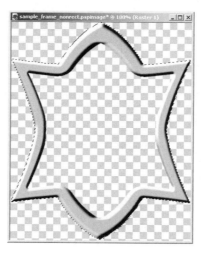

CHAPTER 11

Next, save the selection to an alpha channel by choosing **S**elections > Sa**v**e to Alpha Channel. Turn off the selection with Ctrl+D or **S**elections > Select **N**one, and then export the image as a picture frame just as you do a rectangular picture frame. Figure 11.35 shows the nonrectangular frame with the areas outside the frame set to a color.

Figure 11.35
Picture Frame applied to a photo, with outside areas set to a color.

TIP

Picture Frames stretch or shrink to fit the image that they're applied to. When the aspect ratio of the frame is quite different from the aspect ratio of the image, the frame will be distorted. So you might want to create a couple versions of your frame, each with a different aspect ratio. For example, you might have one that's 1-to-1 (a square) and one that's 2-to-3 (a rectangle).

Keep in mind, too, that the image quality of the frame is maintained best when the frame is shrunk rather than stretched. So try to create your frames about as large as you're likely to use them.

TIP

You can create a rectangular mat that you can colorize on the fly each time you add the frame using the Picture Frame wizard. Create the mat just as you would a rectangular frame, but before exporting the file as a Picture Frame, select the transparent area surrounded by the mat but not the mat itself. Save this selection to an alpha channel, deselect, and then export the frame. When you run the Picture Frame wizard and select the mat, be sure that **Keep transparent** is unchecked. Choose a color for your mat in the **Transparency color** color box.

User Defined Filters

Many Paint Shop Pro users find User Defined Filters baffling. The Paint Shop Pro 7 documentation was overly technical, and the Paint Shop Pro 8 documentation says almost nothing at all on this topic. So you might not even know where to begin with User Defined Filters.

This section leaves most of the technical details aside and concentrates on a few rules of thumb that will help you to make your own Blur, Emboss, Sharpen, and Edge Detect filters. These filters can be used on any greyscale or 16 million color image.

The Technical Stuff

Let's begin by getting some of the technical stuff out of the way. Open the User Defined Filter matrix by choosing Effects > User Defined Filters. The User Defined Filter dialog box appears, as shown in Figure 11.36.

Figure 11.36
A new User Defined
Filter matrix.

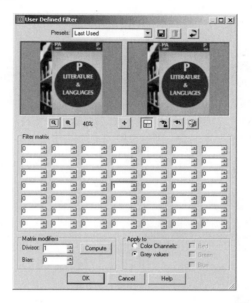

The cells of the matrix represent pixels in an image. The center cell represents the target pixel, and the surrounding cells represent the pixels surrounding the target. The numbers that you place in the cells determine brightness changes in the pixels. A positive number in the center cell increases the target pixel's brightness, and a negative number decreases the target pixel's brightness. Numbers in the surrounding cells combine to further affect the target pixel. The filter examines each pixel in an image separately, calculates how to change each target, and then applies all the results to the image.

In general, you want to keep the overall brightness of the image the same as the original. The total of all the values in the cells helps determine the brightness of the filtered image. If the total equals 1, the filtered image will have the same overall brightness as the original (provided the **Divisor** is kept at 1 and the **Bias** is kept at 0). If the total value is greater than 1, the overall brightness increases; if the total value is less than 1, the overall brightness decreases.

NOTE
If you experiment with User Defined Filters without understanding how the total of the cell values affects brightness, you might very well end up with filters that do nothing more than turn your image solid white or solid black.

You can maintain the original brightness of your image even if the values of the cells don't total 1. You do this by adjusting the **Divisor**. If the total of your cells equals 5, setting the **Divisor** to 5 will maintain the image brightness (because 5 divided by 5 equals 1). Your **Divisor** doesn't have to be equal to the total of the cell values, but other values will change the image's brightness—not always to good effect.

TIP

You don't need to do any math to calculate the proper **Divisor**. Just click the **Compute** button to the right of the **Divisor** box and Paint Shop Pro will compute the value for you and enter it in the **Divisor** box.

As you'll see when you look at a few examples, the Bias is most useful for embossing filters. The **Bias** value is added to the modified pixel's brightness and thus has a big effect on the filtered image's contrast.

Blur Filters

Okay, now you're ready to look at a few examples. Throughout this section, the sample filters are applied to the image in Figure 11.37.

Figure 11.37
Base image to be filtered.

First, take a look at the Blur_More preset that comes with Paint Shop Pro. To see the matrix for this filter, select Blur_More from the **Presets** drop-down list. Figure 11.38 shows the resulting User Defined Filter dialog box.

Notice in this filter that the center cell is set to a positive value and that a symmetric pattern of cells surrounding the center cell also contains positive values. The **Divisor** is set to the total of the cell values. These are the basic characteristics of any blurring filter.

Now we'll make our own Blur filter. Figure 11.39 shows the matrix values and **Divisor** for a more severe Blur filter, along with the effect of applying this filter to the sample image.

Figure 11.38
The Blur_More preset.

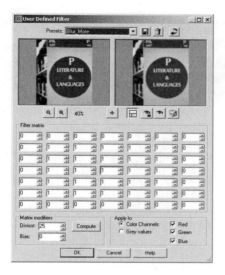

Figure 11.39
A more severe Blur filter.

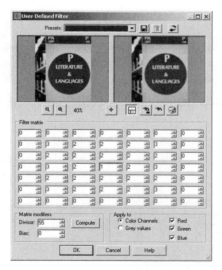

Notice that, again, the center pixel is set to a positive number, and a symmetric pattern of positive cell values is set in the surrounding cells. The total of all the cell values is 55, so to maintain the overall brightness of the original image, the **Divisor** is set to 55.

Emboss Filters Galore

A color Emboss filter makes an image look embossed while generally maintaining the colors of the original image. The matrix values of such a filter (the Emboss_7 preset), and its effect on the sample image, are shown in Figure 11.40.

Figure 11.40
Emboss_7, a color
Emboss filter.

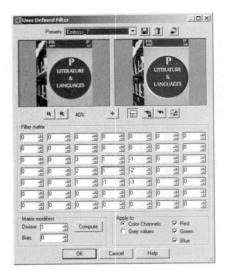

The matrix of this example shows the basic characteristics of color-embossing filters. The center cell value can be either positive or negative. The crucial factor is that cells to one side of the center cell have positive values, and analogous cells to the other side of the center cell are set to 0 or have negative values. The relative position of the positive and nonpositive values determines where the highlights and shadows appear in the embossed image.

Now look at a few embossing filters that more closely resemble Paint Shop Pro's Emboss effect (discussed in Chapter 7, "Paint Shop Pro Effects").

You can create an embossing effect without much color by putting positive values in some of the cells to one side of the center cell and adjusting the Bias. Figure 11.41 shows the matrix and results for one such filter, the Emboss_1 preset.

Figure 11.41
Emboss_1, a basic
embossing filter.

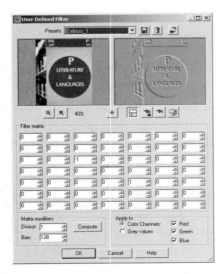

TIP

You can use **Bias** in any User Defined Filter to affect the contrast of your filtered image. For high-contrast effects, enter grid values that yield a relatively large sum, and enter very large positive or very low negative values for **Bias**.

In your embossing filters, you can change where the highlights and shadows appear (and thus change which areas appear raised and which appear recessed) by changing the relative position of the positive and nonpositive cell values. Figure 11.42 shows the result of the Emboss_2 preset, which switches the relative position of the cells of Emboss_1, the basic embossing filter used in Figure 11.41.

Figure 11.42

Emboss_2, the basic embossing filter reversed.

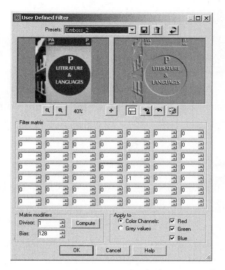

TIP

If you want your embossed image to have no hint of color, apply the filter only to your image's grey values. In the User Defined Filter dialog box, select **Grey values** rather than **Color Channels**.

Sharpen Filters

Now it's time to explore Sharpen filters, which sharpen the focus of a blurry image. For Sharpen, enter a relatively large positive value for the center cell, and enter negative numbers (such as −2 or −1) in a symmetrical pattern in some of the surrounding cells. The smaller the value in the surrounding cells, the more severe the sharpening effect will be. Figure 11.43 displays a basic Sharpen filter (where the central value is 9 and the eight immediately surrounding cells are each set to −1).

Figure 11.43
A Sharpen filter.

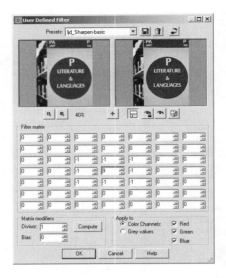

To soften the sharpening effect, increase the value in the center cell and compensate for the increase with the **Divisor**.

TIP

You can make any User Defined Filter effect more subtle by increasing the value of the center cell and compensating for the increase with the **Divisor**.

Edge Detect Filters

An Edge Detect filter enhances the areas of an image in which there are contrasts in brightness or color. For edge detection, the values entered for any cells surrounding the center cell should be positive, and the value of the center cell should be a negative number that when added to the sum of the surrounding cells yields 1. Figure 11.44 shows an example where the central value is –7 and each of the eight immediately surrounding cells is set to 1.

Infinite Filter Possibilities

Experiment with variations on the sample filters covered here. For example, the filter shown in Figure 11.45 is a variation of a basic Sharpen filter, with some added peripheral values and a fairly high Bias.

Other variations to try in your own filters include using 0 as your center cell value and/or using Divisors that don't completely compensate for grid sums that aren't equal to 1. Figures 11.46 and 11.47 are examples of such filters.

Figure 11.44
An Edge Detect filter.

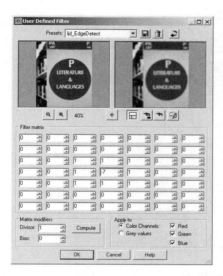

Figure 11.45
A variation on a basic
Sharpen filter.

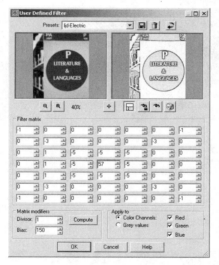

CHAPTER 11

Take a look at the various User Defined Filter presets, and also try out the **Randomize** button (which is sure to generate some pretty wild results). If you prefer to keep to the basics, Table 11.1 summarizes the rules of thumb for simple User Defined Filters.

Figure 11.46
A filter with a center cell value of 0, a **Divisor** that doesn't equal the grid sum, and an extreme Bias.

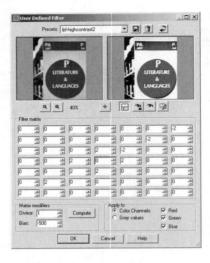

Figure 11.47
A filter with an extreme **Bias** and a **Divisor** that doesn't equal the grid sum.

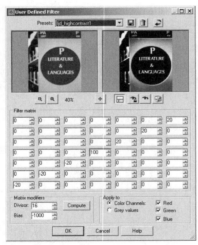

TABLE 11.1 RULES OF THUMB FOR USER DEFINED FILTERS (COMPENSATE FOR SUMS NOT EQUAL TO 1 WITH THE DIVISOR)		
	Center Cell Value	**Surrounding Cell Values**
Blur	Positive	Positive
Sharpen	Positive	Negative
Edges	Negative	Positive
Emboss	Positive	Symmetric positive and/or negative

12
Scripting

One of the most asked-for features in earlier versions of Paint Shop Pro was the ability to record a series of commands and play them back. Now, with its new scripting facility, Paint Shop Pro 8 gives you that and more.

Here's what you'll be exploring in this chapter:

▶ Running scripts (on a single file and in Batch Mode)
▶ Recording and editing scripts
▶ Editing scripts

Script Basics

Scripts can be as simple as a recording of commands, but they're also small computer programs that run within Paint Shop Pro. The scripting language used is Python, and if you're fluent in Python, you can include your own code in your scripts.

You access the script facility either from the **File > Script** menu or from the Script toolbar, shown in Figure 12.1.

Whether you use the menu or the toolbar, you'll be able to select a script and run it, edit an existing script, or record a new script.

Figure 12.1
The Script toolbar.

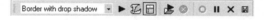

NOTE
File > Script includes one command that's not available from the Script toolbar: Clear Output Window. Scripts that generate error messages or informational text print to the Script Output window, shown in Figure 12.2. Text remains in the window, even after other scripts write to it, until you clear it.

If the Script Output window covers up other windows or palettes in your workspace, read the text, clear the window if you like, and then close the window.

Figure 12.2
The Script Output
window.

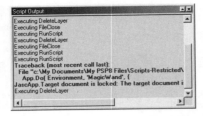

Running Scripts

You run a script either from the Script toolbar or the File menu. To run a Script from the Script toolbar, first toggle the toolbar on with **View** > **Toolbars** > **Script** (if it isn't displayed already). Then select the script you want from the drop-down list, and click the **Run Selected Script** button just to the right of the drop-down list.

NOTE

Scripts listed in the drop-down list on the Script toolbar are those stored in the folders listed in your Scripts - Restricted and Scripts - Trusted file locations preferences, specified on the File Locations dialog box. To access this dialog box, go to **File** > **Preferences** > **File Locations**.

If you want to select a script that isn't in the drop-down list, click the **Run Script** button on the Script toolbar, navigate to the folder that contains the script you want, select the script, and click **Open**.

If you have the **Interactive Playback** toggle on, then by default any command in the script that has settings will open its dialog box to allow you to choose the settings you want. If you have the **Interactive Playback** toggle off, then by default all commands will run silently, without displaying their dialog boxes. (As you'll see later in this chapter, you can adjust a script so that it ignores the **Interactive Playback** setting.)

Recording Scripts

To start recording a script, choose **File** > **Script** > **Start Recording** or click the **Start Script Recording** button. If at any point you want to pause the recording while you do something that you don't want included in your script, choose **File** > **Script** > **Pause Recording** or click the **Pause Script Recording** button on the Script toolbar. When you want to resume recording, again choose **File** > **Script** > **Pause Recording** or click the **Pause Script Recording** button.

When you've finished all the steps that you want included in your script, choose **File** > **Script** > **Save Recording** or click the **Save Script Recording** button. The script is saved in your My PSP Files\Scripts - Restricted folder. (If you instead decide not to save what you recorded, choose **File** > **Script** > **Cancel Recording** or click the **Cancel Script Recording** button. In that case, the script is not saved.)

After you save a script, you'll be able to run it just like any other script.

Editing Scripts

Once you've recorded and saved a script, you can modify it if you like.

Simple scripts can be edited with Paint Shop Pro's Script Editor. You invoke the built-in script editor either by selecting the script you want to edit in the Script toolbar and then clicking the **Edit Selected Script** button or by choosing File > Script > Edit and navigating to the script. The Script Editor dialog box is shown in Figure 12.3.

Figure 12.3
Paint Shop Pro's built-in Script Editor.

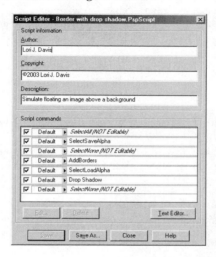

You have the option of inserting script information, including author, copyright, and description. And from within the built-in editor, you can also make simple modifications of script commands. For any of the listed commands, you have several options:

▶ Uncheck any commands that you want to suppress entirely but not delete.

▶ Change the setting in the drop-down list for the command from Default to either Interactive or Silent. With Interactive, the command is always run interactively, no matter what the Interactive Playback toggle is set to. With Silent, the command is always run silently, no matter what the Interactive Playback toggle is set to. With Default, the command is run interactively if the Interactive Playback toggle is on and silently if the Interactive Playback toggle is off.

▶ Highlight a command's name and click the **Delete** button to permanently delete the command from the script.

▶ Highlight a command's name and click the **Edit** button to change the default settings for the command. For commands that have no settings, the **Edit** button will be greyed out and the listing for the command will include "(NOT Editable)" after the command name.

For adding Python code that the built-in editor cannot parse or to make other hand-entered changes to your script, click the **Text Editor** button on the Script Editor dialog box. This calls up Notepad or another text editor that you've specified in the file locations preferences, opening the script you're editing.

Be careful if you edit a script by hand. Python pays strict attention to indenting, for example, and any inappropriate indents will yield unintended results or make the script unrunnable. We won't look at any details here. If you're interested in extensive script editing or script writing, you should consult the script writer's guide available on the Jasc site.

TIP

Never write a script entirely by hand, even if you're a Python expert. Instead, record a script that approximates what you want your script to do, and then edit that script. This is much easier, and yields fewer errors, than coding your script from scratch.

Third-Party Scripts

You're not limited to using scripts supplied by Jasc or that you've recorded or written yourself. You can also share scripts with other people and install other people's scripts. To install a third-party script, you just need to copy the script into one of the Script folders specified in your file location preferences. The script can then be run from the Script toolbar or from the **File** > Script menu.

Scripts that can be understood by the built-in script editor should be stored in one of your Scripts - Restricted folders. Scripts that contain Python code that the built-in editor cannot read must be stored in one of your Scripts - Trusted folders.

CAUTION

Be careful about using scripts that can be run only from a Scripts - Trusted folder. Destructive code can appear in such scripts, either by accident or intentionally. Be sure you know and trust the source of any trusted scripts. (After all, that's why they're called Trusted.)

Running Scripts in Batch Mode

You can run scripts in Batch Mode, running a single script on multiple files in a folder automatically. To run a script in Batch Mode, choose **File** > Batc**h** > **P**rocess and do the following in the Batch Process dialog box, shown in Figure 12.4:

▶ Navigate to the folder that contains the files you want to process, and select the files you want to run the script on.

▶ In the Script pane, click the **Browse** button and choose the script that you want to run. If you like, you can check the **Run script in silent mode** check box.

▶ Choose any other settings that you want for Save Mode and Save Options.

▶ When you're ready, click the **Start** button.

Figure 12.4
The Batch Process dialog box.

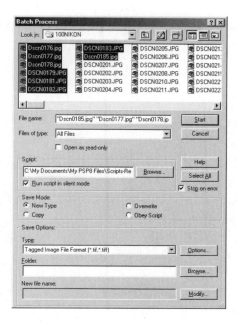

Learning More About Scripting

To learn more about scripting, begin by downloading *Paint Shop Pro 8 Scripting for Script Authors* from **http://www.jasc.com**. To learn more about the Python programming language, go to **http://www.python.org**.

You can also ask questions and share scripts and scripting techniques in the Scripting section of Jasc's Paint Shop Pro forum. To register for the forum and see what's there, head over to **http://forums.jasc.com**, or from within Paint Shop Pro, choose **Help** > **Jasc Software Online** > **User Forums**.

A

Paint Shop Pro 8 Menus, Toolbars, and Palettes

This appendix contains screen captures of Paint Shop Pro 8's major menus, toolbars, and palettes.

If you reconfigure Paint Shop Pro and then want to return to the default workspace, shown in Figure A.1, choose **F**ile > **W**orkspace > **L**oad and choose Default.

Figure A.1
The Paint Shop Pro default workspace (with an image open).

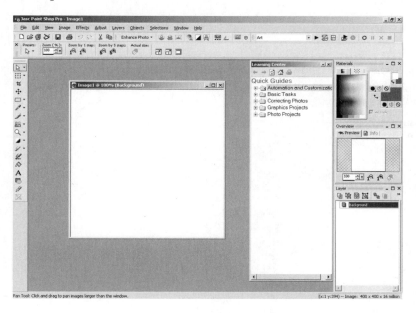

The menu bar shown in Figure A.2 is the one that appears when an image file is open and active. Specialized menu bars appear when no file is open or when the Browser is open and active.

Figure A.2
The menu bar.

By default, the Standard toolbar (shown in Figure A.3) includes buttons for these common operations: New, Open, Browse, Twain Acquire, Save, Print, Undo, Redo, Cut, and Copy.

Figure A.3
The Standard toolbar.

The Photo toolbar (shown in Figure A.4) includes controls for the most commonly used photo adjustment commands, all of which are also accessible from the Adjust menu.

Figure A.4
The Photo toolbar.

The Script toolbar (shown in Figure A.5) includes controls for running, editing, and recording scripts. These commands are also accessible via **F**ile > **S**cript.

Figure A.5
The Script toolbar.

The Tool Options palette that is shown in Figure A.6 is for the Pan tool. The Tool Options palette for any tool includes a drop-down list of presets as well as controls specific to the tool.

Figure A.6
Sample Tool Options palette.

The Tools toolbar (shown in Figure A.7) includes icons for all of Paint Shop Pro's tools. By default, the tools are grouped in families. For example, the Pan and Zoom tools are grouped in one family, and the Paint Brush, Airbrush, and Warp Brush are grouped in another family.

Figure A.7
The Tools toolbar.

You select materials for drawing and painting in the Materials palette, shown in Figure A.8. A material can be a solid color, a pattern, or a gradient. A material can also optionally include a texture.

Paletted images have only 256 or fewer colors. For such images, only the colors present in the palette are displayed in the Materials palette, as shown in Figure A.9.

Figure A.8
The Materials palette (for
16-million color images).

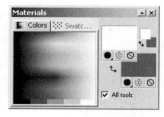

Figure A.9
The Materials palette (for
paletted images).

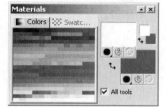

Swatches of materials can be saved and loaded from the Swatch tab of the Materials palette,
shown in Figure A.10.

Figure A.10
The Materials palette
(Swatch tab).

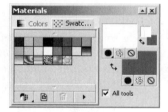

The Overview palette (shown in Figure A.11) displays a preview of the active image. There are
also controls in this palette for zooming in and out on the image.

Figure A.11
The Overview palette
(Preview tab).

The Info tab of the Overview palette (shown in Figure A.12) displays information about the image's dimensions and format. The current cursor position in the image is also displayed. When the Preset Shapes tool is in use, the start and end points of the shape and the height and width of the shape are also displayed dynamically.

Figure A.12
The Overview palette
(Info tab).

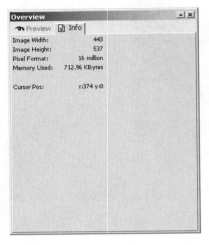

The Layer palette (shown in Figure A.13) makes clear the layer structure of your image, differentiating between the Background layer, raster layers, mask layers, vector layers, and adjustment layers. Vector objects and layer groups are also represented. Commands accessed from the Layer palette are also available in these menus: Layers, Objects, and Selections.

Figure A.13
The Layer palette.

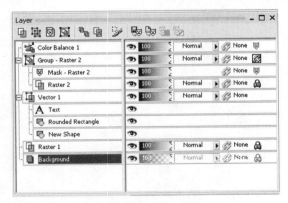

The Status bar is shown in Figure A.14. On the left side of the Status bar, information is displayed about the active tool or about toolbar icons over which the mouse is placed. On the right side, information on cursor placement and file dimensions. Depending on what tool is active, other information might also be displayed on the right side of the Status bar.

The Learning Center, shown in Figure A.15, contains several tutorials (called Quick Guides). To toggle the Learning Center on and off, press F10.

Figure A.14
The Status bar.

Pan Tool: Click and drag to pan images larger than the window.   (x:1 y:394) -- Image: 400 x 400 x 16 million

Figure A.15
The Learning Center
(with some headings
expanded).

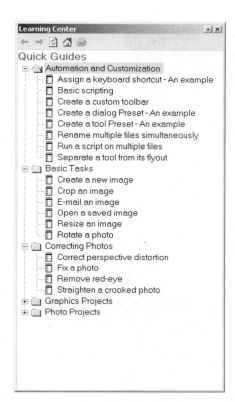

The Brush Variance palette, shown in Figure A.16, provides a powerful means of control of the Paint Brush and Airbrush. To toggle this palette on and off, press F11.

Figure A.16
The Brush Variance
palette.

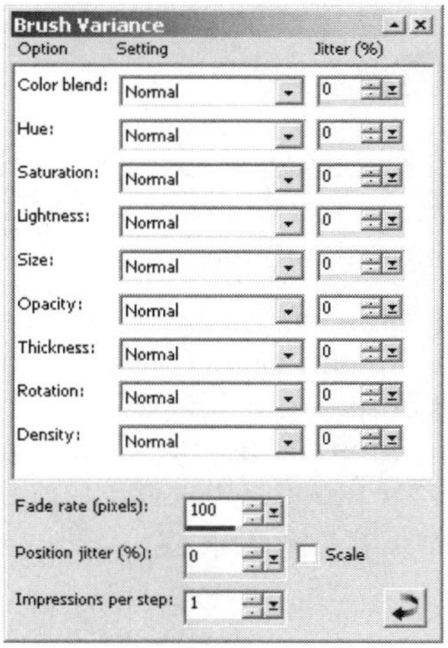

The Script Output window, shown in Figure A.17, displays error messages and output from scripts. It opens automatically when anything is written to it. To toggle this window on and off, press F3.

Figure A.17
The Script Output window.

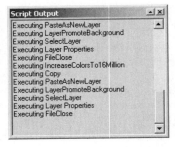

The Histogram, shown in Figure A.18, provides information about the distribution of tones in your image. It is most useful in analyzing digital photos. To toggle the Histogram on and off, press F7.

Figure A.18
The Histogram.

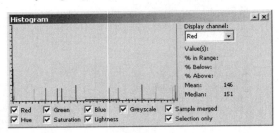

The Effects toolbar, shown in Figure A.19, includes buttons for several commonly used commands available from the Effects menu.

Figure A.19
The Effects toolbar.

The Web toolbar, shown in Figure A.20, includes buttons for several Web-related commands that are also available from the File menu.

Figure A.20
The Web toolbar.

The Browser, shown in Figure A.21, displays thumbnails of your images. Navigate to a particular folder to see thumbnails of the images stored there. You can copy, move, open, and delete images from the Browser. You can also access information about images from the Browser.

Most effects and commands accessed from the Adjust menu make use of a dialog box. In addition to controls specific to the effect or command, a dialog box includes a drop-down list of presets, controls for saving and deleting presets, a reset button, preview windows showing the unaffected image and the processed image, controls for zooming the previews and positioning the previews, a toggle to show or hide the previews, controls for proofing the effect on the actual image, and a randomize button. A sample dialog box is shown in Figure A.22.

Figure A.21
The Browser.

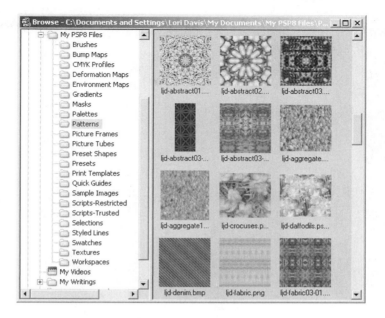

Figure A.22
Sample dialog box.

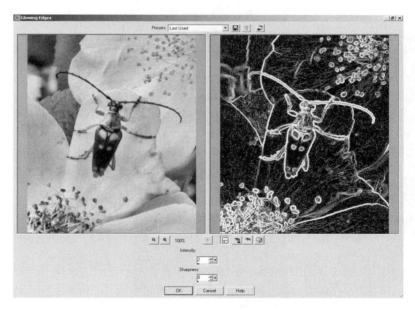

When there is an open image in the Paint Shop Pro workspace, the following menus are available: **F**ile (Figure A.23), **E**dit (Figure A.24), **V**iew (Figure A.25), **I**mage (Figure A.26), Effects (Figure A.27), **A**djust (Figure A.28), **L**ayers (Figure A.29), **O**bjects (Figure A.30), **S**elections (Figure A.31), **W**indow (Figure A.32), and **H**elp (Figure A.33).

Figure A.23
The File menu.

Figure A.24
The Edit menu.

Figure A.25
The View menu.

Figure A.26
The Image menu.

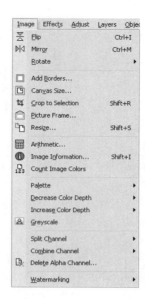

Figure A.27
The Effects menu.

Figure A.28
The Adjust menu.

Figure A.29
The Layers menu.

Figure A.30
The Objects menu.

Figure A.31
The Selections menu.

Figure A.32
The Window menu.

Figure A.33
The Help menu.

B

Configuring Paint Shop Pro 8

Paint Shop Pro 8 provides you a lot of flexibility in setting up your workspace. Besides being able to float, dock, resize, and reposition palettes, toolbars, and menus, you can customize existing toolbars and menus. You can even create your own toolbars and menus. You can bind commands to keyboard shortcuts. And you can modify many aspects of Paint Shop Pro's appearance and behavior.

Customizing Toolbars

To customize a toolbar, choose **View** > **Customize**, or right-click on the title bar of any palette or on an empty space in the menu bar and choose Customize. The Customize dialog box then opens. Click on the Toolbars tab, shown in Figure B.1.

Figure B.1
The Customize dialog box.

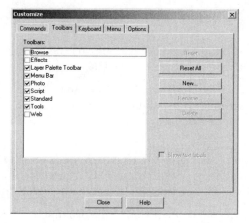

Click the **New** button and enter a name for your new toolbar. A small empty toolbar is then displayed. To add commands to the toolbar, go to the Commands tab, choose the category for the command you want, and select the command from the Commands list. Drag the command onto the new toolbar. Repeat for any other commands that you want to add. If you make a mistake, just drag the unwanted command off the toolbar.

You can also add commands to an existing toolbar by dragging commands onto the toolbar. If you want to delete commands from an existing toolbar, or if you make a mistake, drag the unwanted command from the toolbar.

Customizing Menus

To create a new menu, go to the Commands tab of the Customize dialog box and choose New Menu in the Categories list. In the Commands box, click New Menu and drag to the menu bar or to a displayed palette. When you release the mouse button, a new menu with the name New Menu is displayed (see Figure B.2).

Figure B.2
Creating a new menu.

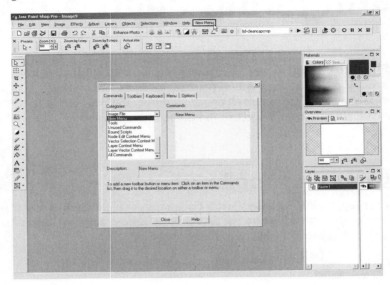

To give the new menu a more descriptive name, right-click on the new menu and choose Menu Text. Type the name you want for the menu, then click **OK**.

To add commands to the menu, highlight the command's menu category in the Categories list, then find the command in the Commands list and drag the command to your menu. Add any other commands that you want in the same way. If you make a mistake, just drag the unwanted command off the menu.

You can also add commands to an existing menu. Highlight the command's menu category, find the command you want, and drag the command to the existing menu. If you want to delete a command from the menu, or if you make a mistake, drag the unwanted command off the menu.

If you want to add commands to a context menu, go to the Menu tab of the Customize dialog box and select the context menu you want to customize. The context menu is then displayed. Go to the Commands tab, find the command you want to add to the context menu, and drag that command to the context menu. Again, you can delete a command from the menu simply by dragging the command off the menu.

Creating Keyboard Shortcuts

The Customize dialog box also enables you to bind commands to a keyboard shortcut. To change an existing shortcut or to create a new shortcut, go to the Keyboard tab of the Customize dialog box, shown in Figure B.3.

Figure B.3
The Keyboard tab of the
Customize dialog box.

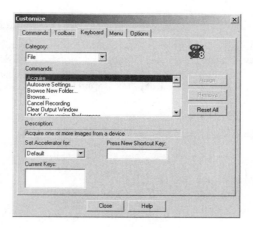

In the **Set Accelerator for** drop-down list, pick Browser if you want the shortcut to apply when the Browser window is active, or choose Default if you want the shortcut to apply when the Browser is not active. Choose a command category, then select the command in the Commands list. Click in the **Press New Shortcut Key** text box, then press the key you'd like to use for your shortcut. If you make a mistake, press another key to use that for your shortcut or press Esc to clear the text box. When you have the key you want, click the **Assign** button.

Saving Workspaces

Paint Shop Pro also enables you to save one or more workspace configurations. You can make any adjustments to the toolbars or menus, position the various palettes where you want them, or even open a specific image file or set of image files, and then save the whole workspace to load again whenever you need it.

To save a workspace, choose **F**ile > **W**orkspace > **S**ave (or press Shift+Alt+S). In the Save Workspace dialog box, navigate to the folder where you want to save your workspace file, provide a name for the file, and click **Save**.

To load a previously saved workspace, choose **F**ile > **W**orkspace > **L**oad (or press Shift+Alt+L). In the Load Workspace dialog box, navigate to the folder that contains your workspace files, select the workspace file that you want, and click **Open**. A few workspaces are included with Paint Shop Pro 8, including one named Default (which returns the workspace to the factory default) and one named Paint Shop Pro 7 (which duplicates, as much as possible, the workspace found in Paint Shop Pro 7).

Setting Preferences

Under **F**ile > **P**references is an option called **G**eneral Program Preferences. Select this menu option to open the Paint Shop Pro 8 Preferences dialog box, shown in Figure B.4. Here you can modify the settings for such things as Undo limits, the appearance of dialog boxes and palettes, and the size of the thumbnails displayed in the Browser.

APPENDIX B

TIP

If you normally perform several very different image-editing tasks, you might want to create workspaces designed specifically for each task. For example, you might want to have one workspace for retouching and enhancing photographs and another workspace for creating Web graphics.

Figure B.4
The Paint Shop Pro 8 Preferences dialog box.

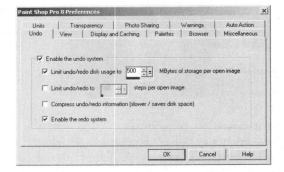

You might also want to tell Paint Shop Pro where to look for various resource files, such as Patterns, Gradients, Picture Tubes, and so on. For this, open the File Locations dialog box (shown in Figure B.5) by choosing **F**ile > **P**references > File **L**ocations. Click the type of resource you want and specify paths for the relevant files.

Figure B.5
The File Locations dialog box.

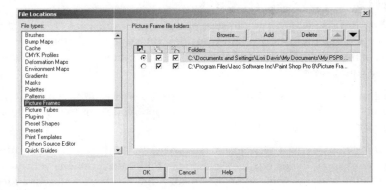

TIP

You can open the File Locations dialog box from any dialog box that makes use of a particular type of resource file. Click the **Edit Paths** button in the dialog box to access File Locations.

NOTE

Preferences are remembered for future Paint Shop Pro sessions. They are not saved or loaded with workspace files.

C

Adjusting Color Depth

Color depth is the amount of color data—and thus the maximum number of colors—that an image can accommodate. Color depth is determined by the number of bits used to store the color information of a pixel in an image.

The lowest color depth is 1 bit, which accommodates only two colors: black and white. The highest color depth in Paint Shop Pro is 24 bit, which can accommodate up to 16.7 million colors.

TIP

If a Paint Shop Pro operation you want to use is greyed out, chances are that the color depth of your image is too low. Many of Paint Shop Pro's operations work only on greyscale images and 24-bit (16-million color) images.

If you want to apply one of these operations to an image with a lower color depth, you can temporarily increase the color depth to 24 bit. Choose **Image > Increase Color Depth > 16** Million Colors (24-bit). Later, you can return the image to its original color depth by choosing **Image > Decrease Color Depth**.

A 24-bit image has three 8-bit color channels, each channel having 256 levels of brightness. A pixel that has 0 as the value of each channel is black, and a pixel that has 255 as the value of each channel is white. Using other values results in colors and shades of grey. Altogether, 256×256×256 (16.7 million) different values can be stored in those 24 bits.

Two basic types of images use a single 8-bit channel: 256-color images and greyscale images. These images are "paletted"—256 fixed colors or shades of grey are used to represent all the colors or brightness levels in the image. The colors or shades of grey are arranged in a palette, with each color assigned a palette index (depending on the color's order in the palette). Figure C.1 shows the Web graphics Safety Palette included with Paint Shop Pro. Notice that in this figure the tile with Palette index 251 is highlighted and that this tile has color channel values of Red 239, Green 240, and Blue 243 (whose HTML value is #EFF0F3).

TIP

To display the palette of an 8-bit image, choose **Image > Palette > Edit Palette**. You can replace colors in the palette by double-clicking a color tile in the palette and then using the Color dialog box to replace the original color of that tile.

Figure C.1
Safety Palette
(Safety.PspPalette).

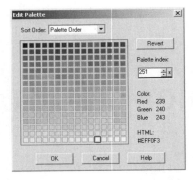

To view an image's color depth, choose **Image** > Image Information, and look at **Pixel depth/colors** in the Image pane. An 8-bit color image will show 8/256, whereas a 24-bit color image will show 24/16 Million.

To increase an image's color depth, choose **Image** > Increase Color Depth, and then choose the color depth you want. Decreasing an image's color depth is a little more involved, however.

NOTE

Typically, the reason you decrease an image's color depth is to optimize its file size. Another frequent use is the obligatory color reduction that occurs when you edit a 24-bit image and then save it in GIF format, which is an 8-bit file format. You can also produce interesting effects by reducing color depth, as can be seen throughout **http://www.campratty.com**, home of Paint Shop Pro's Very Frequently Asked Questions.

To decrease an image's color depth, choose **Image** > **D**ecrease Color Depth. After selecting the color depth you want, you will then see one of the Decrease Color Depth dialog boxes shown in Figures C.2 through C.5, depending on which color depth you chose.

Figure C.2
Decrease Color Depth -
64K Colors (24 bit) dialog
box (the 32K Colors
dialog box is similar).

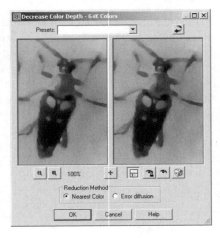

Figure C.3
Decrease Color Depth -
256 Colors (8 bit) dialog
box (the 16 Colors dialog
box is similar).

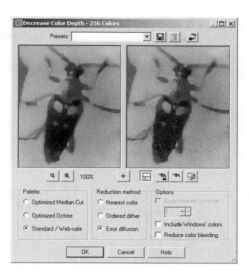

Figure C.4
Decrease Color Depth - 2
Colors (1 bit) dialog box.

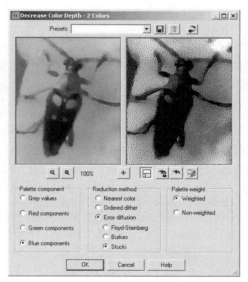

If you choose to decrease the color depth to 64K or 32K, you must choose a reduction method: either **Nearest color** or **Error diffusion**. With **Nearest color**, a pixel's color is replaced with the color closest to it that appears in the reduced color palette. **Error diffusion** also replaces a pixel's color with the closest color in the reduced palette, but the difference from the original color (the error) is passed on to the next pixel, and so on. This method spreads the error in the color replacement across all the pixels in the image. Typically, the Error diffusion method produces an image whose colors approximate those of the original image more closely than the Nearest color method does.

Figure C.5
Decrease Color Depth - X
Colors (4/8 bit) dialog
box.

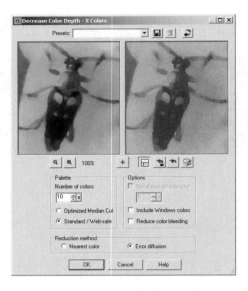

CAUTION

64K-color (16-bit) and 32K-color (15-bit) images are handled in memory as 24-bit images. As a result, their color depth might be inadvertently set to **16 million colors (24-bit)** if you perform any operation on these images other than **Save**, **Save As**, or **Save Copy As**. If you want color depth reductions to 64K or 32K colors, your best bet is to perform the reduction immediately before saving the image.

If you choose to reduce color depth to 256 colors and select **Standard / Web-safe** for the palette, you have a third option for a color reduction method: **Ordered dither**. Dithering is the mixing together of pixels of two or more different colors to create the illusion of a color that doesn't itself appear in the palette. This mixing of colors with **Ordered dither** often produces an obvious pattern, sometimes making your image resemble a color picture on newsprint.

When you reduce to either 256 colors or 16 colors, you must choose a **Palette** and a **Reduction method**. The following are the palette-generation methods to choose from when you reduce to 256 colors:

▶ **Optimized Median Cut** and **Optimized Octree.** Both methods produce adaptive palettes (palettes based on the number and distribution of colors in the original image). They use different algorithms, however, and so can yield noticeably different results. In general, Optimized Octree produces results that include more of the colors present in the original, while Optimized Median Cut favors the most prevalent colors of the original.

▶ **Standard / Web-safe.** This uses a standard palette that includes colors from across the spectrum that display well at a screen setting of 256 colors. Results with this palette are usually far from the best. (Note that with today's video displays, it's not necessary to use the Web-safe palette for your Web graphics.)

NOTE

For color reduction to 16 colors, you'll have **Windows'** in place of **Standard / Web-safe** as one of the reduction methods. Although there was reason to choose this method in the past, it is no longer necessary.

The following are three other options that you can set when reducing to 256 or 16 colors:

▶ When you reduce to 256 colors and choose one of the adaptive palettes—Optimized Median Cut or Optimized Octree—you have the option of including the standard Windows colors in the palette. This is, however, never necessary.

▶ If you choose **Error diffusion** as the reduction method, you then have the option to select **Reduce color bleeding**, which minimizes the bleeding of colors from left to right that the Error diffusion method produces.

▶ You can select the third option, **Boost marked colors by**, to emphasize colors in a selection that you made before initiating the color reduction. Paint Shop Pro will attempt to include in the resulting palette the colors contained in the selection. If you choose this option, you also can set a value for the degree of the color boost, from 1 (least effect) to 10 (greatest effect).

With **Decrease Color Depth - X Colors**, you can reduce the color depth of an image to any number between 2 and 256. You can choose the number of colors to be included in the palette and either the **Nearest color** or the **Error diffusion** reduction method. You can also choose whether to include the Windows colors. If you have a selection in your image, you also can choose **Boost marked colors by**. And if you select **Error diffusion** as the Reduction method, you have the option to select **Reduce color bleeding**.

NOTE

When **Include Windows colors** is selected, the smallest number of colors you can specify is 20.

You also can reduce the color depth of an image to two colors (black and white). Among other things, this can be useful for simulating halftones and other printlike effects. **Ordered dither** and the various **Error diffusion** methods are fun to experiment with here, and don't forget to try both the **Weighted** and **Non-weighted** options under Palette weight.

NOTE

Paint Shop Pro enables you to edit the palette of a 1-bit image. For example, you can change the white palette entry to blue and change the black palette entry to yellow. To try it yourself, choose Image > Palette > Edit Palette (or press Shift+P) when you have a 1-bit image open. In the Edit Palette dialog box, click one of the two palette entries. Then select a new color as you normally would in the Color dialog box.

NOTE

You can decrease the color depth of a 24-bit image to a lower bit depth only if the image has a single layer. If you try to adjust the color depth of a multilayered image, Paint Shop Pro asks whether you want to flatten the image. If you choose OK, the image is flattened and the color depth is adjusted. If you choose Cancel, the image is left alone and the color-depth adjustment is aborted.

D
Printing

Paint Shop Pro 8 provides several means of printing your images or thumbnails of your images. In this appendix, we'll discuss a few printing-related issues and look at the various ways to print your images.

Image Size and Resolution for Printing

Your image's resolution is measured in *Pixels per Inch* (PPI). You can determine the size of your printed image by dividing the number of pixels by the pixels per inch. The higher the image's resolution, the smaller the image is when printed. So, for example, an image that is 200 pixels high and 400 pixels wide and that has a resolution of 100 PPI prints at 2 inches high and 4 inches wide. An image with the same dimensions but a resolution of 200 PPI prints at 1 inch high and 2 inches wide.

Inkjet and laser printers print images by applying dots of ink on paper. A printer's resolution is therefore measured in *Dots per Inch* (DPI). It takes more than a single dot to produce a particular printed color, so DPI is not equivalent to PPI. You can see, then, that the appropriate image resolution for a printer is not the printer's resolution. Table D.1 displays a few recommended image resolution ranges for particular printer resolutions.

You can alter an image's resolution with Image > Resize. As Figure D.1 shows, the Print Size panel of the Resize dialog box has controls for **Resolution**. First, be sure that the check box located near the bottom of the dialog box and labeled **Resample using** is unchecked. Then choose the units (usually Pixels / Inch in the United States) and set the amount. The **Width** and **Height** will automatically be updated. As you'll see shortly, though, you don't need to use Resize in order to print your image at the proper size or resolution, because you can alter the image's resolution temporarily by letting your printer scale the image.

TABLE D.1 IMAGE RESOLUTIONS FOR PRINTING	
Printer Resolution	**Image Resolution**
300 DPI	72 to 120 PPI
600 DPI	125 to 170 PPI
1200 DPI	150 to 200 PPI

Figure D.1
Set the image's size and
resolution using the
Resize dialog box.

CAUTION

If **Resample using** is unchecked, the data in your image is not changed, and its quality will remain unchanged.

However, if **Resample using** is checked, adjusting **Resolution** or **Height** or **Width** changes the data in your image. The image will be stretched or shrunken. Because this stretching or shrinking adds or subtracts pixels, the quality of your image could be adversely affected.

Choosing the Right Paper

When you print your images, you'll get widely different results depending on the paper you use. Porous paper allows the ink to bleed, producing blurry results. Colored paper affects the color of your printed image, with off-white paper reducing the vividness of the image's colors. For this reason, you'll almost always want to use paper that is labeled bright white, coated.

There are all sorts of specialty papers, and your printer manufacturer will recommend different papers for different applications. For example, Epson recommends its Photo Quality Inkjet Paper or Photo Quality Glossy Paper for business graphics, but for photographs you want to frame, Epson's Photo Paper, Matte Paper Heavyweight, or Premium Glossy Photo Paper is recommended. Papers differ in characteristics such as porosity, brightness, weight, and acid content (this last being particularly important for photographs that you want to last for years and years). Be sure to consult your printer manufacturer's recommendations before choosing a paper for a particular application.

Printing an Image

To print a single image, you can begin by opening the image in Paint Shop Pro and choosing **File > Print**. In the Print dialog box (Figure D.2), you choose the number of copies to print, the orientation of the paper, the position of the image on the page, and any scaling that you want. On the Options tab, you can choose a few other options, such as whether to print in color or greyscale or whether to print a negative of your image. (If you have more than one printer and want to switch printers, you can press the **Printer** button to call up another dialog box that includes a drop-down list of your available printers.)

Figure D.2
The Print dialog box.

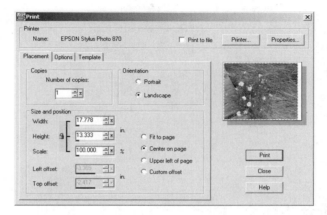

Most of these controls are self-explanatory, but let's take a brief look at **Scale**. What scaling does is stretch or compress the data of your image so that you can get a different printed size. Scaling doesn't affect your actual image, only the printed image. Scaling your image to a smaller size than its actual size will usually yield satisfactory results. However, scaling up to a larger size can be pretty disappointing, because the pixels of the image are likely to show up as noticeable individual rectangles of color. The result of scaling is similar to the result you'd get with Resize with **Resample using** unchecked.

After you've chosen the settings you want on the Placement and Options tabs of the Print dialog box, you can click the **Printer** button or the **Properties** button. Clicking the **Printer** button opens a dialog box in which you can choose what printer to use (if you have multiple printers), as shown in Figure D.3.

Figure D.3
The printer selector
dialog box.

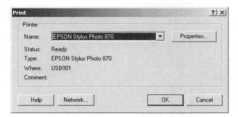

Clicking the **Properties** button brings up a dialog box for your particular printer. Figure D.4 shows the Properties box for the Epson Stylus Photo 870.

Your printer's Properties box probably has more than one tab of controls. In this example, the Main tab has controls for choosing the media type, whether to print in color or black and white, and what mode to use, along with an indication of the current ink levels. Which controls you have available and the tabs they're found on will depend on the make and model of your printer. Consult your printer's documentation for more information.

Figure D.4
Choose the paper or other media type in your printer's Properties dialog box.

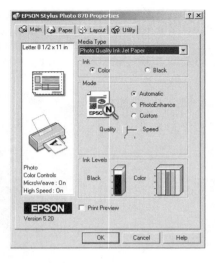

Using Paint Shop Pro's Print Layout

Paint Shop Pro also enables you to print multiple images or copies of an image. For this, try Paint Shop Pro's Print Layout. First, open all of the images you want to print, and then choose File > Print Layout. Paint Shop Pro's workspace is then temporarily replaced with the Print Layout workspace (Figure D.5).

Figure D.5
The Print Layout workspace.

Thumbnails of the open images appear on the left, and a representation of the page to print appears on the right. To add an image to the page, simply double-click the image's thumbnail or click and drag the thumbnail to the page. Click inside the image on the page and drag it to position it where you like. You can also resize an image in the page by clicking on the image to select it and dragging on one of the selection handles that appear in the image's corners or by dragging one of the image's edges. To move the image, click it and drag. To add another image, just click its thumbnail and drag it onto the page. (You can also add the same image again and again simply by repeatedly dragging its thumbnail onto the image canvas.) To remove an image from the page, click the image to select it and then press the Del key or choose **I**mage > Remo**v**e.

You can also use a printing template to print multiple copies of an image or a series of images. To load a template, choose **F**ile > Open **T**emplate, then select one of the categories listed in the Templates dialog box and choose one of the templates. Figure D.6 shows the Wallets template selected from the Standard Sizes catalog.

Figure D.6
Choosing a template.

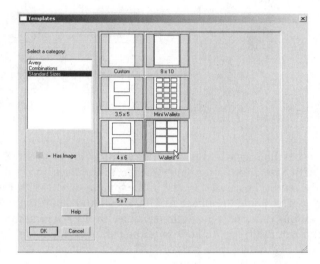

Once you've selected a template, click **OK** to load the template to the page on the workspace. Then drag your image onto the page, where it will snap into position when you release the mouse button.

You can fill the entire template with a single image (as in Figure D.7) by pressing the Fill Template with Image icon on the Print Layout toolbar or by choosing **T**emplate > Fill Template **w**ith Image.

If the image doesn't fill the template or isn't placed correctly, select the image and choose one of the placement options available through the toolbar or under **T**emplate > **C**ell Placement. Here are the available options:

▶ **Free**
▶ **Size and Center**
▶ **Fit Cell**
▶ **Fit to Cell Centered**
▶ **Fit to Cell Left**
▶ **Fit to Cell Right**
▶ **Fit to Cell Top**
▶ **Fit to Cell Bottom**

Figure D.7
Filling the template with a single image.

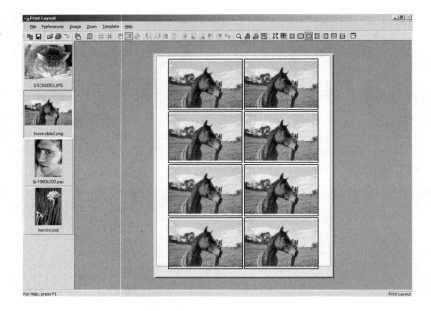

With **Free**, you can resize the image and position it with the cursor just as you can when no template is loaded. With **Size and Center**, you can select the image and resize it, but Paint Shop Pro will automatically center the resized image in the template cell. With **Fit Cell**, Paint Shop Pro does all the work for you, resizing the image to fill the cell and centering the resized image in the cell. The other five options do exactly what their names imply, pushing the image over so that an edge lines up with the left, right, top, or bottom of the cell or so the image is centered in the cell.

TIP

All of Print Layout's commands available in the File, Preferences, and Zoom menus are also available from a context menu. Right-click in an empty area of the workspace or print page to access this menu.

In another menu, you can access all the commands available under Image, Zoom, and Template. Right-click in an empty template cell or on an image placed on the print page to get this menu.

If your image has a different orientation than the template cell's, don't despair. Just select the image's cell and choose **I**mage > **R**otate +90 or **I**mage > **R**otate –90 (or select their icons on the Print Layout toolbar). Figure D.8 shows an example. Here the template is filled with a single portrait. The upper-left cell shows the result of rotating the image in the cell and applying **Fit Cell**. The upper-right cell shows the result of rotating the image only.

When everything's placed, sized, and positioned as you like, press the Print icon or choose **F**ile > **P**rint.

To exit the Print Layout workspace and return to the Paint Shop Pro workspace, choose **F**ile > **C**lose Print Layout or click the Print Layout window's **Close** button on the extreme right of its toolbar.

Figure D.8
Rotating and fitting the
image to the cells of the
template.

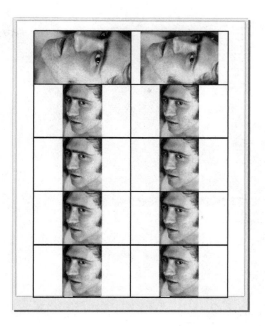

TIP

If you need to change the printer, set printer properties, or make other printing
changes such as adding crop marks while you're in Print Layout, choose **F**ile >
Print Set**u**p. (The dialog box for Print Setup will give you access to various printer
controls.)

For more information on the handy Print Layout feature, consult Paint Shop Pro's documentation
and Help.

Printing from the Browser

Paint Shop Pro's Browser (Figure D.9) is great for browsing images on your hard drive or other
storage media and for opening, copying, or moving your images. Another handy feature of the
Browser is that it provides you with a quick and easy way to print a digital "contact sheet" of all
the images in a folder.

To print the image, open the Browser by choosing **F**ile > **B**rowse (or press Ctrl+B), navigate to the
folder you want, and choose **F**ile > **P**rint (or press Ctrl+P). You're then presented with the Browser
Print dialog box, shown in Figure D.10.

In the Browser Print dialog box, you choose the orientation of the paper, whether to use the
Browser thumbnails, whether to use the standard Browser template or any of the templates
available with Print Layout, and what pages to print. This dialog box also shows you a preview
of what your printed page will look like.

Figure D.9
Use Paint Shop Pro's
Browser to print a digital
"contact sheet."

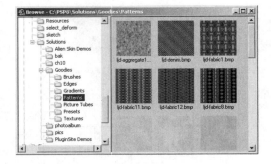

Figure D.10
The Browser Print dialog
box.

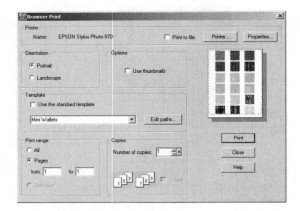

A Note on Printing Services

A thorough treatment of professional printing is far beyond the scope of this book. However, here are a few things you should know if you want to send your images to a printing service:

▶ Some printing devices measure resolution in lines per inch, and this resolution measure is called the screen frequency. The resolution of your images should typically be about one and a half to two times the particular device's screen frequency, but check with your printer to be sure.

▶ Flatten any layered image before sending it to a print service.

▶ Choose a file format that is generally used for printed images. *Tagged Image File Format* (TIFF) is common, but you should check with your print service to see what its needs are. Whatever the file format, be sure that your image is saved in the format's uncompressed mode (or at the lowest level of compression if there is no uncompressed mode).

▶ If the print service requires *Cyan-Magenta-Yellow-Kohl* (CMYK) color separations for your image, you can print them by choosing CMYK Separations in the Print Setup dialog box available in Print Layout (**F**ile > Print Set**u**p).

Be sure to consult your particular printing service to see what its requirements and recommendations are.

E
Resources

This appendix lists URLs for a number of resources that can help you create graphics with Paint Shop Pro. The list is far from exhaustive, but it's sure to be helpful. Please think of this as just a starting point—you're certain to find many other helpful sites. And keep in mind that things on the Web are quite unstable, so these URLs might change or disappear altogether.

PSP Tips, Tutorials, and Resources

Here are a few sites dedicated to Paint Shop Pro. Many also have link pages that will lead you to other useful sites.

► Lori's Web Graphics
http://loriweb.pair.com

► Camp Ratty (home of Paint Shop Pro's Very Frequently Asked Questions)
http://www.campratty.com

► Diana's Free Tubes
http://www.freetubes.com

► Digital Arts Resources
http://www.digitalartresources.com/PSP/ArtResources.htm

► Paranormal PSP8
http://jpkabala.com/paranormal

► Pixelnook
http://pixelnook.home.comcast.net

► PSP-X
http://www.psp-x.com

► Ron's Toons Dot Com
http://www.ronstoons.com

► State of Entropy Webgraphics and Design
http://www.state-of-entropy.com

For collections of more links to Paint Shop Pro tutorial sites, head over to Jasc Software at **http://www.jasc.com** and to PSP Tutorial Links at **http://www.psplinks.com**.

Filters

Many commercial and free plugins are available on the Web, either to order or to download. Here are a few sources to get you started.

- ▶ Alien Skin Software
  http://www.alienskin.com
- ▶ Auto FX Software
  http://www.autofx.com
- ▶ Flaming Pear Software
  http://www.flamingpear.com
- ▶ The Plugin Site
  http://www.thepluginsite.com
- ▶ Steve's Desktop Photography
  http://stevesdesktopphotography.com/plugins.htm

Newsgroups, Newsletters, and Discussion Boards

There are lots of places you can go for information on Paint Shop Pro. Here's a sample.

- ▶ Jasc User Forums
  http://forums.jasc.com
- ▶ Paint Shop Pro Users Group
  http://www.pspusersgroup.com
- ▶ PSP Interactive Zone
  http://www.pspiz.net
- ▶ *pspPower* newsletter
  http://www.psppower.com

Freeware and Shareware Fonts

Commercial fonts can be expensive. Here are a few places where you can find free or inexpensive fonts.

- ▶ Astigmatic One Eye Typographic Institute
  http://www.astigmatic.com
- ▶ Brain Stew Font Archive
  http://members.aol.com/MCGRAFIX/archive.html

▶ The Dingbat Pages
  http://www.dingbatpages.com

▶ Emerald City Fontwerks
  http://www.speakeasy.org/~ecf

▶ Font Freak
  http://www.fontfreak.com

▶ Font Garden
  http://www.fontgarden.com

▶ Fonts & Things
  http://www.fontsnthings.com

Scanning, Printing, and Digital Photography

Be sure to visit the sites of the manufacturers of any graphics-related hardware or media that you use or are considering for purchase.

▶ Avery Office Products
  http://www.avery.com

▶ Canon
  http://www.canon.com

▶ Hewlett-Packard
  http://www.hp.com

▶ Epson
  http://www.epson.com

▶ Kodak
  http://www.kodak.com

▶ Microtek
  http://www.microtek.com

▶ Nikon
  http://www.nikon.com

▶ Pentax
  http://www.pentax.com

If you have equipment from a manufacturer other than those listed here, be sure to check out the appropriate manufacturer's site for helpful information and the latest drivers.

For advice about scanning, look at Wayne Fulton's scanning tips at **http://www.scantips.com**.

Index